# Political Pressures on Educational and Social Research

*Political Pressures on Educational and Social Research* draws upon a variety of theoretical and methodological approaches to consider the problems that can arise when research findings diverge from political directions for policy. Chapters explore the impacts this can have on the researchers, as well as the influence it has on the research, including the methodology and the publication of results. The book offers innovative ways of seeing how these connect, overlap and interact, revealing particular issues of concern for researchers and evaluators in the context of research internationally. Key topics include the power and positioning of research, evidence-based policy development, ethics and the importance of research that seeks to explore and discover knowledge.

The book is divided into two sections. The first presents chapters from international academics, which provide a theoretical underpinning and discussion of power, policy, ethics and their influence on research resourcing, autonomy, purpose and methodology. The second section explores specific case studies and instances from the authors' own experiences in the field.

This book offers an interesting and enlightening insight into the sometimes political nature of research and will appeal to researchers, evaluators and postgraduate students in the fields of education and the social sciences. It will be of particular interest to those studying research methods.

**Karen Trimmer** is Associate Professor with the University of Southern Queensland. With extensive experience in education, her research interests include decision-making by school principals; policy and governance; social justice impacts of policy; Indigenous participation in higher education and quantitative methods.

# Political Pressures on Educational and Social Research

International perspectives

Edited by Karen Trimmer

LONDON AND NEW YORK

First published 2016
by Routledge

2 Park Square, Milton Park, Abingdon, Oxfordshire OX14 4RN
711 Third Avenue, New York, NY 10017

*Routledge is an imprint of the Taylor & Francis Group, an informa business*

First issued in paperback 2017

Copyright © 2016 selection and editorial matter, Karen Trimmer; individual chapters, the contributors

The right of Karen Trimmer to be identified as the author of the editorial material, and of the authors for their individual chapters, has been asserted in accordance with sections 77 and 78 of the Copyright, Designs and Patents Act 1988.

All rights reserved. No part of this book may be reprinted or reproduced or utilised in any form or by any electronic, mechanical, or other means, now known or hereafter invented, including photocopying and recording, or in any information storage or retrieval system, without permission in writing from the publishers.

Notice:
Product or corporate names may be trademarks or registered trademarks, and are used only for identification and explanation without intent to infringe.

*British Library Cataloguing in Publication Data*
A catalogue record for this book is available from the British Library

*Library of Congress Cataloging in Publication Data*
Names: Trimmer, Karen, editor.
Title: Political pressures on educational and social research / edited by Karen Trimmer.
Description: New York, NY : Routledge, 2016. | Includes bibliographical references.
Identifiers: LCCN 2015046892| ISBN 9781138947122 (hardcover) | ISBN 9781315670263 (electronic)
Subjects: LCSH: Education—Research—Political aspects. | Education—Research—Methodology. | Social sciences—Research—Political aspects. | Social sciences—Research—Methodology. | Education and state. | Social policy.
Classification: LCC LB1028 .P54427 2016 | DDC 370.72—dc23
LC record available at http://lccn.loc.gov/2015046892

ISBN: 978-1-138-94712-2 (hbk)
ISBN: 978-0-8153-6065-0 (pbk)

Typeset in Bembo
by Swales & Willis Ltd, Exeter, Devon, UK

# Contents

*List of figures* x
*List of tables* xi
*List of contributors* xii
*Acknowledgements* xiii

**PART I**
**Contexts surrounding policy, ethics, power and resources** 1

1 The pressures of the political on rigorous and ethical research 3
   KAREN TRIMMER

   *1.1 Introduction 3*
   *1.2 Definitions 4*
   *1.3 Sponsored research by universities 6*
   *1.4 Journey through the chapters in this book 7*
   *1.5 Conclusion 9*

2 The problem of the policy agora: how power differentials, methodological naivety and the ideological preferences of policy-makers affect the development of government policy 10
   CHRIS BROWN

   *2.1 Introduction 10*
   *2.2 Power and policy development 11*
   *2.3 Michel Foucault 12*
   *2.4 The policy agora 14*
   *2.5 Discourse in relation to evidence-use in educational policy development 16*
   *2.6 The discourse of marketisation 17*

*2.7 The implications of the policy agora for policy development 19*
*2.8 Evidence misuse 20*
*2.9 Conclusion 24*

## 3 'What works?': from health to education, the shaping of the European policy of evidence 25
ROMUALD NORMAND

*3.1 Introduction 25*
*3.2 The epistemology of evidence-based technologies 26*
*3.3 The development of the US evidence-based policy in health and education 27*
*3.4 The structure of a European network between science and policy in education 34*
*3.5 Conclusion 39*

## 4 Ethical drift in educational research: understanding the politics of knowledge production 41
PATRICK M. JENLINK AND KAREN EMBRY JENLINK

*4.1 Introduction 41*
*4.2 Origins of ethics in educational research 42*
*4.3 Ethics and politics in/of educational research 43*
*4.4 Ethical dilemmas in educational research 44*
*4.5 Ethical drift in educational research 46*
*4.6 Negative effects of ethical drift 50*
*4.7 Addressing ethical drift 51*
*4.8 Final reflections 52*

## 5 Play the game or get played? Researchers' strategies around R&D policies 55
SOFIA VISEU

*5.1 Introduction 55*
*5.2 Methods 57*
*5.3 Results: play the game or get played by it 58*
*5.4 Final remarks 63*

## 6 On relevance and norms of science in times of restructuring: educational research in Sweden 66
RITA FOSS LINDBLAD AND SVERKER LINDBLAD

*6.1 Introduction 66*
*6.2 Norms of science: why and how they (still) matter for educational research 67*

*6.3 Educational research in Sweden: trajectories of relevancing and funding 69*
*6.4 A periodization: from conquered trust to contested relevance for educational research 70*
*6.5 Institutionalization: aspiring academic relevance 70*
*6.6 Expansion: taking advantage of given academic relevance 71*
*6.7 Contraction: competing in a period of contested relevance 72*
*6.8 Different periods – different organizations, relevancing and research positions 73*
*6.9 Concluding comments on educational research in an era of contraction 75*

### 7 Is the Emperor naked? Experiencing the 'PISA hysteria', branding and education export in Finnish academia 77
FRED DERVIN

*7.1 Introduction 77*
*7.2 Marketization, branding and the 'PISA hysteria' in Finnish higher education 79*
*7.3 Marketization and branding in practice: actors, (hidden) agendas and impact 83*
*7.4 Discussion and conclusion 91*

### 8 Making an impact: politics and persuasions in 21st-century higher education 94
JOANNE DOYLE AND LISA McDONALD

*8.1 Introduction 94*
*8.2 Understanding impact 95*
*8.3 Research to 'make a difference' 97*
*8.4 Assessment not evaluation 98*
*8.5 The complexity of research impact 98*
*8.6 Communicating and translating research 100*
*8.7 The future of research 101*
*8.8 Conclusions 102*

### 9 The impact of managerial performance frameworks on research activities among Australian early career researchers 104
EVA BENDIX PETERSEN

*9.1 Introduction 104*
*9.2 The larger study 105*
*9.3 Theme 1: objectionable research practices 107*

*9.4 Theme 2: the grant game 110*
*9.5 Discussion 112*
*9.6 Conclusion 114*

## PART II
## Case studies from the field     117

### 10  Ethical dilemmas in program evaluation     119
CARINA CALZONI

*10.1 Introduction 119*
*10.2 Ethical dilemmas in evaluation 119*
*10.3 Case study: evaluation of a mental health court program 120*
*10.4 Ethical considerations around involving mental health consumers in evaluations 121*
*10.5 The ethical trade-offs in selecting evaluation participants 122*
*10.6 The limitation of accepted ethical principles 122*
*10.7 Applying evaluation theoretical approaches to these ethical dilemmas 123*
*10.8 Conclusion: the need for more open discussion on ethical dilemmas in evaluation 124*

### 11  Surfacing the implicit     126
KEVIN GAITSKELL

*11.1 Introduction 126*
*11.2 The paradox of boards 126*
*11.3 Evaluating boards 128*
*11.4 Conclusion 135*

### 12  Balancing relationships and intellectual rigour in research for government agencies     136
GRAEME GOWER AND GARY PARTINGTON

*12.1 Introduction 136*
*12.2 The student wellbeing study 138*
*12.3 The attendance book 140*
*12.4 Interdepartmental cooperation? 141*
*12.5 The aspirations project 143*
*12.6 Teacher assistants' project 145*
*12.7 Conclusion 148*

## 13 When research, policy and practice disconnect: an educational leadership policy example  150
VICKI FARWELL

13.1 Introduction  150
13.2 Background: the re-emergence of Instructional Leadership (IL)  151
13.3 A snapshot review of Queensland government policy focused on IL  153
13.4 Disconnect through the implementation of policy  161
13.5 Policy disconnect  163
13.6 Conclusions  166

## 14 The politics and complexity of research utilisation in the central education policy arena in Taiwan  167
HUNG-CHANG CHEN

14.1 Introduction  167
14.2 MoE research commissioning in Taiwan  168
14.3 The salience of political considerations in research utilisation  168
14.4 Meanings of research use  169
14.5 Qualitative multiple-case study design  171
14.6 Political constraints and researchers' pressure  172
14.7 The dynamics and complexity of research utilisation  174
14.8 Discussion  177
14.9 Conclusion  178

## 15 The pressures within: dilemmas in the conduct of evaluation from within government  180
KAREN TRIMMER

15.1 Background  180
15.2 The politics of research and evaluation  180
15.3 Case studies of political influence and associated strategies for research and evaluation  184
15.4 Conclusion  191

*References*  192
*Index*  217

# Figures

| | | |
|---|---|---|
| 2.1 | The policy 'agora': the wider environment that determines which evidence is considered by policy-makers | 15 |
| 5.1 | FCT applications and approved calls evolution in all scientific areas (2000–2012) | 59 |
| 5.2 | Researchers' network | 60 |
| 5.3 | Research centres' rating in all scientific areas (1996–2007) | 61 |
| 5.4 | Educational research centres' rating (1996–2007) | 62 |
| 13.1 | The Bowe, Ball and Gold Policy Cycle (1992, p.20) | 164 |

# Tables

| | | |
|---|---|---|
| 6.1 | Summary of periods in relevance and position of educational research in Sweden 1900–2015 | 74 |
| 13.1 | Instructional Leadership expectations: Queensland Government reports and policy documents | 155 |
| 14.1 | The flow of research-use models | 174 |

# Contributors

| | |
|---|---|
| Dr Eva Bendix Petersen | *Roskilde University, Denmark* |
| Dr Chris Brown | *Institute of Education, University of London, UK* |
| Carina Calzoni | *Director, Clear Horizon Consulting* |
| Hung-Chang Chen | *Institute of Education, University of London, UK* |
| Professor Fred Dervin | *University of Helsinki, Finland* |
| Joanne Doyle | *University of Southern Queensland, Australia* |
| Vicki Farwell | *University of Southern Queensland, Australia* |
| Kevin Gaitskell | *Independent Consultant* |
| Dr Graeme Gower | *Edith Cowan University, Western Australia* |
| Professor Karen Embry Jenlink | *Stephen F. Austin State University, Nacogdoches, Texas* |
| Professor Patrick M. Jenlink | *Stephen F. Austin State University, Nacogdoches, Texas* |
| Professor Rita Foss Lindblad | *University of Borås, Sweden* |
| Professor Sverker Lindblad | *University of Gothenburg, Sweden* |
| Dr Lisa McDonald | *University of Southern Queensland, Australia* |
| Professor Gary Partington | *Edith Cowan University, Western Australia* |
| Professor Romuald Normand | *University of Strasbourg, France* |
| Associate Professor Karen Trimmer | *University of Southern Queensland, Australia* |
| Professor Sofia Viseu | *University of Lisbon, Portugal* |

# Acknowledgements

The editor is very grateful to the following individuals without whom this book would not have been published:

The editorial team at Routledge for all their work in getting this publication to press.

The chapter authors for their respective chapters, for their contributions to the writing workshops that facilitated the chapter writing, and for engaging wholeheartedly with feedback from the editor and peer reviewers.

The scholars who provided double blind peer reviews of submitted chapters:

- Betty Adcock, University of Southern Queensland, Australia
- A/Professor Dorothy Andrews, University of Southern Queensland, Australia
- David Axworthy, Department of Education, Western Australia
- Dr Malcolm Brown, University of Southern Queensland, Australia
- Professor Tracey Bunda, University of Southern Queensland, Australia
- Professor Simon Clarke, University of Western Australia, Australia
- Professor Geoff Cockfield, University of Southern Queensland, Australia
- Dr Pauline Collins, University of Southern Queensland, Australia
- Professor Rick Cummings, Murdoch University, Australia
- Professor Patrick Danaher, University of Southern Queensland, Australia
- Dr Mark Dawson, University of Southern Queensland, Australia
- A/Professor Scott Eacott, University of New South Wales, Australia
- Yvonne Findlay, University of Southern Queensland, Australia
- Professor Christine Forde, University of Glasgow, Scotland
- Associate Professor Andrew Hickey, University of Southern Queensland, Australia
- Professor Lyn Karstadt, University of Southern Queensland, Australia
- A/Professor Graeme Lock, Edith Cowan University, Australia
- Dr Johnathon Mendel, University of Dundee, United Kingdom
- A/ Professor Peter McIlveen, University of Southern Queensland, Australia
- Dr Stewart Riddle, University of Southern Queensland, Australia
- Nerida Spina, Queensland University of Technology, Australia

- Dr David Thorpe, University of Southern Queensland, Australia
- Dr Sheila Trahar, University of the West of England, Bristol, United Kingdom
- Dr Anna Traianou, Goldsmiths University of London, United Kingdom
- Professor Sally Varnham, University of Technology Sydney, Australia
- Professor Gina Wisker, University of Brighton, United Kingdom

My colleagues in the University of Southern Queensland, particularly Professor Patrick Danaher and Associate Professor Warren Midgley for their continuing encouragement and interest, and Katrina Wilson for her support and work in editing and preparation of the manuscript.

My family and friends for their inexhaustible love and support.

# Part I

Contexts surrounding policy, ethics, power and resources

# Chapter 1

# The pressures of the political on rigorous and ethical research

*Karen Trimmer*

## 1.1 Introduction

When researchers and evaluators encounter political influence during the conduct of their work, it creates a source of tension for them. Political influence may be felt during the design stage in formulating questions and methodology, during the conduct of the research or evaluation, and during the concluding stages when reports are written and recommendations proposed (Mohan & Sullivan, 2006). Researchers and evaluators are trained through study and practice to seek objective and ethical approaches to their work, so the intrusion of politics poses problems (Palumbo, 1987).

Many authors (O'Brien, Payne, Nolan & Ingleton, 2010; Patton, 2008; Slattery, 2010) argue that research and evaluation is inherently political. They contend that research and evaluation processes involve politics at micro and institutional levels, in multiple ways, and at multiple points. This is because it engages complex social relations about rules and resources between various interest groups, all of whom have vested interests in the outcomes. The current Australasian perspective held by the Australasian Evaluation Society is that evaluators view themselves as facilitators of inquiry conducted in a political environment that involves multiple players and perspectives (Markiewicz, 2008). In other words, the Australasian Evaluation Society recognises and acknowledges the political milieu in which evaluators carry out their work.

The chapters of this book explore the impact of politics on the work of the researcher and evaluator in the broad field of social science. This chapter commences with an examination of definitions of key terminology and then outlines the ways in which politics impinges upon research and evaluation work. Subsequent chapters discuss theoretical aspects of power, including funding; they examine the areas of sponsored or commissioned research, issues around evidence-based policy development and ethics, provide and discuss examples of where politics has become involved in research and evaluation, and explore a range of strategies that may be employed by researchers and evaluators to counter political impact.

## 1.2 Definitions

Research and evaluation are similar in their approaches but somewhat different with respect to their purpose. Research is considered to be a process that seeks and provides 'new knowledge' (O'Brien et al., 2010) whereas evaluation is the process of identifying information or generating knowledge about policies and programs that can then be used to improve them or make decisions about their effectiveness and whether they should continue (Slattery, 2010; Torrance, 2010). Generally, evaluation should: provide a service to decision makers; be responsive to the information needs of a range of stakeholders; be democratic rather than autocratic; and be informative (Torrance, 2010). Essentially, evaluation is concerned with determining the value, merit or significance of a program, policy or project (Abma & Schwandt, 2005). Audiences for the reports of evaluations vary, but may include the client commissioning the evaluation, stakeholders with vested interests in the success or failure of programs and policies, program developers and managers, government officials, politicians, and the general public. Research has traditionally been more focussed on generating theoretical knowledge in an independent context.

While there are some distinct conceptual differences between the practices of research and evaluation, there is considerable overlap between the two and the distinctions between them appear to be blurring further with changes to funding, priorities in higher education governance, and performance agreements for academics. Evaluation and research share many of the same methods of social science research such as: clarifying the purpose of the task; addressing principles of research design; formulating questions; choosing methodologies; choosing data collection instruments; identifying samples; analysing data and interpreting and reporting results (Cohen, Manion & Morrison, 2011). Their differences though, for the purpose of this book, generally relate to the following:

- audience: evaluations are often commissioned and therefore become the property of the sponsor;
- scope: evaluations tend to have a limited scope due to various constraints;
- purpose: evaluations are conducted to make judgements;
- agenda setting: evaluators work within a given brief;
- uses to which the results are put: evaluations may be used to increase or withhold resources, continue or cease programs, or modify policies;
- ownership of data: the evaluator generally surrenders ownership of the data to the sponsor upon completion;
- project control: the commissioning body can sponsor the evaluation but not control the independence of the evaluator;
- power: the evaluator may have power to control the operation of the evaluation but not the project brief;
- politics: the evaluator may not be able to stand outside any politics related to the purposes or uses of the evaluation (Cohen, Manion & Morrison, 2011).

In comparison, intellectual property, ownership of data and publishing rights of research are usually retained by researchers or their employing universities. Agendas, scope and purpose for research vary considerably, and whilst traditionally may have been based on development of knowledge and theoretical contribution to academe, chapters within this book will provide evidence that the nature of research and the work of academic researchers is being impacted by a range of political influences within and external to higher education institutions globally. References in the literature regarding the political influence that researchers and evaluators may be subject to therefore relate both to work in the field of evaluation and also more recently upon pure research work as a consequence of funding policies for research. As such, the person conducting the work will be referred to as a researcher or an evaluator throughout this book.

Politics is defined in various ways. Simons (1995, p. 436) defines politics as it relates to research and evaluation as 'the contest for power between groups with different vested interests in the practice and outcome of research' while Kelly (1987) defines the term as relating to bargaining transactions and negotiations that maximise action. Palumbo (1987, pp. 18–19) defines the word in a more inclusive manner as 'the interactions of various actors within and among bureaucracies, clients, interest groups, private organisations and legislatures as they relate to each other from different positions of power, influence and authority.' Each of these definitions involves references to interactions between people, that may be negotiated, but involve some element of power or control over some issue. Politics are situated in, and refer to, the sometimes complex interactions of individuals and teams involved in research or evaluation (Simons, 2000). Aspects of the power differentials, the influence of politics, and their impact on evidence-based policy development by those wielding this power are explored in Chapters 3 and 6.

Ethics as defined by Simons (1995, p. 436) is 'the search for rules of conduct that enable us to operate defensibly in the political contexts in which we conduct educational research.' Ethical practice is generally considered to be 'doing no harm' (Piper & Simons, 2005) when conducting research or evaluation and is concerned with conducting research and evaluation objectively and properly (Simons, 1995). Ethical practice relates to the principles and procedures that guide appropriate action during the course of conducting research and evaluation. Ethical principles include such behaviours as honesty, justice and respect (Shaw, 2003) on the part of researchers and participants, and ethical procedures involve maintaining confidentiality, respecting participants' rights to privacy and anonymity, adopting sensitivity towards participants and ensuring that participants provide informed consent (Cohen, Manion & Morrison, 2011; Piper & Simons, 2005; Shaw, 2003). In many instances, ethics committees have been established to manage and ensure that researchers have considered a range of ethical issues that might arise during their research and that they have developed protocols to protect participants from harm (Piper & Simons, 2005). Ethical principles and procedures are central to all research and evaluation and for qualitative and quantitative methodologies (Shaw, 2003).

A recent consideration in the field of ethics is that which relates to the researcher. Ethical principles and guidelines are generally formulated with a view to protecting participants from harm during the research process and little attention is paid to the protection of the researcher. Piper and Simons (2005) consider that this situation may be changing somewhat with the research community becoming increasingly aware of some risks and ethical dangers that researchers may face when studying in certain contexts. These have tended to be physical risks to the researcher when studying in remote areas of the world or in some large urban contexts. Little consideration has been given so far to any potential emotional risk to the researcher in the conduct of their work (Piper & Simons, 2005). Simons (1995) purports that ethics and politics are linked in research and evaluation and indicates that 'different political contexts call for different strategies in the enactment of ethical principles. Jenlink and Jenlink introduce the terminology of 'ethical drift' in Chapter 4 to explore these issues in greater depth.

Tensions may arise for the researcher and evaluator when politics intervenes in their work. In the case of a commercial provider, the evaluator may struggle to balance their intent to remain objective and independent with their business interests in undertaking paid work (Bridges, 2003; Markiewicz, 2008). For an internal evaluator in an organisation, they may experience a conflict of interest with political pressures and may feel compelled to produce anticipated findings, highlight positives and downplay any negatives (Markiewicz, 2008). The chapters in Part I consider the theoretical issues surrounding power and resources, policy and ethics, Part II considers case studies in relation to evaluations conducted by private contractors, government evaluators, and universities via tender arrangements. For a researcher in a university, there may be considerations with regard to breaking paid research contracts, an issue that may have later implications for the institution seeking further research funding. Chapters throughout the book explore the impacts of funding and higher education policy. In all facets of research and evaluation, researchers increasingly need to build up a relationship of respect with those who commissioned the research and who may be affected by the publication of any adverse findings (Bridges, 2003).

## 1.3 Sponsored research by universities

In recent years, a fiercely competitive research market has developed in the United Kingdom, Europe, the United States, Australia and New Zealand in which universities have found that a significant element of their success is their capacity to attract contract research funding (Bridges, 2003; Czarnitzki, Grimpe & Toole, 2011). This shift from a situation of conducting pure research to conducting what may be considered as entrepreneurial activity enables universities to continue to employ research staff, maintain equipment and facilities, establish a national and international research standing, and attract further research funding. Villani and Normand (2015) refer to the 'Schumpterian' idea of the academic researcher as an entrepreneur and the social, moral and political ways of being an academic entrepreneur. This, according to Bridges (2003), has compromised the academic freedom of universities in those countries. This trend, the consequences for and responses by academic researchers are explored in Chapters 5, 6, 7, 8 and 9.

University researchers, of course, engage in 'traditional research' under publicly funded posts. Involvement with corporate funding, however, may lead to: the steering of research resources through the designation of particular centres of excellence; the identification of a preferred theme and encouragement of academics to forward research proposals relating to the theme; the selection of researchers based on their perceived merit; and funders creating in-house research establishments (Bridges, 2003). From Bridges' (2003) perspective, these possibilities see a move towards 'business' having a potential impact on the more traditional avenues of research conducted by universities.

Corporate funding of research has an additional impact, especially with regard to the publication of research findings (Czarnitzki, Grimpe & Toole, 2011). A study undertaken in Germany by Czarnitzki, Grimpe and Toole (2011) found that the levels of industry sponsorship of research had an impact on the public disclosure of that academic research. In particular, academic researchers who accepted industry-sponsored research reported significantly more delays and greater secrecy around the publication of their work. The authors reported that, in OECD countries, the proportion of industry-sponsored research is rising. Notably, in 2007, Australia ranked second behind Germany in terms of the proportion of industry-sponsored higher education and government research and development it undertook. The findings of Czarnitzki, Grimpe and Toole's study in a German context are likely to be similar in Australian and international contexts. Case studies in Part II provide examples of these pressures in Asia and Australia.

## 1.4 Journey through the chapters in this book

The introductory chapter sets the scene for the book. It maps the landscape of political influence within a range of environments including policy development and higher education research. The chapter provides definitions of key terms and maps the progression of all proceeding chapters, which are divided into two parts. The first part includes chapters from international academic authors to provide a theoretical underpinning and discussion of power, policy, ethics and their influence on research resourcing, autonomy, purpose and methodology. The second part presents chapters from a broad range of authors who explore specific cases studies and instances from their own experience in the field. It includes academics working within higher education and those conducting commissioned research. It also includes experienced voices from outside the academy who are impacted in their conduct of research and evaluation within private consultancy and within government.

Chapter 2 considers the problem of the policy agora and how power differentials and their manifestation through discursive dominance interact to override evidence-informed approaches in the development of government policy in the United Kingdom. The theme of evidence-based policy development is followed into Chapter 3 which explores its influence on epistemic governance in the European context and the impact this in turn has on humanities and social sciences in academe. Chapter 4 moves to consideration of how political forces impact on knowledge production and the potential outcomes of research. This chapter discusses the issue of ethical drift and the dilemma of navigation through these tensions by academic researchers whilst maintaining ethical positions and practices.

The next group of chapters explore how these political forces impact on higher education research at an individual researcher level and at organisational and systemic levels in a range of international contexts. In Chapter 5 readers are led to ponder the impact on researchers who may be motivated to position themselves to play the research game as an alternative to encountering frustrations and barriers to their research and career progression through consideration of an empirical study conducted in Portugal. Chapter 6 is based on the Swedish perspective and ventures closer to the core of the issue of the changing relevance of educational research as an international dilemma. The position of the global education superstructure is explored in Chapter 7 via an autoethnography of the influence of the political marketisation and branding on work as scholars. Through consideration of the case of Finnish education in relation to PISA (Programme for International Student Assessment), this chapter exposes the complex ways in which today's universities are integrated into local, national and global political economies and the economisation of higher education which influences universities' approaches to sustainability and in turn research. The Australian perspective on the competitive nature of research in relation to a highly competitive pool of available funding resources is explored in Chapter 8. The influence on research priorities, outcomes and impacts is discussed. The Australian context is continued as a focus in Chapter 9 which considers the impact these neo-liberal influences have had on the managerial performance frameworks of universities and consequently has on early-career researchers' experience in academia.

The next part of the book, through Chapters 10 to 15, takes a different perspective and introduces the voices of practitioners exploring case studies of their experience. A consultant program evaluator considers the dilemmas in negotiating rigorous and ethical approaches to commissioning in Chapter 10. This theme is continued in Chapter 11 where an independent consultant, who is an experienced board member and evaluator, explores the power of boards and the dilemmas of negotiating these forces in conducting rigorous and ethical evaluation in such a politically charged environment. As seen in Part I, universities are not immune to these influences in conducting rigorous and ethical research and these dilemmas are investigated through consideration of a series of cases undertaken by academic researchers conducting commissioned program evaluations for government in Chapter 12. Another academic who has significant experience as a secondary principal considers the particular case of the divergence between politics, research evidence and policy implementation in the context of instructional leadership of schools in Queensland, a State of Australia, in Chapter 13. Chapter 14 moves to the context of Taiwan and the differences between policy positions and purposes in commissioning research and evaluation, and the position taken in utilising the results and outcomes following its completion are mapped through an analytical framework for a series of cases. The position of a researcher conducting program evaluation from within government is explored in the final Chapter 15. This chapter also links back to themes and dilemmas explored in previous theoretical and case study chapters.

## 1.5 Conclusion

The sequence of chapters outlined is, of course, just one possible pathway through the chapters of this book. The reader may choose a completely different path through the chapters and parts presented, allowing exploration of the impact of politics and the incorporated power differentials, including funding, on the work of researchers and evaluators, and of universities, at each stage of the process, from the decision of what are the priority areas of research, impacts on methodology and ethics, outcomes and impacts of research. In addition to exploring the dilemmas, issues and contradictions that arise in a range of international contexts, the personal and professional understandings, beliefs and experiences of a broad range of researchers and evaluators are explored. The negotiation and navigation of these domains provides insight into how potential risks, agendas and stakeholders may be managed to ensure that rigorous and ethical positions and approaches can be maintained in the conduct of research and in the development of evidence-based policy and its implementation based upon it.

Chapter 2

# The problem of the policy agora
How power differentials, methodological naivety and the ideological preferences of policy-makers affect the development of government policy

*Chris Brown*

## 2.1 Introduction

The notion of using evidence to aid policy is not without controversy or debate (see, for example, Hargreaves, 1996; Hillage et al., 1998; Tooley and Darby, 1998; Biesta, 2007; Nutley et al., 2007). Notwithstanding these issues, this chapter is grounded in the idea that engaging with evidence is socially beneficial. This premise is explicated through the work of advocates such as Oakley, who argues that there exists a moral imperative for policy-makers to only make decisions, or to take action, when armed with the best available evidence; also described by Alton-Lee (2012) as the 'first do no harm' principle. Similarly, it is acknowledged that failing to employ the best available evidence can lead to situations where public money is wasted (for example if vulnerable members of society are not offered treatments or interventions at points in their lives where doing so might provide most benefit). This is typified in the work of Scott et al. (2001) who, in their analysis of the financial cost of social exclusion, note that acts of antisocial behaviour (ASB) at the age of 10 are accurate predictors of the cost of public services consumed by a given group at age 28; typically a cost 10 times that of those with no ASB issues. Yet such costs could be avoided by policy-makers adopting effective and timely intervention strategies.

Nonetheless, facilitating the meaningful or sustained use of evidence is no simple matter: assuming that we believe it is beneficial to do so, evidence use is not something that can be effectively introduced into policy development simply by researchers providing a catalogue of 'tips and tricks'. On the contrary, policy-making is a socially situated activity; correspondingly I argue that, if it is to be 'evidence-informed', we are required to engage with the complexity of the social world and to take this complexity into account. Policy-making, for example, often represents a tension between 'optimal' decision-making (i.e. that which might lead to the best improvements for the most numbers of people) and short-lived, ever-changing ideologies or perspectives, with decisions on the education system being made under public scrutiny. It also presents a situation within which it is acknowledged that differentials in power can affect or limit interactions between policy-makers and research/ers (e.g. Hargreaves, 1996; Davies, 2006; Brown, 2013); despite these complexities, however, there have only been few theoretical or empirical examinations of policy development which have directly considered how power affects the use of evidence by policy-makers (existing examples include Ball, 2008 and 2012).

In order to augment extant theory and empirical analysis in this area, the effects of power inequalities between researchers and policy makers were explored in Brown (2011), which sought to answer two broader questions: What factors affect the adoption of research within educational policy making?; and: How might a better understanding of these factors improve research adoption and aid the development of policy? Data from the project (a literature review and 24 in-depth, semi-structured interviews) have been used within this paper to explore four key areas. First, I outline current conceptualisations of how power operates in society. Second, I use the notion of the policy 'agora' to spotlight the implications of power inequalities for the use of evidence in the development of policy. Third, I define what I consider as evidence 'misuse', before finally finishing with an analysis of why evidence misuse materialises and also how its enactment might be minimised.

## 2.2 Power and policy development

I use this first section of the chapter to outline contemporary conceptualisations of how power operates in society; whilst also situating this within and in relation to policy-making. I do so by juxtaposing the work of Jürgen Habermas and Michel Foucault. Both Foucault and Habermas have examined notions of power and governance, and both have developed very different perspectives. At the same time these perspectives can broadly be seen as representing the two dominant schools of thought relating to evidence-informed policy (e.g. Brown, 2009; 2014): that is, they can be seen to represent the ideal vs. the reality. Correspondingly, the conclusions reached by Foucault and Habermas, and so the implications of their work for how evidence might impact on policy development would appear to be in tension and, as a consequence, they are unable to both exist simultaneously. In order to explore power and it implications for policy development we therefore need to argue for one or the other to act as our theoretical frame.

I begin by examining the work of Jürgen Habermas, who is principally concerned with how rational decision-making can be facilitated in modern democratic societies. Habermas's thesis is dependent on his theory of 'communicative action'; action oriented towards reaching agreement, which, Habermas contends, is the fundamental type of social action. In turn, communicative action depends on a further premise; the notion that discourse is used by people as an everyday process of making claims to validity. These two premises enable Habermas to conceive of civic life as comprising networks of relationships that display two principle characteristics: first they are cooperative – this is because the success of any interaction depends upon the interdependent activity of both narrators and audiences (respectively as producers and receivers of the communicative act); second that discourse must have a rational dimension: a narrator will seek to provide reasons for the validity of their communicative act, knowing that their counterpart (the audience) may either accept it or counter it with a better argument. Habermas's twin premises of mutual agreement and discursive validity also allow him to set out a vision which positions valid and rational arguments as the basis for all major decisions. In other words, in a Habermasian-based society, public acts of praxis are ultimately determined by what Habermas describes as 'the force of the better argument', which represents a 'cooperative search for *truth*' (1990, p. 198: my emphasis). Habermas thus conceives of power as something that can be constantly ameliorated by rationality: power is only afforded to individuals or institutions in instances where they can successfully argue their case. The notion of the better argument, meanwhile, is required to be 'policed' by rules established by Habermas to uphold the validity of arguments (Habermas' five 'tenets' of discourse ethics: Habermas & Cooke, 1999).

The Habermasian approach would appear to reflect much of the essence of the rhetoric of being 'evidence-informed'. For example, the consequence of Habermas's analysis emphasises decision-making that is informed by: widespread public participation; the extensive sharing of information that might inform decisions; consensus reached through public dialogue rather than the exercise of bureaucratic power; a reduction of the privilege afforded to policy-makers based solely on their position; and the morphing of the role of policy-maker from policy technician to that of the reflective practitioner (Argyris and Schön, 1974). As such, Habermas argues that the legitimacy of praxis cannot simply be viewed in terms of whether individuals (undertaking public roles) have acted intra vires, but also on the nature and the quality of the deliberation that preceded this action. Evidence therefore has a key role to play in shaping decisions via actions such as informing citizens with regards to particular issues, or providing decision-makers or social actors with a myriad of perspectives with which to inform their decisions/actions. Researchers in a Habermasian system are thus afforded pivotal positions as both gatekeepers to and interpreters of knowledge whilst using this to uphold the freedoms of individuals.

## 2.3 Michel Foucault

A counter position to Habermas's democratic approach is provided by Michel Foucault. Habermas's notion of power and its amelioration by legal and democratic frameworks contrasts significantly with that of Foucault, who argues that his own analysis is only possible because it has 'abandon[ed] the juridical model . . . [that] makes the law the basic manifestation of power'

(Foucault, 2004, p. 265). Whilst Habermas argues for a system governed by universally accepted and applicable democratic principles, Foucault argues that such principles do not exist. Instead, Foucault suggests that the worldviews of social groups are contextually grounded (and so truth, 'perspectival and strategic': 2004, p. 268). Such a position not only rules out Habermas's invocation of the general principle of 'the better argument', since there is no neutral or a priori way in which this can be judged. It also negates the possibility of social groups or institutions operating in ways that might be considered 'value neutral' or in accordance with any universal imperative. Subsequently, rather than concern himself with the construction of mechanisms which provide a blueprint for how utopian government might operate, Foucault's work is 'genealogical'; it describes the genesis of a given situation in order to illustrate how it was arrived at. This enables Foucault to demonstrate that what is often taken for granted has not always been so and that alternatives are possible. Foucault specifically describes the task of laying open norms and the identification of alternatives as: 'criticiz[ing] the working of institutions which appear to be both neutral and independent; to criticize them in such a manner that the political violence which has always exercised itself obscurely through them will be unmasked, so that one can fight them' (Chomsky and Foucault, 1974, p. 171).

A natural extension of this line of argument is that those in power are better placed to promote their perspectives as 'normal'. Foucault describes this notion as the 'will to knowledge'; the desire by social groups to advance their version of events. Key to the successful operation of the 'will to knowledge' is how knowledge might be disseminated: this affects how power is enforced or maintained and how it is undermined. Foucault suggests that this role is played by discourse. For instance, in terms of maintaining power, Foucault (1980) argues that each society has a 'regime of truth': discursive realities which are not only accepted as true, but which are also made to function as true (e.g. via affording status to those charged with pronouncing the truth). In such cases, the dissemination of discourse facilitates control over what those in power wish to promote as the truth: power is synonymous with the promotion of the 'true' knowledge of the status quo and the discourse that results is specifically designed to uphold the current, specific 'regime of truth'. Foucault (1978, pp. 100–101) also notes, however, that: 'discourses are not once and for all subservient to power . . . discourse can be both an instrument and an effect of power, but also a hindrance, a stumbling block, a point of resistance and a starting point for an opposing strategy'. Discourses formed as part of the appropriation of knowledge can also be used, therefore, to seek to undermine existing power relations through the promotion of alternative 'truth regimes'. Foucault (1988) also suggests that a powerful way to achieve this is through the idea of 'practising criticism': a genealogical approach that involves dismantling the assumptions and the tacit unchallenged thinking on which particular arguments or discourses rest.

## 2.4 The policy agora

The analysis above opens the possibility that the use of evidence use by policy-makers is unlikely to be dependent on how well researchers have argued the case for its inclusion (the Habermasian approach). Instead, the topics of investigation, the methods researchers employ and the way in which evidence is communicated and/or married to policy issues, can potentially all be affected by the discourse of government; i.e. by any given government's 'regime of truth'. Should this be true then a logical consequence is the suggestion that, if researchers wish to influence policy, they will need to ensure that their subject areas, approaches and narratives are compatible with either current or nascent dominant political philosophy and/or ideas that are currently privileged (by government or those in opposition), or risk their work being excluded. Ideological and epistemological salience (both in terms of methodology and in terms of 'surface-level' concerns) are thus likely to be key drivers in determining which evidence policy-makers are likely to adopt.

By including in this analysis the notions of 'Mode 2' knowledge and the agora, however, I am able to formalise this analysis by establishing the notion of the 'policy agora' and to use it as a tool to illustrate how power operates with regards to evidence adoption: Gibbons et al. (1994) use the notion 'Mode 2' knowledge to represent research designed to be applied to specific problems right from its very inception. Gibbons et al. (1994) also posit that the validity of any knowledge produced will, in part, be determined by its users; this is referred to as the 'social robustness' of knowledge. In addition to the concept of 'Mode 2', Nowotny et al. (2003) and Gibbons (1999) also posit the idea of the 'agora' or the market place in which 'Mode 2' knowledge is both produced and 'traded', and suggest that within the agora sit numerous evidence 'experts', both academic and non-academic, with whom policy-makers might engage to help find solutions to such problems.

As a resultant entity, the policy agora therefore represents the conjoin of the discursively established, ideological and epistemological preferences of policy-makers. The boundaries of the agora are thus defined by the range of ideas that are currently ideologically acceptable to policy-makers (as determined by the political priorities of the government of the day), juxtaposed against their epistemological concerns; for instance, whether a 'what works'-type methodological approach has been employed and/or whether outputs have been designed to be 'policy-ready' (Brown, 2013). Within these boundaries of ideology and epistemology sits a space filled with the gamut of evidence that policy-makers are most likely to consider when developing policy (bearing in mind that they may not consider any evidence at all). Conversely, studies or ideas outside of the agora are more likely to be criticised and rejected: Ouimet et al. (2009) argue, for example, that if evidence is seen as politically irrelevant, then government departments are unlikely to spend significant resources attempting to engage with its findings. Censure or exclusion will also relate to the method employed by a research study and the type of evidence or suggestions such studies can provide to policy-makers. Likewise, within the agora will also sit numerous evidence providers, both academic and non-academic, with whom policy-makers might engage to help find solutions to such problems. The proposed nature of this 'wider' environment that determines which evidence is considered by policy-makers is illustrated diagrammatically in Figure 2.1, below.

Based on the Foucaultian position, I argue that any given agora is established and will be held in position by the discourse employed by policy-makers. Whilst discursive dominance results in the normalisation of a particular ideological or epistemological position, the boundaries or the policy agora are, however, capable of shifting and changing. One cause for such a shift will be through the political process; for example, the election of a new party (or coalition of parties) to government is almost certainly likely to lead to shifts or changes in the ideological or political paradigm as new policy commitments are introduced, based on new ideologies, evidence or ideas which had, hitherto, existed outside of the agora (an example of this in relation to 'restorative justice' is given in Brown, 2011). Another way a policy agora might be shifted is via a growing weight of evidence for alternative viewpoints (see Brown, 2013). As a result, the nature of the ideological and epistemological paradigms that form the agora will also be a function of the existence of a wider corpus of knowledge or perspectives. Thus, policy agoras will be broadly centred on dominant points of view (which form the mainstay of discursively promoted social realities) until these are shifted by the force of any consensus. I now set out to validate the concept of the agora and to suggest its nature, and 'shape' or areas of content, based on my abductive thematic analysis of interview data and current literature. I begin by looking at what interview data revealed regarding extant discourse on evidence use.

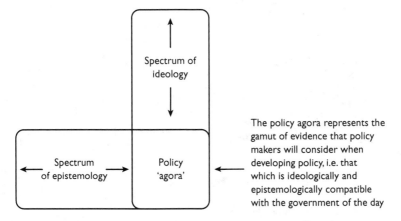

Figure 2.1 The policy 'agora': the wider environment that determines which evidence is considered by policy-makers.

## 2.5 Discourse in relation to evidence-use in educational policy development

In my interviews with researchers and policy-makers, I witnessed and recorded a wealth of interesting discourse concerning the interaction between policy and evidence/policy-makers and researchers. At a macro level, this discourse seemed to be directed at three main areas: first, the level of sympathy evidence exhibits with regards to any currently dominant ideology (and the need for it to be so in order for it to be considered by policy-makers in the formation of policy); second, the need for evidence to conform to the epistemological concerns of policy-makers (typically the positivist in nature, see Brown, 2013); last, also ensuring that policy-makers' 'surface level' epistemological concerns were met: for instance, with regards to how evidence is presented and how findings are equated or married with policy issues.

For example, of those I interviewed, all (both policy-makers and researchers) agreed, suggested or concurred that policy-makers require research inputs (i.e. topics of investigation) to be compatible with the residing political beliefs of the day and with the current direction of policy travel. In addition, that those responsible for policy will challenge or attempt to squash findings which are seen to run counter to given policy, or even to undermine the researchers providing them. One interviewee, a former government minister, recounted the following example:

> When we launched the . . . strategy [a respected academic researcher] . . . said that the . . . strategy was rubbish . . . [their own research undermined it], . . . we'd got [second respected academic] to work on it and we felt that it was evidence-based. [The critique came] . . . at a very difficult time for us politically. What we . . . did was try and undermine it and never spoke to [the researcher providing the critique] again.

One academic respondent described the following two situations where particular evidence was seen to run counter to the government of the day's beliefs and chosen policies and the subsequent reaction by policy-makers to this:

> I had a . . . run-in with [a former Secretary of State] . . . where we described evidence which was very solid against [the direction the government were taking with policy 1]. . . . we had an absolutely vituperative letter back . . . it was quite extraordinary and obviously [prompted by] knowledge . . . 'actually the research might be right but I don't want to hear it and I'm going to rubbish anybody who says so'.

And second concerning a second policy:

> the research hit the headlines and it wasn't just our research, there was a number of other pieces of research showing that [policy 2] didn't have

much effect on primary standards but obviously that was against the policy [direction]. So . . . I had kind of public dressing-down for that.

Those I interviewed also noted that methodological approaches must be considered 'robust', and sit within policy-makers' preferred epistemological paradigm. Civil service respondents, for instance, illustrated how studies viewed as incompatible with favoured epistemologies were handled in order that findings might be 'legitimately' dismissed or ignored. Preference was also regularly afforded to larger-scale studies and meta-analyses:

> Where the research is slight [it] wouldn't pass [our] quality control test . . . there's lots of little research [projects] in the system. We're big fans of systematic reviews.

## 2.6 The discourse of marketisation

Researchers and evidence were also positioned, however, by discourse that made reference to other 'ideals' that needed to be met, or to deficits that needed to be overcome. For example, my interviews with policy-makers and researchers spotlighted that a nascent trend in evidence use is the requirement by educational policy-makers for 'policy-ready' research findings (see Brown, 2013). Other trends included the growing plethora of think tanks seeking to influence policy and the notion of 'socially robust' knowledge. I also argue in Brown (2011, 2014) that, in acting as choice-laden consumers and in picking and choosing from the multitude of knowledge providers which now provide outputs that are 'policy-ready', policy-makers have implicitly begun to 'marketise' the practice of research. As a process, marketisation thus serves to introduce competition amongst evidence producers, with those organisations able to deliver the 'ideal' of 'policy-ready' findings (or whose ideologies are most compatible), patronised and privileged over others.

During my interviews I was able to directly observe 'policy-ready' marketisation in action, via the ways in which evidence was described and discussed. Trowler (2003) suggests that, as a phenomenon, marketisation will involve the distillation and appropriation of discursive repertoires from business or marketing and from the language of consultancies or think tanks. For the policy-makers I interviewed, this initial permeation could be easily observed where, for instance, 'policy-ready'-related phrases or words such as: 'solutions', 'ideas', 'applications', 'implementation', 'impact', 'rendered fit for policy use' were all used when making reference to evidence. It also could be seen, however, in the discourses employed by those researchers who actively attempt to influence policy or produce 'policy-ready' outputs (i.e. these researchers had incorporated and were acting in response to a discourse that had been originated by policy-makers). This is illustrated in the following example:

> If you don't have that work in the middle to translate basic research into [policy applications] then it's very unlikely that research is going to influence anything.

The researchers not making this type of attempt, however, continued to employ more traditional academic phrases when describing what their research output might reveal about the empirical world, for example by using terms such as: 'perspectives', 'critique', 'inform', 'complexity' and so on.

In theory at least, the process of marketisation, as it relates to 'policy-ready' findings, can be considered a positive phenomenon. This is because it serves to improve the output of researchers/universities by relating them to customer/public need (Shore and Wright, 1999). Outputs thus become spurred by what is required by society (via government) rather than by the whims or desires of individuals (i.e. outputs become more efficient uses of resource); as a result, the behaviours and actions of social actors become more efficient by being linked to these outputs. The discourse of 'policy-ready' can also operate to the detriment of researchers, however; with policy-makers expecting researchers to go beyond their traditional skill sets and spend more resources in producing specific types of evidence output but without either assisting this process or administering any reward for researchers doing so. For example, an examination of what was *not* said by policy-makers concerning 'policy-ready' outputs also proved poignant: policy-makers made no suggestion, for instance, that 'policy-ready' outputs should be born out of acts of partnership or that they (policy-makers) had a role in transforming research outputs. These omissions came despite the practical experience of policy that is required in order to produce 'policy-ready' output; the proven effectiveness of partnership working in such situations (Sylva et al., 2007; Taggart et al., 2008); the obligations on policy-makers to explicitly specify their requirements from research so that they might be met by researchers (Rickinson et al., 2011), as well as the benefits to policy-makers themselves.

In addition, on the flipside of such discourse, policy-makers were also prone to promote a 'deficit' model of research(ers). For example, in my interviews, most policy-makers put forward comments in a similar vein to the following:

> The way research is presented isn't helpful. It's presented, not interpreted . . . fit for policy use . . . it doesn't say . . . what the applications are . . . Researchers often . . . say, 'that's not my job. My job is to report the world as it is' . . . Well thanks, but we pay . . . for that privilege.

Researchers also set out the argument from their side of the fence:

> lot of emphasis on improving communication from research side . . . but . . . nothing like the same attention given to policy-makers'

receptiveness... to even engage with the research findings... emphasis is on research deficits, not on policy-makers themselves, how they might be stimulated to take into account the work that is out there.

As a consequence, as well as promoting 'policy-ready' outputs, policy-makers would both castigate those who failed to provide such outputs whilst simultaneously giving primacy to the argument that researchers communicate evidence poorly. In other words, they hold up notions of researcher 'deficit' in preference to other possibilities, for example, with regards to the extent of their [policy-makers'] ability to work in partnership with researchers, or any lack of capacity on the part of policy-makers to take on board academic evidence. The result of such additions to, or omissions from, the discursive lexicon employed by policy-makers is, therefore, that [some] academic researchers change their behaviour to meet that which is required; in other words, they act alone/ without policy-maker assistance in the production of 'policy-ready' (or 'what works') type outputs. Correspondingly, this supersedes the ability for researchers more generally to be able to engage with policy-makers in preferred, alternative ways, for example, through the process of policy 'enlightenment' (Weiss, 1980; 1982), where evidence serves to inform the medium- to long-term policy environment, rather than provide a direct steer on a particular issue (often, however, enlightenment may be the only realistic course available to researchers: for instance, where their research comprises complicated and complex messages that are not prone to an easy distillation into simple recommendations).

There is also no guarantee that policy-makers will subsequently adopt any output that is produced (and so such efforts lead to only nominal benefit for the researcher themselves). An academic response to this 'push' isn't inevitable and this is confirmed by the responses of those interviewed. But, at the same time, the 'move away from traditional expertise' spotlights that, should researchers not wish to succumb to the forces of marketisation, the value of their contribution may be systematically ignored or downgraded (in other words excluded from the agora) and alternative knowledge providers such as 'policy-ready' researchers, think tanks or consultancies privileged instead.

## 2.7 The implications of the policy agora for policy development

Both politics and policy-making is fundamentally ideological in nature. As such, it may appear 'natural' that evidence which is incompatible with the views of the government of the day (i.e. that which sits outside of the agora) should be ignored. However, it was also suggested in my interview sessions that dogmatic adherence to a given set of ideological ideas will, by definition, lead to policy-makers failing to hear alternative views which might add value when attempting to solve a particular issue:

> Well I think if you look at it across educational research you will find a range of different perspectives on many of the issues that policy-makers are concerned about and I think that educational research can be of great value precisely in providing those different perspectives.

In addition, the ideological paradigms for education favoured by both the previous New Labour and the current Conservative government (preceded by the Conservative–Liberal Democrat coalition) have within them common assumptions concerning how education should be structured and enacted in order for it to best serve the interests of the economy. These include, for example, the inclusion of specific subjects within the curriculum and the importance of continuously improving academic exam results (e.g. Ball, 2008, 2012; Eurydice Network, 2012 – this last source specifically looks at the efficacy of entrepreneurial education within schools). One academic researcher I interviewed, however, noted that this focus might not be the most effective approach in terms of meeting economic means:

> Everything is [currently] judged in terms of grading examination papers and that itself is then taken to be an indicator of effectiveness in terms of economic [performance] in the global economy. Yet clearly . . . a lot of research suggests that the sort of learning going on . . . is not [what] the economy [or the knowledge economy] actually requires.

Thus the narrowed and selective view of evidence implied by the existence of the agora is likely to mean that issues at the heart of the policy problem and, importantly, potential ways to address those issues, will not be fully considered. An effective insight, for example, may exist at point 'A', well outside the boundaries of what is being contemplated. Narrowing the 'epistemological infrastructure' (Atkinson, 2000) in this way is therefore likely to impact upon the efficacy of any proposed policy solution to meet its desired aims and move policy-making away from the more effective, efficient and equitable outcomes it is suggested can accrue from considering an evidence base (Oakley, 2000; Oxman et al., 2009). Were policy-makers to consider alternative perspectives, however, this might aid them in preventing instances of 'policy failure': as Hargreaves and Harris (2011) note, the organisations that successfully perform beyond expectations are those that can successfully marry pragmatism (i.e. seeking alternative but effective solutions) with ideology.

## 2.8 Evidence misuse

The notion of the policy agora and its function as an instrument of/tool to maintain power (i.e. through its role in normalising particular ideological and epistemological positions) provides a platform from which I am able to develop the idea of evidence 'misuse'. It is clear from the analysis above that discursive power enables the powerful to successfully determine whether an idea will be privileged or not. That they might champion an idea, however, requires us to make certain assumptions about what motivates policy-makers to act and in turn, this requires us to assume a certain level of rationality exists within the policy system. Specifically, there are three assumptions that must hold here: i) that politicians are driven simultaneously both by ideology (and a desire to perpetuate this ideology through their re-election) and a desire to improve outcomes for at least certain subgroups of the population; ii) that sometimes ideology and tranches of evidence overlap (i.e. evidence is situated within the agora) and government can pursue evidence-informed policies should it wish. On other occasions, however, tranches of evidence will exist outside of what politicians might normally consider and so are most likely to be ignored and excluded by them; and iii) that the type of exclusion described in ii) may be overridden if civil servants (who, unlike their political masters, are required to act in an apolitical way: see Mountfield, 1999; Brown, 2013) are able to identify and then subsume the key messages from such research within the government's current agenda. In other words, to find ways in which pertinent or salient points may be incorporated to improve the efficacy of the government's preferred course of action, without necessarily adopting them as wholesale changes to policy direction (i.e. ensuring a policy is as optimal as it can be, within the aims, desires and constraints of political ideology).

As a consequence, I suggest that evidence misuse should be regarded as a situation in which any policy optimum is suppressed. Especially so if this suppression is a function of political unacceptability, rather than where an action or direction is actually unachievable. In defining this situation, I therefore regard evidence misuse as a strategic discursive position, comprising instances of policy-makers successfully developing and implementing policy that ignores the perspectives suggested by a compelling weight of research evidence.

Evidence misuse may be regarded as occurring in a number of situations. For example, when evidence is not used or selective evidence is used post-hoc, and any resultant decision flies in the face of what a corpus of evidence existing within the agora recommends; or when evidence is only selected from within the agora but where pertinent alterative perspectives exist beyond its borders and could be used to enhance a policy decision. Unlike in a Habermassian system, where this situation would be regarded as a result of government's failure to install systems to facilitate argument; or via Lukes's (2005) conception of power, where researchers are directly coerced or forced to comply; my notion of evidence misuse is something which flourishes because the existence of discursive control on the part of policy-makers allows its enactment to be normalised and reproduced. In other words it exists and is allowed to exist because policy-makers can: i) appeal to notions of 'common sense' in order to rubbish alternatives to their solutions (or the ideas held most dearly within their given constructed reality); and; ii) can draw down on the deficit argument to argue that evidence is not timely in its production, has not been well communicated or that it fails to provide solutions.

Clearly, the occurrence of evidence misuse is co-dependent on the absence of justifiable cause: evidence misuse should not be considered to occur every time policy-makers fail to implement evidence as policy. Exceptions as to what might be considered as evidence misuse comprise, for example, where what evidence suggests is unaffordable or is simply unachievable, due to a lack of extant infrastructure. My definition does, however, include instances of where alternatives are dismissed simply due to ideological considerations. A quote by one former Secretary of State for Education I interviewed when exploring this topic nicely summarises a hypothetical example of what I consider to be evidence misuse with regards to education policy development. This example refers to the consideration of grammar schools by an incumbent New Labour Government:

> Even in opposition you tend to ignore the research that is counter to your political values . . . so if somebody comes to us and says 'all the evidence says selection works' we are still not going to adopt it [selection], it's just counter to what we do.

Thus if, in theory, a substantial tranche of evidence did indicate that 'selection worked', then civil servants could make attempts to ascertain the social drivers 'selection' activates/invokes. They could then seek to reproduce these drivers in a way more sympathetic to the ideological perspectives of the government of the day. The quote above, however, suggests that any such attempt would have been ruled out or findings dismissed by the Secretary of State at the time: as such I regard it as highlighting how the potential optimality of education policy might be suppressed.

My definition of evidence misuse should not be seen as one which decries value-based politics, however I believe that in a democratic society it is both unfeasible and undesirable to employ a fully technocratic approach to policy development. Politicians will quite rightly want to follow their convictions and/or what they feel they have been given a mandate to carry out by the electorate. They are also required to react in the face of media pressure to specific short-term crises. The voters who elected them will also have been driven by party allegiance (which is often ideological or conviction based) and/or personal experience and/or media spin. As such, it is not my suggestion that politicians must be guided by the force of the better argument (which in the Habermassian system is thus seen to result in the truth), but should, at least in part, be driven by a desire to make their policies as effective as possible by considering what a diverse range of perspectives have to offer.

Defining the concept of evidence misuse in this way should also not be confused with any adoption of a technical, rationalist perspective with regards to the role of research in policy-making. I argue (Brown, 2013) that research serves to aid policy development by allowing policy-makers to make sense of the social world and to anticipate the likely reaction of social actors to policy initiatives. In this sense then, evidence, rather than detail of any objective reality, merely illuminates the range of perspectives that exist in relation to (or behaviours that might occur as a result of) given policy areas/programmes. The potential optimality of a given policy will thus be enhanced as salient perspectives are engaged with. Conversely, refusing to engage with alternative perspectives simply on the basis of dogma or partisanship serves to act as a boundary to the optimality of policies: the smaller the agora the more likely its optimality will be constrained.

In part, limiting the enactment of evidence misuse depends upon an effective differentiation between the roles of politicians and civil servants in the policy process and correspondingly, a re-specification of their respective domains. For example, the effects of evidence misuse will be particularly pronounced in areas such as education where these roles have become 'overlapped'. In other words, in areas where politicians, rather than simply specifying the outcomes they require, also specify the inputs; the particular policies and programmes that might serve to achieve these outputs. This occurs when, for instance, politicians specify particular modes of pedagogy (for instance teaching via specific types of phonics) or the exact subjects that should form part of the curriculum (as opposed to stating that reading and writing skills need to be improved, or that children should receive a broader curriculum or one which works to reduce the instances of them developing extremist attitudes, etc.). One example of this type of prescription is the Secretary of State for Education Michael Gove's attempted reform of the national curriculum in England and Wales. In June 2012, *The Guardian* newspaper announced that Gove's proposals had been decried as 'fatally flawed' by Professor Andrew Pollard, a member of the expert panel involved in advising on the changes.[1] The reasons for this, it would seem, include Pollard's view that Gove and Schools Minister Nick Gibb had already decided upon a desired course of action. Pollard argues in his blog,[2] for example, that 'the voice that has really counted from beginning to the end has been that of an American educator, Ed Hirsch . . .' and that 'When I first met Nick Gibb, Hirsch's Core Knowledge Sequence was open on his desk, heavily stickered with Post-It notes'. Subsequently, Professor Pollard suggests that: 'it is Hirsch's very detailed year-on-year model that has prevailed. This was one of the main issues which caused the Expert Panel as a whole to withdraw from the development of programmes of study, leaving only Tim Oates [the head of the review team] to work with Ministers'. In other words, Ministers had decided on a specific course of action and on detailed changes that they had wished to make, leaving very little scope for expert advisors, or others, to suggest alternatives.

That this might comprise evidence misuse is highlighted in *The Guardian's* article when it is noted by Christine Blower, General Secretary of the National Union of Teachers, that: 'It is extraordinary that the secretary of state would establish an expert panel to look into the national curriculum and then choose to ignore their advice. This government seems determined to impose its vision of education regardless of the evidence or professional opinion.' Likewise, comments by Stephen Twigg (Labour's current shadow Education Secretary), also point to Gove's proposals constituting a misuse of evidence: 'It now seems that after commissioning an in-depth review, the government is ignoring many of its recommendations in favour of its own prejudice. [The government] should put evidence ahead of dogma when it comes to education. The curriculum mustn't be prey to political ideology.'

## 2.9 Conclusion

Over the course of this chapter, I have examined extant notions of power, presented a definition of evidence misuse and illustrated its negative consequences. In particular, I have juxtaposed the ways in which Habermas and Foucault tackle notions of power, arguing that whilst both focus on how civic society does or might function, they employ fundamentally opposing approaches. In doing so I have highlighted the tension between the ideal of evidence-informed policy, where decisions are made in keeping with the 'force of the better argument' and the often-experienced reality, where discourse serves to influence what this better argument might be. Combining this analysis with my data, I have set out the notion of the policy agora, a concept grounded firmly in Foucaultian notions of discursive control and 'regimes of truth' and have illustrated how a narrowly defined policy agora will serve to prevent the development of policy that is perhaps 'truly' effective, efficient and equitable in nature (with the resultant notion of evidence misuse applying to actions which seek, because of dogmatic concerns, to narrow the agora at the cost of optimality).

I have also suggested, however, that in a democratic society it is both unfeasible and undesirable to employ a fully technocratic approach to policy development (also see Brown, 2013). The process of policy-making requires more than an ability to read evidence, judge its quality and then enact its findings; policy-makers whether politicians or civil servants must employ both values and a wealth of skills when deciding what is right for the education of a nation. This leads me to conclude that evidence misuse, while detrimental to the optimality of policy development, cannot and should not be totally eliminated from the policy process. At the same time, however, it is exactly because policy development based on dogmatic ideological adherence is unlikely to result in truly effective solutions that instances of evidence misuse should be kept to an appropriate level. To do so requires balance; the establishment of an appropriate mix between the development by politicians of ideological, strategic, choices on educational outcomes (which should be considered an integral part of the democratic process) and the employment of evidence to help inform the most effective ways to meet these outcomes by civil servants.

## Notes

1 The full article may be accessed via: http://www.guardian.co.uk/education/2012/jun/12/michael-gove-curriculum-attacked-adviser.
2 The blog entry may be accessed via: http://ioelondonblog.wordpress.com/2012/06/12/proposed-primary-curriculum-what-about-the-pupils/

Chapter 3

# 'What works?'
## From health to education, the shaping of the European policy of evidence

*Romuald Normand*

## 3.1 Introduction

Evidence-based policy (EBP) seeks to answer one question: what works as a public policy in the areas of health, education, justice, and welfare? It is imposed as a "gold standard", claimed for its experimental robustness. This "political experimentalism" is at the crossroads of science, expertise and policy and it has been institutionalised as a discourse of truth addressing criticism of current educational research. It legitimises institutions and technologies supporting other intervening modes of the Welfare State.

EBP can also be considered as an epistemic regime defined as transforming explicitly or implicitly stable forms of knowledge and evaluative instruments while it legitimises new actors sharing the same norms, interests and conventions regarding a certain vision of the relationship between science and policy. This epistemic regime introduces a new division of labour while it transforms modalities of evidence and standards in the production of knowledge in a time of information systems, big data and digital economy. In this chapter, evidence-based policy trajectories in health and education areas are described at international and European levels. Beyond the translation and hybridisation of some international norms, we analyse some mechanisms of policy borrowing and knowledge transfer in national contexts as well as the way this epistemic and instrumental regime is built as a science of government (Lascoumes & Le Gales, 2007a).

As it has been proved in the case of international indicators (Normand, 2009; Lawn & Normand, 2014; Henry, Lingard, Rizvi & Taylor, 2001), technologies of evidence are transferred and borrowed between countries. The chapter focuses on policies which introduce and institutionalise these technologies at the core of the State, particularly with the development of New Public Management and the restructuring of the Welfare State. In taking some examples from education and health, we analyse some arguments, devices and types of mobilisation which have contributed to the success of these new technologies. The chapter also describes the changing conditions of educational sciences and the emergence of a "regulatory objectivity" producing hierarchies of evidence in research (Cambrosio, Keating & Bourret, 2007; Jasanoff, 2011).

In the following pages, the epistemological foundations of technologies of evidence are set out. They legitimise a new mode of production of scientific knowledge while educational sciences are accused of being incapable of adopting the same quality.[1] This new "experimentalism" has been first introduced in evidence-based medicine and US health public policies. We show how it has been extended in the area of education. In the second part of the chapter, we characterise the use of this political technology within the UK Third Way policies, particularly in public evaluation programmes focused on "at risk" populations. The last part is devoted to studying the international circulation of evidence-based technologies from local configurations in New Zealand to transnational networks linking and associating local actors into worldwide collaborations and international projects.

## 3.2 The epistemology of evidence-based technologies

The epistemology behind evidence-based technologies strongly challenges the academic tradition of educational sciences. First, it institutionalises a "hierarchy of evidence" for which Randomised Controlled Trials (RCTs) are positioned at the first rank above upper quasi-experimental devices, systematic reviews of research literature, and meta-analyses. Ethnography and case studies based on interviews and observations are positioned at a minor rank.

Technologies of evidence legitimise the Mode 2 of knowledge production (Gibbons, Limoges, Nowotny, Shwartzman, Scott & Trow, 1994). The latter considers that the production of knowledge must be improved by ending the compartmentalisation of academic disciplines, the heterogeneity of methods, and the fragmentation of research findings. New standards and criteria have to be developed to organise a breakdown with the interpretative pluralism. The "functionalist" model, so criticised in social sciences during the 1980s–1990s, gains a certain legitimacy (Weiss, 1979). Assuming a direct link between the production of evidence and decision-making, and considering the model of natural sciences as a standard, it proposes to reduce the gap between scientific knowledge and social problems faced by reformers.

The experimental approach is praised for bringing closer producers and users of knowledge in a function of "mediation" inspired by health monitoring systems. Research findings have to be translated into platforms, websites, and other media to better inform policy-makers and practitioners and to associate them into knowledge production and transfer. This function of "brokerage" is now developed by the creation of numerous "portals". One of the best known devices is the UK Educational Evidence Portal. International organisations like Cochrane and Campbell, the EPPI-Centre (Evidence for Policy and Practice Information Coordination-Centre), the Social Care Institute for Excellence, the National Institute for Clinical Excellence, are active brokerage agencies in the areas of health, education and social welfare.

## 3.3 The development of the US evidence-based policy in health and education

To understand the creation and dissemination of the US evidence-based policy, it is necessary to come back to changes in the evaluation of federal programmes during the 1970s. These occurred in an ideological climate hostile to social sciences. In health as well as in education, randomised control trials (RCTs) and hierarchy of evidence have been promoted to challenge usual techniques of evaluation and assessment.

### *3.3.1 The return of positivism in public evaluations*

At the beginning of the 1970s, a science of evaluation had emerged in the US, but with different theoretical currents. The psychologist Donald T. Campbell had published a paper noticed by specialists in this area of research (Campbell, 1969). Campbell made claims for adopting a new experimental approach in social reforms. Some "true" experiments required subject groups of individuals to be treated and compared with control groups. The evaluation of public policy, to be validated, had to expose some individuals to different randomised treatments corresponding to the experimental approach principles. Campbell's book proposed to extend "the logic of laboratory" to the whole of society. With the statistician Julian C. Stanley, he also published another book claiming for a new standard in social sciences by which the social scientist would become the "methodological servant of the experimental society" (Campbell & Stanley, 1963).

This strengthening of methodological requirements in public evaluation was made in a conservative climate against social sciences. While the federal state's empowering capacities were reduced because of the economic crisis, social programmes were put under pressure to increase their performance and effectiveness. The Government Accountability Office, in charge of evaluation and audit for the US Congress, wanted to promote controlled experiments, and this was supported by members of the parliament, governmental agencies, and the federal administration. Consequently, randomised controlled trials (RCTs) were extended into economic and social policies, and even into the areas of police and justice. For example, the Spouse Assault Replication Program has developed controlled experiments to assess the impact of warrants for arrest on the diminution of offences.

Controlled trials served also to assess incentives of social reforms on "at risk" young people's behaviours. Different programmes were launched: New Chance, the LEAP (Learning, Earning, and Parenting Program) in Ohio, Learnfare in Wisconsin, and the Teenage Parents Demonstration Project in New Jersey and Illinois. In the area of education, one of the most important experiments was an evaluation conducted in Tennessee. From 1985 to 1990, the project STAR (or Tennessee Student/Teacher Achievement Ratio Experiment) has been a large-scale controlled experiment measuring the effect of class-size reduction on school achievement (Mosteller & Boruch, 2002). Its findings have been used to persuade teacher trade unions that additional public expenses in education would be a source of waste. This evaluation has also remained a landmark for economists of education promoting human capital theory and controlled experiments.

### 3.3.2 Evidence-based medicine and international metrology

Evidence-based policy principles were developed in the medical world under the influence of pharmaceutical industries (Marks, 2000). During the 1990s, the epidemiologist David Sackett, one of the eminent representatives of evidence-based medicine, had noticed the variety of treatments used by physicians, and proposed new methods to test medical interventions, to evaluate their clinical and scientific validity, and to educate physicians in the use of systematic reviews of research literature. He considered "controlled randomised trials" as a methodological "gold standard" for medicine (Timmermans & Berg, 2003). In addition to these works, official reports ordered by foundations and governmental agencies pointed out the failure of medical care, the problems generated by the increase of medical expenditures, and the necessity to use RCTs in diagnoses (Berg, 1997).

For some professionals and policy-makers, evidence-based medicine provides a lot of advantages. It reassures practitioners about the effectiveness of treatments and associated risks. Government agencies can define recommendations and design guidelines of best practice to improve the effectiveness and quality of care. Epidemiologists defend the extent of health monitoring systems to alert public authorities about problems faced by "at risk" populations. US courts use the findings of evidence-based medicine to make judgements about good or bad medical practices in conflicts between opposing physicians and patients (or their associations).

During this period, the Agency for Health Care Policy and Research was created. Its objectives are to promote and disseminate guidelines provided by evidence-based medicine. Centralised by an agency, the National Guideline Clearinghouse, the agency has to transform the knowledge of physicians and medical practice. At the same time, in the UK, the National Health Service (NHS) launched a R&D programme to change the production of evidence in medical care. British authorities offered Iain Chalmers and his colleagues the task of developing RCTs in the area of natal and prenatal clinics. From this experience, they created the Cochrane Collaboration to develop systematic reviews at a global scale (Timmermans & Kolker, 2004). Some collaborative review groups (CRGs), organised in networks, gather todays' experts and scientists in charge of quality in protocols of evaluation, compilation of resources, and training of other colleagues. In a few years, the Cochrane Collaboration has created several dozen world-wide centres and it has developed big data banks as well as a register of RCTs to deliver recommendations of best practice. An infrastructure, similar to the Cochrane Collaboration, was also created in the area of education, welfare, crime and justice: the Campbell Collaboration. Born in the US, in the wake of Donald T. Campbell's ideas, the Campbell Collaboration has developed its own data bank named C2-SPECTR, or Campbell Collaboration Social, Psychological, Educational and Criminological Trials Register, from RCTs and systematic reviews of literature extended to the area of welfare policies: education, justice, crime, social work, etc.

### 3.3.3 The extension of evidence-based policy in education

During the 1980s, after several cuts in budgets for education, and in a climate of scepticism towards large programmes, the US Office of Educational Research and Improvement (OERI) played an active role in restructuring educational research. Researchers were accused of being insufficiently trained in evaluation, contrary to physicians linked to pharmaceutical industries. Consequently, the OERI influenced the Academy of Sciences which produced a damning report about the quality of educational sciences and made claims for adopting more rigorous methodologies related to coherent, explicit and more understandable modes of reasoning for practitioners and policy-makers. This criticism, addressed at educational research and sciences, was supported by complex networks of neoconservative think tanks and foundations able to diffuse numerous ideas taking place at the same in the neoconservative political agenda (Spring, 2005). Through these networks, some policy-makers like Chester Finn or advisers like Diane Ravitch, because of their long stay at the federal government or in US foundations, were successful in influencing the media beyond the capacities of educational academics and researchers. In 1982, they created the Educational Excellence Network within the Hudson Institute, a network supported by the Thomas B. Fordham Foundation. The Educational Excellence Network flooded the public space with incessant political recommendations, briefs, bills, and reports. Finn and Ravitch argued that federal programmes were under the control of a federal elite and that the financial support of educational research centres was leading to an excessive leftist politicisation. From these assumptions, they were very active in developing evidence-based policy.

In 1998, under the influence of interest groups, the US congress voted for an annual budget of $150 billion to fund education reforms based on evidence. At the beginning of the 2000s, a bill calling for more rigour in educational research and the development of RCTs, was examined.[2] Even though it was not adopted, it gave birth to a coalition of experts and researchers, close to the US New Right, defending the policy of evidence (the Coalition for Evidence-Based Policy).

Robert Boruch (a well-known expert in the technologies of evidence at the origin of the creation of the Campbell Collaboration), Diane Ravitch (spokeswoman of the neo-conservatives), and Robert Solow (the economist representing the economic orthodoxy) were all members of the coalition. It had lobbyists close to US policy-makers and members of the parliament, but also to the National Science Foundation, to promote technologies of evidence in welfare and health policies. The No Child Left Behind Act (2001), which has defined the new objectives of federal policy in education, has resumed these recommendations. This act stipulates that educational research has to test hypotheses and to use experimental or quasi-experimental devices such as RCTs. In 2002, the Institute of Education Sciences (IES[3]) was created, and it continues to prescribe some evidence-based standards and "best practices".

### 3.3.4 Evidence as a political technology in the UK Welfare State

The story of US evidence-based policy in education and health shows that these technologies have succeeded in persuading policy-makers seeking short-term answers and eager to reduce public research budgets. Evidence-based technologies have transformed the UK Welfare State. New measurement tools have been used to assess individual and collective risks in social intervention programmes in health and education. In putting away pluralistic modes of evaluation, which did not fit urgent decision-making and short-term political mandates, British authorities have privileged new modes in the production of evidence. They have facilitated the mobilisation of "stakeholders" for elaborating consensuses and techniques aiming to reach a certain "objectivity" in the treatment of social issues. In doing so, evidence-based policy-making (EBPM) has redefined the relationships between science and policy.

### 3.3.5 The "Third Way" experimental and social policy

Over the 2000s, National Health Service's policy-makers thought that issues of education, welfare and crime were related to public health. International organisations like Campbell and Cochrane Collaborations were invited to participate in a large project, the Wider Public Health Project, to collect evidence on health policies. This evidence-based policy was largely included in New Labour's modernising agenda. Researchers, analysts and policy-makers wanted to identify "what works". In 1997, the White Paper The New NHS proposed reform to the public health system while the Labour government were explaining that health services and treatments of patients had to be profitable and to lay on evidence.

Then, the government facilitated the creation of a set of official organisations to explore and disseminate "what works" in health, education and social welfare. The National Institute for Clinical Excellence made evaluations and formulated national guidelines. In the area of welfare, the Social Care Institute for Excellence produced similar data and tools. The Evidence for Policy and Practice Information and Coordinating Centre, created in 1993, launched a journal, *Evidence & Policy*, to promote widespread use of new modes of evidence. The objective was to conduct systematic reviews of research literature, to develop methodological tools, to implement procedures and training sessions about assessment and to maintain a data bank for users and policy-makers.[4] Methods were borrowed from the Cochrane Collaboration and the Campbell Collaboration. In education, the EEPI-Centre focused its actions on schools and students, and managed knowledge according to different standards to make research findings accessible and conform to the criteria defined by evidence-based research. Each review of literature has to precisely meet the chosen protocol and criteria of inclusion/exclusion on the basis of which data are collected from data banks. The review of literature is generally made in two steps: a first step of mapping the research area analysed with key-words to obtain a first descriptive account, then a second and more detailed exploration extracting the most important studies. They include numerous areas: teaching, evaluation and learning, leadership, gender, inclusion, student skills, professional development of teachers, etc.

Though the notion of "evidence" did not directly appear in the White Paper Modernising Government (Cabinet Office, 1999), evidence-based technologies have been disseminated since 1999 in conferences and publications under the supervision of the Economics and Social Research Council. The idea that policy has to be led by evidence of "what works" has progressively appeared in governmental reports (Cabinet Office, 2001; National Audit Office, 2001, 2003). The notion of evidence-based policy-making (EBPM) gained remarkable success amongst policy-makers while public services were transformed to better respond to the users' needs in terms of effectiveness and quality (Davies, Nutley & Smith, 2007; Sanderson, 2002). This technocratic and instrumental conception of public action has then been narrowly related with accountability policy and performance management.

Progressively, EPBM took a place in the strategy of Tony Blair's cabinet and the National Audit Office in charge of social policies evaluation, relevance, cost, and effectiveness inspired by the principles of new public management (Parsons, 2002). The introduction of comprehensive spending reviews (CSRs) or public service agreements (PSAs) was a means to "galvanise" the provision of public services and to lead to "major improvements of results". This new logic of evidence was aimed at replacing a partial and short-term vision of politics among ministerial cabinets for a more rigorous and systematic approach of public expenditures. These hopes were largely unmet (Wells, 2007). However, a profound change in the political culture of national policy-makers occurred: they put away political values to replace them with a "scientific objectification" of "what works" to legitimate decision-making. This new orientation broke with the British political model (or "Westminster model"). Instead of a centralised exercise of power shared with the members of parliament according to traditional mechanisms of political representation, the dispersion of the state's authority among networks and non-governmental agencies reinforced expectations for evaluation and evidence.

### 3.3.6 The UK evidence-based research policy in education

In 1996, during the annual conference of the Teacher Training Agency, David Hargreaves,[5] eminent researcher in education, gave a lecture which had a great echo in the UK scientific community (Hargreaves, 1996). As Professor of Educational Sciences at the University of Cambridge, he resumed some criticism he had addressed to the sociology of education, and this extended his reasoning to education research which was accused of being incapable of serving the UK education system. To support his arguments, he established a comparison with the area of health, in which evidence-based medicine was emerging. Then, he asked the Teacher Training Agency to improve the dissemination of research findings to teachers and to give them the possibility of conducting their own projects instead of relying on academic research with few direct and beneficial impacts on teaching practices. David Hargreaves defended the idea that educational research, contrary to medicine, had no prestige and could not adopt the same technical language. The majority of research projects were not cumulative, while small-scale surveys produced no relevant or conclusive findings.

Alis Oancea analysed the discourses of the new orthodoxy of evidence and the criticism addressed towards educational research, in distinguishing topics and levels of analysis of this denunciation (Oancea, 2005). It is organised in three categories: the diagnosis of the quality, the explanation of dysfunctions, and the solutions to be implemented. The arguments in favour of reform called for a clarification of concepts, a better methodology to prevent biases, some programmes of training for researchers, some changes in the research agenda with a stronger involvement of users, the dissemination of best practices, the strengthening of partnerships and links between research and practice, some changes in the process of funding, the development of systematic reviews, the transformation of evaluation by peers, and the creation of structures for coordination and steering of research.

The debate between the pros and cons was embedded in oppositions related to the accumulation of scientific knowledge (reproduction, dissemination, interdisciplinarity), the needs of a harmonisation of research procedures (in terms of coordination, commensurability, codes of best practices), the rationality in linking policy, practice and research, and the adoption of a teleological or normative vision (improvement of practices, prescriptions, planning, scientific determinism). Researchers opposed to the evidence-based policy denounced this "new orthodoxy" which relies on a linear and cumulative vision of knowledge and a truncated conception of "accountability". Some of them qualified this policy as hidden "instrumentalism", "positivism" or attempt to reinstall "strong sciences" and "rationalism". Others criticised the "maximisation of objectivity" which undermines values, emotions, and subjectivity; the centralism of methodologies to assess quality; the uselessness of lists of criteria to be accountable; the behaviourist description of practices; the "diktat" of the UK Department of Education; and the adoption of a scientific language.

Other criticism was made against the evidence-based policy in education. Maggie Maclure has analysed in detail the systematic reviews conducted by the EPPI-Centre and strongly supported by the UK policy-makers (MacLure, 2005). She shows that the language used to describe and justify this methodology is a mix of old scientific positivism (systematisation, reliability, rigour, and reproduction) and of rhetoric from the culture of audit (transparency, quality, insurance, standards). But the approach of the EPPI-Centre maintains a discourse of mistrust towards academics and researchers accused of being not sufficiently cautious, undemocratic, furtive, unskilled, chaotic, egocentric, etc. However, the work of the technicians/experts who design these systematic reviews has been closely studied by MacLure. They follow very tight protocols and use tools to extract key words from data to synthesise and make an account in an online report. They have not only to conform to the epistemology of evidence, they are also subjected to a neo-Taylorist regime and a managerial discipline which characterise the work within the EPPI-Centre.

Hargreaves's statements have interested policy-makers, however, particularly Chris Woodhead, who was Chief Inspector of Schools and head of the OFSTED, the UK agency of inspection. He also criticised the claimed value of sociology of education and affirmed that academics were only producing bad and poorly written research findings. Two reports were published at the request of the UK Department of Education. The first one, led by James Tooley,[6] considered, from the review of research articles, that a lot of them were faulty (Tooley & Darby, 1998). Chris Woodhead, in the introduction, claimed that the majority of articles were second-hand findings and that a lot of money had been wasted to fund them. Funded by the OFSTED who wanted to raise standards in classrooms, the study resumed the criticism of Hargreaves and defined the good criteria for the evaluation of research: a serious contribution to the theoretical knowledge, a relevance for practice, an upstream and downstream coordination. The second report, the Hillage report, written by researchers from the Institute for Employment Studies at the Sussex University, went further in discussing the quality and utility of research (Hillage, Pearson, Anderson & Tanmkin, 1998).

Following the suggestion of Hargreaves, who called for the creation of an independent forum and a national strategy, the authors of the last report considered that educational research was too often disconnected from teaching practices and inaccessible to teachers. They recommended that research be made more relevant for the members of the education community, to better disseminate good quality results towards users and the public, to contribute to solidifying the existing body of knowledge, to strengthen links between research, policy and practice, to give a greater coherence to research programmes, to require a better relevance and reliability, and to implement quality insurance mechanisms to master public expenditures. The report detailed what should be implemented as new modes of relationships between policy and research: more partnerships and mediations, and quality improvement by evidence-based policy.

The UK government took a series of initiatives to make educational research able to identify the most effective practices to raise standards. It sought to promote "centres of excellence" in allocating special funds to institutions involved in priority areas, in supporting the systematic review and randomised controlled trials to better fit these new strategic objectives. In 2001, after the creation of the EPPI-Centre, the National Educational Research Forum (NERF) was launched to define priorities in funding educational research to better respond to users' needs. The NERF had produced an ambitious document for its national strategy. The Forum had to demonstrate that R&D could play a major role in responding to the needs of education policy, to anticipate changes, and to strengthen the links between research and educational programmes. According to Stephen Ball, this document was "ridiculous and depressing" because of its caricatured conception of research and its apparent ignorance of its main constituents, whilst it wanted to be the starting point of the national consultation (Ball, 2001). The document proved the political will to implement "governance by quality" and to strengthen the steering of research by non-governmental agencies for accountability. It proposed to standardise the objectives and procedures of research, but did not however recognise the diversity of types of educational research and of objectives pursued by different programmes. The NERF also aimed to set up national priorities and to assess researchers' skills. During this period, the Economic and Social Research Council created the Teaching and Learning Research Programme (TLRP) to better respond to the expectations of policy-makers about the effectiveness of research and its capacity to be accountable to "what works". The aim was to federate and to fund researchers focused on the improvement of learning and outcomes involving stakeholders. It was the result of strong political pressure to better articulate teaching practices to evidence-based research and to strengthen accountability. The programme has concentrated a large part of public funds devoted to educational research.

## 3.4 The structure of a European network between science and policy in education

Up to this point, we have considered the emergence and development of evidence-based policy in the US and the UK, in demonstrating how, in health and education areas, new technologies have redrawn modes of the State's social interventions and challenged social and educational sciences. However, these configurations are extended worldwide. The third part of this chapter aims to describe these global scales from the local to the global (Dale & Robertson, 2009). Globalisation is not only a simple interdependence between states. It articulates actors and intra-statist processes with global networks that promote a government-by-numbers and standardised technologies guiding decision-making at local level (Ozga, Dahler-Larsen, Segerholm & Simola, 2011). This multi-scalar globalisation creates transnational dynamics which are embedded in local policies and devices. I present here the space of evidence-based policies' circulation in the area of education. I study the connections by which policy-makers and experts are involved in translation and transfer processes supported by an international organisation like the OECD. Topics of evidence have been gradually included in the European strategy for Lifelong Learning. To illustrate some of these connections, I begin with the case of New-Zealand which has served as a political laboratory in the design and implementation of evidence-based technologies and which has become a model for international organisations. Then, I describe the New-Zealand policy's extension into a project funded by the European Commission which has gathered a great number of experts, stakeholders and policy-makers.

### 3.4.1 New Zealand as a political laboratory

In the beginning of the 2000s, the New-Zealand evidence-based policy was developed from the design of indicators for the education system and the definition of a new strategy for education policy. A Strategic Research Initiative was initiated by the Ministry of Education to make commissions working together from systematic reviews of research literature with the aim of better informing decision-making. These first reviews have helped to identify leading topics and to show that some data and research findings were lacking to adjust the national strategy, in terms of learning and raising student outcomes. The ministry wanted to strengthen the relevance of these works in using more rigorous methodologies. The idea was to adopt a method to capitalise on knowledge produced by research at a global level and to develop regular syntheses to inform practitioners and policy-makers.

From 2002, the NZ Ministry of Education implemented a project named Iterative Best Evidence Synthesis Programme (BES) which aimed to reinforce the access to and the use of evidence-based research by practitioners (Alton-Lee, 2007). The objective was to identify, assess and synthesise "what works" in education, particularly for the improvement of effectiveness and student outcomes. Syntheses have been regularly worked out from a capitalisation of international research findings. While the project was under the responsibility of its Chief Education Adviser, Adrienne Alton-Lee, the NZ ministry has created a national group including writers of syntheses, quality insurers and methodologists, representatives of teachers, researchers, and political advisers. Some more specialised groups have been institutionalised to developed evidence-based methodologies.

The BES programme has been well supported by teachers' trade unions while syntheses were applied to various areas, such as teaching and learning, training, and school management. Today, the programme continues to develop online resources and propose support for professionals in research and training by linking difficulties in student learning with health and welfare issues. This explains why this policy has been focused on the relatively poor and marginalised Maori people. Some practical guides and recommendations have been addressed to the whole of NZ educational stakeholders. Collaborations between researchers, policy-makers and professionals have been strongly supported according to the principles held by mode 2 of production of knowledge. The NZ Ministry of Education still assumes a function of brokerage in the implementation of evidence-based policy.

This programme has benefited from a strong worldwide recognition, whilst New Zealand has demonstrated very good scores in international surveys like PISA. Consequently, the NZ experience has influenced the OECD which has promoted international expertise on evidence-based policies.

### 3.4.2 The creation and dissemination of international expertise by the OECD

In April 2004, the OECD expressed its interest for evidence-based technologies by organising a first workshop in Washington DC under the aegis of the Centre for Education Research and Innovation (CERI), the US Institute of Education Sciences, and the Coalition for Evidence-Based Policy. The OECD/CERI was defending the idea that policy-makers need relevant and rigorous educational research. The seminar proposed to reflect on needs and constraints addressed by the "policy of evidence", to explore sources and reasons of resistance against experiments, and to study the practical results obtained in different countries. The discussion was focused on randomised controlled trials. On the US side, the OERI had coordinated research syntheses of "what works" (OERI, 1985) and the Institute of Education Sciences had been very active in the development of randomised controlled trials and systematic reviews. Among the papers discussed, one was an excerpt of the lecture given by Phil Davies, a member of Tony Blair's cabinet, during the first annual conference of the Campbell Collaboration, while another document presented three examples of the use of randomised controlled trials synthesised by Ann Oakley, the future head of the EPPI-Centre (Oakley, 2003).

The next meeting was held on the 14th–15th September 2005 at The Hague (Netherlands). Its aims were to explore some possible "bridges" between researchers, policy-makers and practitioners, in using evidence-based research to improve education policies. Participants were required to design an analytical framework and to discuss brokerage agencies, as the EEPI-Centre in the UK was seeking to improve the links between research and political expectations. Participants were invited to talk about experiments led by different national agencies and programmes: the EPPI-Centre, the What Works Clearing House in the US, the Iterative Best Evidence Synthesis led by Adrienne Alton-Lee in New Zealand, and the work of the Campbell Collaboration in its project C2-SPECTR. During the welcome session, Tom Schuller, head of CERI, gave a lecture with David Gough, then the new head of EPPI-Centre. The working document resuméd the conclusions of the CERI about knowledge management (OECD, 2003).

The final meeting was organised in London (6th–7th July 2006) under the auspices of the UK Department of Education and the Teaching and Learning Research Programme (TLRP), 19 representatives of OECD countries and David-Pascal Dion, then responsible for the European Network of Economists of Education (ENEE) for the General Directorate Education and Culture at the European Commission (http://www.tlrp.org/conference/oecd/document.html). The objective was to reflect on the implementation of "evidence-based policies", the extent of and support to experimental programmes and to make general recommendations. In his introduction, Tom Schuller (OECD, 2007) resumed the issues worked out by CERI to demonstrate the utility of evidence-based research in improving the performance of education systems with regard to international surveys. David-Pascal Dion shared the ideas of introducing technologies of evidence within the European strategy for Lifelong Learning (OECD, 2007).

The OECD report *Evidence in education: linking research and policy* (OECD, 2007) has resuméd different contributions from experts involved in its seminars, without producing recommendations to member states. Taking distance from the strongly controversial "evidence-based" work within the educational research community, it justifies the necessity to develop an "informed-based research policy", e.g. a policy better "informed" by research. Beyond these semantic differences, the two authors evoke the problems raised by the lack of quality and effectiveness of educational research and its incapacity to improve the performance of education systems. The report invites researchers to bypass the split between quantitative and qualitative methods and to use evidence-based research in decision-making and the implementation of reforms.

In March 2007, the Directorate General for Education and Culture (DGEAC) of the European Commission organised an international conference with the German Ministry of Education and Research titled *Knowledge for action: research strategies for an evidence-based education policy* (DIPF, 2007). While the head of the DGEAC, Odile Quintin, was attending the meeting with other lecturers presenting successful evidence-based policies, Tom Schuller was remindful of the set of seminars and the last report from the OECD. During the same year, the DGEAC wrote a report titled *Towards more knowledge-based policy and practice in education and training* (European Commission, 2007) which valorised the work done by the OECD on "evidence-based policies". The document of the DGEAC concludes that some ideas have to be disseminated amongst state members to develop evidence-based policies and practices in their education systems. It also provides some examples of programmes and experiments: the UK Teaching and Learning Research Programme, the EPPI-Centre, and some other agencies and European institutions involved in similar approaches.

### 3.4.3 The EIPPE project and its developments

Since 2009, the General Directorate of Education and Culture has funded a project titled *Evidence Informed Policy in Education in Europe* (EIPEE) in collaboration with the UK Institute of Education and the EPPI-Centre. The EIPEE has mobilised different European partners to develop networks and mechanisms of knowledge brokerage in the area of education and training to reinforce the links between research, policy and practice, and the attention of policy-makers and practitioners to research findings (Gough, Tripney, Kenny & Buk-Berge, 2011). Beyond the study of activities, and the networking and the development of European centres, the project (which has obtained the support of the Campbell Collaboration, the OECD-CERI, and the US Clearing House for Educational Research) has scheduled data collection and analyses to improve the quality of procedures and to inform professionals and policy-makers.

The creation of websites and data banks has been considered as a means to classify the most relevant activities and research findings and to provide on-line resources and training tools produced during international seminars for dissemination through different networks. Some experts have been mobilised under the leadership of the EPPI-Centre to develop a common understanding of the evidence-based policies while European stakeholders have associated to promote new relations between research and policy in the area of education. An analytical framework has also been designed.

This framework promotes three logics: the production of evidence, e.g.: relevant research findings to be produced, disseminated and accessible to practice; the mediation bringing producers and users closer according to a function of brokerage; the use of evidence or how it directly transforms decision-making or indirectly shapes knowledge, understanding and attitudes of policy-makers. Stakeholders have been involved in the process (media, professionals, social partners, civil society organisations, trade-unions, employers, etc.). The information system has to assure not only coordinated and effective interventions, but also a visibility and a sufficient capacity to produce relevant evidence for policy-making.

Progressively, the European Commission has adopted the idea of evidence-based policy-making (EBPM) for its strategy of Lifelong Learning in declaring that EPBM is a good means to gather and share evidence of the understanding of life conditions, youth attitudes and values in relation to other areas of public policies. But the European recommendations for the adoption of evidence-based technologies go far beyond the areas of education and health to be applied to the whole area of social sciences and humanities. To foster its communication about evidence-based research, the European Commission has recently designed a practical guide for researchers in human and social sciences (European Commission, 2010). It defends the idea that EBPM contributes to stimulating interactions between researchers, policy-makers and stakeholders in the world and inside European institutions. In making research more available and relevant to support policies, particularly through new framework-programmes, this rhetoric proposes to move beyond the model in which researchers present their research as an "accomplished fact" and to engage them in activities of dissemination and transfer for the most relevant target-groups. The guide presents a set of best practices for research to gather data, to improve capacities in the measurement and evaluation of public policies, and to attract the attention of media and stakeholders.

Before the publication of this practical guide, the European Commission, through its Directorate of Research for Humanities and Socio-Economical Sciences, produced a synthesis (2008) titled *Scientific Evidence for Policy-Making* in which it proposes, after several in-depth interviews and questionnaires addressed to policy-makers and European scientific advisers, improvement of the links between science and policy. The questionnaire positions the knowledge produced by the academic world and the knowledge delivered by think tanks or interest groups on the same level. To bring arguments into the report, some of the interviewed and selected experts and policy-makers had to identify obstacles preventing links between the two worlds: jargon, juridical barriers, and gaps in the agendas. Some proposals have been formulated to increase the utility of research by framing and better evaluating public policies. The Directorate General for Research and Innovation has affirmed its will to support the development of EBPM and will play a role of mediation in the new framework-programmes developed by the European Union.

## 3.5 Conclusion

As shown by the European research agenda, evidence-based policy-making, as a political experiment, legitimises some new areas of effectiveness and mediation between policy, research and practice. It also establishes a hierarchy in the modes of evidence.

The mode 2 of production of knowledge, or the model of a networking science, became the great principle shared by policy-makers in international organisations within the European Commission. It reflects the reconfiguration of relationships between science and policy in social and educational sciences. The demand for expertise in the design of new instruments of government relates to an assumed policy connecting experts, research units, agencies, and think tanks, capable of producing the metrology required for the restructuring of education policies. Creating networks, building sites and connecting spaces of calculation are political operations implemented today by supranational organisations to capitalise, totalise and classify knowledge and tools of measurement more and more independently from the State's power. In parallel, the democracy of sciences and technologies is valued as a legitimate principle of regulation for research activities, modes of funding and evaluation.

These new figures of international expertise, rehabilitating a positivist vision, tend to legitimate an objectivity away from the attachment to the State and its traditional tools of knowledge and action. The criticism is made difficult because devices and agencies developing measurement worldwide are distributed between different groups of agents with a weak level of explicit coordination. So, it is problematic to identify some forms of solidarity and complicity between experts whose activity is always plotted and technically guided while it generates global effects in the restructuring of statist structures and cognitive representations. The expertise acts at the earliest stages because it produces knowledge and instruments which directly serve decision-making before it is made public. If educational sciences, and particularly sociology, wish to maintain a certain critical reflexivity, they have to take into account the transformation of their cognitive and metrological environment. In being aware of their relative position among new sciences of government, and by taking account of some asymmetrical effects created by the extension of international expertise beyond the academic field, they have to rebuild a survey method capable of simultaneously describing the implementation of evidence-based policy at the European or international level and its normalising effects in different situations, devices and experiences of local social actors.

## Notes

1 This research was achieved through a participation to an expertise programme EIPEE (Evidence-Informed Policy in Education in Europe) coordinated by the l'EPPI-Centre of London in cooperation with the French Institute of Education and the French Ministry of Education (its Generate Directorate of Schools). I participated in several meetings with experts, ministries of education, agencies and stakeholders working for the European Commission. I also studied the official reports of the OECD and the European Commission and analysed several official websites of national and international organisations. This work gave the opportunity to write a thesis for the accreditation to supervise research in France titled *En quête d'évidence: Les sciences sociales et la mesure de l'État dans l'éducation et la santé* (In *Quest of evidence: social sciences and the measurement of the state in education and health*) (2011, Sciences Po Paris).
2 Scientifically Based Education Research, Evaluation, and Statistics and Information Act (2000).
3 The IES replaced the National Institute of Education (NIE) and the Office of Educational Research and Improvement (OERI).
4 EPPI-Centre, or Evidence for Policy and Practice Information and Co-ordinating Centre, is a part of the Social Science Research Unit of the Institute of Education at the University of London. Since 1993 it claims to advance the implementation of systematic reviews in the area of social sciences and public policies.
5 Former Chief Inspector of London's schools, he was one of the leaders criticising teacher training as unadjusted because of its academic orientation.
6 James Tooley, Professor of Educational Sciences at the Manchester University and Head of Education in the most important New Right think-tank (the Institute of Economic Affairs).

# Chapter 4

# Ethical drift in educational research

## Understanding the politics of knowledge production

*Patrick M. Jenlink and Karen Embry Jenlink*

## 4.1 Introduction

Writing on ethical dilemmas in research, Sultana (2007), has noted there are varied critical disjunctures between aspects of everyday ethical behaviour in the field and the university's institutional frameworks that aim to guide/enforce sound ethical practice, "as the conduct of fieldwork is always contextual, relational, embodied, and politicised" (p. 374). Ethical drift in research has become increasingly problematic; political and economic tensions often result in ethical drift in undertaking research, from the Institutional Review Board (IRB), also known as an independent ethics committee, process to the implementation of the study to the reporting of findings.

In large part, ethical drift is related to interpersonal reasons caused by the influences of others' control (external governmental entities, institutional entities such as universities, funding entities, etc.). Simply stated, interpersonal processes that contribute to ethical drift in research originate in varied social interactions (Moore, Detert, Treviño, Baker, & Mayer, 2012). The thesis of this chapter is that it is important for educational researchers to pay greater attention to issues of reflexivity, positionality and power relations in the field in order to undertake ethical research.

Understanding the politics of knowledge production requires that researchers look beyond the antecedents of unethical behaviour and focus on possible interventions rather than descriptions of the status quo, thereby recognizing the political forces in play rather than allowing ethical practice to drift. Navigating the politics of knowledge production is concerned, in part, with how politics play a role in determining research outcomes, control knowledge and its dissemination, and determine whose agenda is in control. Making moral judgements in research is a translation of behavioural ethics. Similarly, understanding ethical judgement and dishonesty are prerequisites to ethical research practice and behaviour (Bazerman & Gino, 2012; Gino & Bazerman, 2009; Shalvi, Dana, Handgraff, & De Dreu, 2011; Weber, Kopelman, & Messick, 2004).

The first section in the chapter presents a discussion of the origins of ethics in educational research, followed by a section that discusses ethics and politics in/of educational research. Next, the nature of ethical dilemmas in educational research is discussed, followed by discussion of ethical drift in educational research. The chapter closes with final reflections.

## 4.2 Origins of ethics in educational research

The origins of ethics in research takes direction from the history of medical research, which has been at the forefront of the ethics of research involving humans, both with respect to the development of vocabularies and frameworks and with respect to the formulation of federal policy. Social research in general, and educational research in particular, has evolved from the early history of medical research. Unfortunately, the history of the development of the field of ethics in research has largely been built on egregious and disastrous breaches[1] of humane ethical values (Annas, 1992; Beyrer & Kass, 2002; Bledsoe, Sherin, Galinsky et al., 2007; Mitscherlich & Mielke, 1949; Moreno, 1997; Schuman, 2010; Shamoo & Resnik, 2009; Smith, 2006).

Formal consideration for ethics in research is predicated on the rights of research or human subjects. Ethics in this sense grew out of the Nazi medical experiments during World War II. These atrocities prompted the creation of the Nuremberg Code of 1947 (Annas & Grodin, 1992; Mitscherlich & Mielke, 1949),[2] a code of ethics that begins with the stipulation that all research participation must be voluntary. Other codes of ethics soon followed, including the Declaration of Helsinki (1964),[3] which mandated that all biomedical research projects involving human subjects carefully assess the risks of participation against the benefits, respect the subject's privacy, and minimize the costs of participation to the subject. The Council for International Organization of Medical Sciences (CIOMS) was created for those researching in developing nations (Beyrer & Kass, 2002).

In the history of ethics, accounts of research misconduct reveal the terms of political debate and conflict and the stakeholders relevant at a given time and place. Misconduct serves as object lessons – shared memories with a moral, which are meant to teach people entering the research profession a common ethical sense in the present day. Carefully examined histories of misconduct also demonstrate how difficult it is to identify the intersection of ethics and politics. Such accounts are important in that they can prompt political change and indicate the contours of a collective conscience, recognizing the importance of carefully articulated research ethics that inform research practice (Bledsoe, Sherin, Galinsky et al., 2007; Moore, 2009; Messick & Tenbrunsel, 1996; Shamoo & Resnik, 2009; Smith, 2006; Stark, 2012; Steneck, 1994).

The regulatory architecture underlying the protection of human research subjects that informs research practice in contemporary society has drawn on lessons of history derived from experiences such as the Holocaust and from the 1947 Nuremberg Code governing human medical experimentation and the 1964 Helsinki Declaration governing biomedical research on human subjects. Noted in this architecture is a realization of how political ideologies have historically guided (or misguided as the case may be) research on human subjects. The need for ethics in research as a counter balance to politics is a reality that history has taught.

## 4.3 Ethics and politics in/of educational research

Education in today's society "is by its very nature a profoundly political enterprise because it is the means and the message by which worldviews are transmitted, cultures are reproduced, a way of life is passed on, and a person is created" (Randall, Cooper, & Hite, 1999, p. 2). Education at the same time is an ethical enterprise by its very nature and function within society. The overarching belief systems become the lens through which a reality takes shape and by which ethical and political decisions are rendered. They contain prescriptive views of what constitutes the just society, ethical behaviour, and legitimate social institutions and structures. By its nature and function in society education is not an impartial activity; it is inherently value-laden (Randall et al., 1999). While educational research is often confounded by political ideologies, the "politics" of educational research is much more complex. Politics in this context means the contest for power between groups with different vested interests in the practice and outcome of research, whereas ethics in this context means the search for rules of conduct that enable researchers to operate defensibly in the political contexts in which they have to conduct educational research (Simons, 1995). Understanding the politics of educational research and examining the ethical stance that one must take as researcher reflects a level of complex interaction between politics and ethics necessary to conducting defensible research. Understanding the "risk" factor in educational research requires understanding the politics and ethics of research.

Educational researchers, "to do engaged research" against the backdrop of the politics of educational research, "and to do so ethically" (p. 50), as Kumashiro (2014) has argued, "must expand not only how to define risk, but also for whom 'risk' is being defined." Educational researchers must ask, "Who still bears the burden of risk in the current ways of conceptualizing ethics?" (p. 50). Educational research in relation to risk and to contested educational issues in society "simply cannot remain antiseptically objective – particularly when differing ideologies are pitted against one another in field of social science data" (Babbie, 2014, p. 79).

Therein, research by its very nature of being situated in education becomes political. The cloak of neutrality in both research and education was discarded as educational researchers began to acknowledge the political nature of their work. To a large degree, educational research theorists and methodologists have become the arbitrators of which knowledge and truth claims are considered acceptable within normative parameters of inquiry, and the importance of understanding the larger political context of knowledge production and use has influenced the nature of educational research and the ethics that govern it (Randall, Cooper, & Hite, 1999).

Ethics[4] and politics[5] are implicit in undertaking educational research. Ethics and politics are integral and indispensable elements of any examination of the social issues and problems confronting education. Babbie (2014) argued that ". . . ethics and politics hinge on ideological points of view" (p. 62). What is acceptable from one point of view will be unacceptable from another. A corollary in educational research is that ethical considerations are not always apparent to the individual researcher. As a result, the researcher often enters into a research study "without seeing ethical issues that may be apparent to others and may even be obvious to us when pointed out" (Babbie, 2014, p. 62). Likewise, the researcher, upon entering into the research process, may not be self-aware of the political underpinnings of the problem or issue serving as the focus of the study.

Thus, being attentive to the politics of knowledge production and processes of research has become important to educational researchers; being analytical and reflexive about their fieldwork and research process. This attentiveness includes challenging pre-given categories and narratives, and being attentive to power, knowledge and context. Concomitantly, ethics in research practice is equally important to the educational researcher. Being attentive to "ethics in practice" (Emihovich, 1999; MacLean, 2006; Romano, 2006; Woliver, 2002) matters ". . . for the simple reason that [educational researchers] can bring real harm to study participants and collaborators" (Fujii, 2012, p. 717).

Although political and ethical issues are often closely intertwined, they are distinguished in two ways. First, the ethics of educational research ". . . deals mostly with the methods employed; political issues tend to centre on the substance and use of research" (Babbie, 2014, p. 75). The second distinction between the ethical and political aspects of educational research "is that there are no formal codes of accepted political conduct" (p. 75). However, some ethical norms have political aspects – for example, IRB "guidelines for not harming subjects clearly relate to Western ideas about the protection of civil liberties – no one has developed a set of political norms that all social researchers accept" (p. 75). It is noted that one exception to the lack of political norms in relation to educational research is ". . . the generally accepted view that a researcher's personal political orientation should not interfere with or unduly influence his or her scientific research" (p. 76).

## 4.4 Ethical dilemmas in educational research

Ethical dilemmas present the educational researcher with difficult decisions. Ethical dilemmas in educational research are the result of conflicts between potential benefits or harms for two or more competing interests. Therefore, ethical decision-making for the researcher implies a responsibility to identify those interests, harms, and benefits (see duToit, 1980; Girvan & Savage, 2012; Lincoln & Homes, 2007; Sultana, 2007; Tenbrunsel & Messick, 2004).

The complex and multi-faceted nature of the work of educational researchers forces them to deal with a multiplicity of dilemmas related to research ethics.

Researchers have responsibilities to the research, the subjects of research, other researchers, the institution, society, the environment, and self. Ethical dilemmas emerge in relation to the rights of subjects, conduct of research, cultural and social differences, reporting of research, and politics of research.

Educational researchers, whether in designing, implementing, or reporting research, may find themselves in an ethical dilemma, a conflicting situation with choices between right and wrong decisions, or variations of right decisions, or variations of wrong decisions. Such conflicts may deal with risk to the researcher or the researched, or may be political conflicts of interest between funding entities and researchers, where the source of funding has particular expectations that may or may not be aligned with ethical conduct in research (Carpenter, 2012; González-López, 2011; Guillemin & Gillam, 2004; MacLean, 2006; Woliver, 2002).

One of the major sources of ethical dilemmas can occur within the power imbalance between researchers and the researched. This imbalance may be further exacerbated by internal and/or external political tensions. Fujii (2012) explained that the ". . . magnitude and direction of asymmetry will vary by project, researcher, and research setting; so, too, will the areas where the researcher or participant exerts more power over the process" (p. 718). In this sense, ethical dilemmas require of the researcher the use of "mindful ethics" as a counterweight to professional or political incentives that may sway the researcher's decision (González-López, 2011). With respect to the existence of a power imbalance, one of the central responsibilities that researchers have is "to obtain voluntary, informed consent" (Fujii, 2012, p. 718). Such consent presumes that individual's participation in the research is voluntary.

An exemplar of ethical dilemma is presented in Baez's (2002) study, "Confidentiality in qualitative research: reflections on secrets, power and agency." Baez (2002) examined the dilemma of confidentiality through a personal account he experienced in maintaining the confidentiality of his respondents. Baez interviewed 16 minority faculty members to understand how those faculty members experienced tenure and promotion at a private university. His research highlighted how the convention of confidentiality influenced both his (as researcher) and the respondents' actions, and how it thwarted transformative political goals. He noted that maintaining confidentially could be a double-edged sword. Keeping the interviews confidential, especially for untenured faculty, allowed him to obtain candid data regarding racism and sexism within the university. On the other hand, confidentiality prevented him from reporting "serious contradictions within an institution that, through institutional documents and public comments by key administrators, purported to be supportive of racial and cultural diversity" (Baez, 2002, p. 39). For Baez personally, he stated, "I could not do so without feeling that I would be identifying my respondents to others in the institution," (p. 39) although he reflected a desire to call attention to what he perceived as contradictory, even racist transgressions and patterns he uncovered in his research. Ethical dilemmas of this nature may cause the educational researcher to "... struggle along with such thick layers of bias and rationalization, compartmentalization and denial, that [his or her] choices suffer immeasurably" (Bok, 1989, p. 71).

Just as power hierarchies, such as those that exist between the researcher and the researched, give rise to dilemmas around consent, "... the researcher's social proximity to participants and interlocutors can give rise to dilemmas about how to maintain people's privacy and confidentiality. When researchers insert themselves, even as observers, they alter the social landscape" (Fujii, 2012, p. 720). Researchers "do so by drawing attention to those in their orbit, such as key informants, research assistants, and interpreters. Such attention may be a boon to some, but a threat to others" (p. 720).

Given the intersection of ethics and politics in educational research, it is argued that a consideration of ethics needs to be viewed as a critical part of the substructure of the research process from the inception of the researcher's problem to the implementation of the research design forward to the interpretation and publishing of the research findings. Ethics play a critical role in educational research and when applied to research practice can offset the possibility of ethical drift.

## 4.5 Ethical drift in educational research

Educational researchers are confronted with ethical dilemmas each day in the research setting, and they experience the ebb and flow of tensions that impact ethical decision-making. With the ebbing of ethical conduct in concert with the challenges of ethical research practices, researchers are confronted with yet another challenge, that of ethical drift[6] in the behaviour of others that are primary to ethical research practice (Bledsoe, Sherin, Galinsky et al., 2007; Sternberg, 2012a, 2012b; Tenbrunsel & Messick, 2004). Kleinman (2006) has argued this point forcefully:

> The importance of ethical drift cannot be overestimated because of people's universal susceptibility to it and the gravity of its potential consequences. The very essence of ethical drift is that it occurs before the seriousness of the dilemma takes shape or before the conflict is even perceived. People make an imperceptible adjustment to the situation or make a minor exception to their ethical code due to the pressure of the situation, most often with no awareness that this has occurred. It is not apparent to them that the farther they go down a new path, the farther they get from their original course. (p. 75)

There are many factors that challenge educational researchers in adhering to ethical values. Ethical drift is the erosion of ethical behaviour that occurs in individuals below their level of self-awareness. Kleinman (2006) noted that ethical drift is when good people do bad things. Sternberg (2012a, 2012b, 2012c) explained ethical drift as the gradual ebbing of standards that occurs in an individual, a group, or an organization as a result of pressures internal and external to the social content of an organization, such as a school. Drift typically occurs when: there is intense competition for resources; people start to feel that they are in a zero-sum game; people perceive, or think they perceive, others acting in ways that are ethically compromised; or people see no other viable way out of the quandary; they feel they just can't leave the situation (Sternberg, 2012a, p. 59).

Ethical drift in educational research is provoked by at least four environmental forces. First, it typically occurs when there is intense competition for resources, such as federal, state, or private sources of funding; resource allocation is political by nature. Second, individuals working in research who are competing for academic and professional recognition begin to feel that they are in a zero-sum game, the politics of reward directs actions; the political and ethical represent interdependent choice at one extreme, the extreme of diametrically opposed interests. Third, people perceive, or think they perceive, others are acting in ways that are ethically compromised. At times, when individuals or organizations compete (internally and/or externally), individuals and/or members actually may encourage an individual to act in ethically compromised ways. Finally, people may see no other viable way out of the dilemma. They feel they cannot just leave the situation, exit means losing one's position and professional identity (see Bledsoe, Sherin, Galinsky et al., 2007; Sternberg, 2012c; Whitney, Alcser, Schneider, McCullough, McGuire, & Volk, 2008).

Kleinman (2006) explained that ethical drift is "an incremental deviation from ethical practice that goes unnoticed by individuals who justify the deviations as acceptable and who believe themselves to be maintaining their ethical boundaries" (p. 73). Often, ethical drift occurs below a level of awareness, to the individual and to others, and "facilitates doing that which fosters self-serving needs" (p. 73). Ethical drift occurs when the perceived costs to the researcher outweigh adhering to principled ethical conduct, and the researcher elects to place the needs of "self" above the ethical responsibility to the research, the subjects, the institution, and society. Ethical dilemmas and concerns are part of the everyday practice of doing research.

Tenbrunsel and Messick (2004) explained that the basis of unethical decisions, in part, is self-deception, which allows "individuals to behave incomprehensibly and, at the same time, not realise that they are doing so" (p. 224). In educational research, self-deception can lead "to coding, or framing of decisions that either eliminate negative ethical characterizations or distort them into positive ones. Self-deception helps to disguise violations of our ethical principals" (p. 232). In matters of human subjects, confidentiality, reporting findings, and authorship researchers may drift ethically in their decisions, deceiving the self and masking violations of ethical principles.

Ethical violations in educational research are a concern for all researchers. When the researcher (and others involved and/or invested, i.e., funding entities, institution, etc.) believe everything is going as expected in the research endeavour, taking risks and violating ethical conduct is not perceived as a viable option; it is not attractive. However, when the researcher (and involved and/or others invested, i.e., funding entities, institution, etc.) perceives that the research endeavour is not going as expected, ethical violations may be more attractive. The steps taken to violate ethical conduct is a form of ethical drift; one drifts ethically when the consequence of one's actions are not perceived to be as costly as the potential gains of ethical violations.

The educational researcher working to resolve political, economic, or cultural tensions may find that the point of origin for these tensions and/or its intensity is predicated on or exacerbated by ethical drift in various social actors that are embedded in the context of the institution granting IRB approval and/or the content within which the research is conducted. The very essence of ethical drift is that it occurs before the seriousness of the ethical dilemma takes shape or before the value conflict is even perceived (Kleinman 2006; Sternberg 2012b, 2012c).

An exemplar of a significant problem for education research has been what experts term "mission creep" or "ethics drift" (Bledsoe, Sherin, & Galinsky, 2007; Gunsalus, 2004), in which IRBs are unable to clearly delineate and employ the exempt or expedited categories for work that is extremely low risk to human subjects. Even more concerning are reports that university IRBs have required proposal review and approval for routine academic activities, such as interviews performed by students for a class on investigative journalism (Gunsalus, 2004). The notable expansion of IRB review since the late 1990s, experts have argued, is due more to fears of losing federal funding than to true concerns regarding human abuses (Bledsoe, Sherin, & Galinsky, 2007).

Ethical drift may also arise when strong pressure (often implicit) leads to inaccurate data collection. For example, such pressure may occur when a research assistant believes that significant results must be obtained and either consciously or unconsciously alters the data. Other circumstances may have the same net outcome. The data collection process is often laborious, boring, or even extremely difficult. This has led to incidents in which research assistants actually record fictitious data rather than conscientiously observe participants.

A breach of integrity during the development, execution, or dissemination of results, whether it be intentional or unintentional, may be recognized as ethical drift, which will seriously weaken or even invalidate a research study (Bledsoe et al., 2007; Keller & Lee, 2003; Pittenger, 2003). Tenure track assistant professors seeking to obtain both institutional tenure and promotion to associate professor may find themselves under pressure to publish as a requirement for tenure and/or promotion. They may drift away from grounded ethical practice in order to survive the "publish or perish" climate of the university. In this case, the placing of the researcher "self" above the ethical responsibility to the research, subjects, institution, etc., creates a drift in ethical decision making (Cole, 2000; Fujii, 2012; Kleinman, 2006). The non-tenured professor may be pressed by the institutional politics and/or the desire to obtain tenure, and therefore take shortcuts to completing a research study, including treatment of human subjects, conduct of the actual study, falsifying data, and reporting findings. The politics of educational research often presents pressures, both internal and external, that result in self-deception about the right and wrong of decisions in the conduct of research.

Ethical drift can be interpreted as moving away from one's moral compass, so to speak. Given the political nature of educational research and the complex and dynamic nature of research problems, compounded by external tensions from government agencies (i.e., funding entities, consumers of research, standards and accountability, etc.) and internal tensions (i.e., cultural and political resistance to research-based decisions), the research practice and decision-making processes are subject to those tensions and therefore subject to "ethical drift". The consequences of "ethical drift" include research dropped altogether, major portions of research removed, diversion of research topic or population to one more likely to pass easily through IRB review, choosing new research themes according to the likelihood of swift IRB approval above inherent importance of the research itself, and choosing methods, such as meta-analysis, rather than new data collection to avoid IRB review (Whitney, Alcser, Schneider, McCullough, McGuire, & Volk, 2008).

Ethical drift may emerge as a result of self-deception. Tenbrunsel and Messick (2004) identified four reasons why self-deception, which lies at the root of ethical drift, is perpetuated. These include language euphemisms, decision-making, error in perceptual causation, and constraints induced by representations of the self. Self-deception in this sense ". . . allows one to behave self-interestedly while, at the same time, falsely believing that one's moral principles were upheld" (p. 223). Self-deception and decision frames are part of the sequence linking socialization cues to unethical behaviour, with socialization cues acting as prompts for self-deception. The educational researcher does not "see" the moral components of an ethical decision, not so much because they are morally uneducated, but because psychological processes fade the "ethics" from an ethical dilemma (p. 224, emphasis in original). Central to ethical drift is the ". . . art of self deception . . ." which is unclear as to whether ". . . such deception is the result of a conscious act or an unconscious act" (p. 225).

Messick and Bazerman (1996) explained that self-deception results when the educational researcher is unaware that this leads him or her to make decisions or judgements. Ethical drift begins as ethical decisions are made as a trade-off between self-interest and moral principles. By avoiding or disguising the moral implications of a decision in the research experience, individuals can behave in a self-interested manner and still hold the conviction that they are ethical persons. Ignorance and false beliefs about oneself can create errors in judgements concerning moral responsibility and in estimates of the amount of harm that is caused, as well as obscure means to reverse an immoral decision (Bok, 1989). Messick and Bazerman (1996) further explained that to counter self-deception the educational researcher must condition him or herself to be self-aware of the enablers of self-deception; furthermore, he or she must be more critical of judgements and motives driving both actions and judgements of others' behaviours. Failing to engage in critically questioning ethical decision frames and the political motives for decisions and actions in conducting educational research can lead the researcher and the researched to fall victim to socialization into ethical drift.

Moore and Gino (2013) noted that ethicality "... is bounded, such that we cannot reliably know when our moral compass is deviating from true North..."(p. 3). When educational researchers socially identify with individuals who engage in unethical behaviour, their own ethical behaviour will likely degrade as well. In a study by Gino, Ayal, and Ariely (2009), college students were asked to solve simple math problems in the presence of others and had the opportunity to cheat by misreporting their performance and leave with undeserved money. Once the researcher makes concession to socializing pressures over values, the researcher finds it "... easier and easier to make further concessions, particularly if there are no immediate negative consequences. Those engaged in ethical drift go blithely along believing nothing has changed and do not appreciate their descent down a very steep and slippery slope" (p. 75).

Socialization as denoted may result in deviation from one's ethical foundation as an educational researcher. In many instances, the researcher grounded in sound ethical principles realizes the blatant nature of the drift from his or her ethical foundation and rejects the socializing behaviour. Blatant lapses in ethical behaviour, as Kleinman (2006) has explained, "... take many forms. In some cases, these lapses are immediately identifiable as they appear suddenly and represent a major deviation while in other cases, such lapses represent slow erosion of boundaries that only retrospectively appear blatant" (p. 73).

Socialization to unethical practices can happen either consciously, when a researcher resists objectionable practices until finally *surrendering* to them as inevitable, or unconsciously, when the researcher becomes *seduced* by the positive material or psychological benefits of participating in corrupt behaviour (Moore, 2009, emphasis in original). In either case the consequence is ethical drifting along a path that becomes increasingly easier to follow.

## 4.6 Negative effects of ethical drift

The cornerstone of educational research is trust. The public and other professionals must be able to trust that research being reported is honest, accurate, and as free from bias as possible. The immediate and long-term effects of ethical drift include harm to human subjects, a priority concern in all educational research. As well, ethical drift, the intentional or unintentional act of not meeting one's responsibility to the research, to the subjects of the research, to the other researchers (or vested parties), to the institution (researcher's university, funding entity whether government or NGO), to society, and self, leaves deep imprints across all levels (see Alvino, 2003; Israel, 2014; Polonsky & Waller, 2010; Seals, 2013). In many cases, the negative effects of ethical drift are cross-generational and the identity and integrity of individuals and institutions are permanently damaged.

The list of questionable research practices in education in particular and social science in general is long and ever-expanding, and can include things like poor data management, failing to share data, questionable data selection methods, fiscal mismanagement, or inadequate supervision of research assistants, graduate students or post-doctoral fellows. When issues of ethical misconduct are discovered, the researcher's credibility of current and future research may be called into question. It could lead to greater scrutiny and oversight in the future. It may also limit the acceptance of publications in certain journals, depending on the nature of the unethical act. Falsification, fabrication, and plagiarism are examples of research misconduct that are adjudicated based on institutional, professional, and governmental policy.

Effects of ethical drift may include, but not be limited to, research being dropped or banned, major portions removed, diversion of research topic or population, funding being restricted or revoked, dismissal from research position, legal action, sanctions on the researcher (debarment from receipt of funding for a period of time), and related decisions and actions that are viewed as appropriate and necessary to atone for ethical misconduct and its impact and/or harm to human subjects (see Babbie, 2014; Bazerman & Gino, 2012; Bledsoe, Sherin, Galinsky et al., 2007; Gunsalus, 2004; Moore, Detert, Treviño, Baker, & Mayer, 2012). Depending on the nature of research being conducted, the funding agency and/or the academic institution have the ability to halt the research, particularly if the research might have safety implications for the research participants or the general public. Acts of research misconduct also tend to reach the media and threaten public trust in research.

## 4.7 Addressing ethical drift

The phrase 'responsible conduct of research' is important to addressing ethical drift. Ethical drift can be either intrapersonal (caused by cognitive limitations) or interpersonal (influenced by others) (Moore, Detert, Treviño, Baker, & Mayer, 2012). Intrapersonal drift reflects individual researcher biases and cognitive failings that affect one's ethicality. Interpersonal drift originates in the social interactions of the researcher. Mediating ethical drift first requires an understanding of the origin or factors affecting ethicality. The researcher (and other individuals drawn into the ethical drift), whether due to intrapersonal or interpersonal factors, must first become self-aware that ethical misconduct has taken place; self-awareness precedes and is integral to mediating the negative effects of ethical drift.

It is difficult for the educational researcher to develop self-awareness related to ethical drift when the process is most often unrecognized and then only retrospectively. Self-awareness, as an educational researcher, is paramount to ethical research conduct. Retrospectively recognizing that ethical drift has negatively influenced research in its design, execution, or reporting, and that human subjects may have been harmed, does not rectify the failure to follow ethical guidelines. There is both a social and psychological element to mediation. If the factor dominant in ethical drift is interpersonal, the researcher (and others influencing the researcher) must recognize and critically question the social interactions that culminated in ethical misconduct. However, if the factor dominant in ethical drift is intrapersonal, the researcher (and others influenced by the researcher) must become self-aware of the deception or contributing influences that culminated in ethical misconduct (Moore, Detert, Treviño, Baker, & Mayer, 2012; Tenbrunsel & Messick, 2004).

Learning retrospectively from the past is difficult and important, but not sufficient to address ethical drift. As Kleinman (2006) explained, ". . . other strategies must be implemented to prevent deviation from ethical practice" (p. 5). Offsetting ethical drift requires "Ongoing peer support groups and leadership development sessions to allow managers and administrators to reflect, review, and reconsider in a safe environment in which others may see what they themselves do not" (pp. 75–76).

The ethics and politics of knowledge production have become increasingly important to educational researchers. Current tensions – political, economic, cultural, and methodological – draw into specific relief the changing dynamics of conducting research, from the IRB phase to the reporting of findings phase. By being analytical and reflexive about their fieldwork and research process, challenging pre-given categories and narratives, and being attentive to power, knowledge and context, researchers can counter ethical drift and mediate the political tensions in educational research (Sultana, 2007). Recognizing and working with multiple positionalities of researchers and research participants as well as working within and across institutional and external contexts requires constantly negotiating ethical relationships. To address ethical drift, what is needed is an institutionalized ethical framework sufficient to address "ethical drift" in the course of conducting educational research.

## 4.8 Final reflections

If, as educational researchers, we are uncomfortable with navigating the many ethical challenges that arise when conducting research, we must remind ourselves that to enter another's world as a researcher is a privilege, not a right. Wrestling with ethical dilemmas is the price we pay for the privileges we enjoy. Being self-aware when ethical drift presents is integral to ethical practice. It is a responsibility, not a choice, to engage in ethical research practices, and when taken seriously, it may be one of the most important benefits we have to offer those for whom our research endeavours is carried out.

Although the ethical and political dimensions of research are in principle distinct, they do intersect. Ethical challenges are ever-present and the force of self-deception alongside internal and external political pressures often present difficult decisions and daunting challenges. There are inevitably shades of grey in interpretation of the ethics of research and what constitutes ethical responsibility, but any single act of deviation or deception should result in redressive steps. If these steps are not taken, the researcher, and by relationship the institution or governing bodies concerned with ethical research, has essentially failed in its obligations, rendering the researcher, the research, and all parties involved noncompliant (Bledsoe, Sherin, Galinsky et al., 2007). Learning from past experiences is important, but the ethical researcher understands the necessity of embracing other strategies, implementing those strategies to prevent deviation from ethical practice.

Those researchers who engage in what is defined as IRB-relevant research will find they are more vulnerable than those who do not, because of the multitude of additional rules they must commit to follow in order to conduct their research. To the extent that researchers have trouble adhering to these rules because of their disciplinary philosophies, they are even more exposed.

As ethical researchers we are bound by a moral covenant to protect human subjects (Babbie, 2014). Ethics exist within a bounded social context. Ethical rules cannot possibly account for all events that may arise in a given research project. By agreeing to comply with ethical rules, a researcher is not absolved from adhering to the underlying ethical values contained in these rules. In this sense, ethical drift is a choice that educational researchers must consistently avoid.

## Notes

1 Concerning the evolution of the research ethics, egregious and disastrous breaches of humane ethical values hallmark human history, globally, and the failure to protect human life. The Nazi war crimes and the Nuremberg trials resulted in the Nuremberg Code established in 1948, which provided a historical baseline. The Nuremberg Code provided a clear statement of standards for research on human subjects. Unethical research programs continued to be designed and conducted. The Willowbrook hepatitis study, Jewish Chronic Disease Hospital case, and Tuskegee Study of Untreated Syphilis in the Negro Male, among others, represent part of the history of why research ethics are necessary. Each of these infamous examples of egregiously unethical research was designed and conducted long after the Nuremberg Code was in place. In 1964 the World Health Association established the Declaration of Helsinki to guide doctors in biomedical research involving human participants. In contemporary society today, responsible conduct of research focuses on human subjects, plagiarism, falsification of data, and a myriad other forms of ethical misconduct. The Nuremberg Code and the Declaration of Helsinki are historical cornerstones in human history concerning research. The need for ethical guidelines in educational research takes direction from the history of ethical misconduct in research (see Bledsoe, Sherin, Galinsky et al., 2007; Howe & Moses, 1999; Stark, 2012).
2 See Trials of War Criminals before the Nuremberg Military Tribunals under Control Council Law No. 10, Vol. 2, pp. 181–182. Washington, D.C.: U.S. Government Printing Office, 1949.
3 World Medical Association, Declaration of Helsinki (1964). Available at http://www.fda.gov/ohrms/dockets/dockets/06d0331/06D-0331-EC20-Attach-1.pdf
4 Ethics as presented in this chapter is a process; a process for making good, justified, defensible decisions, personally, professionally, and in the public square. Ethics involves systematizing, defending and recommending concepts of right and wrong behaviour.

It is concerned with the justification of actions and practices in specific situations. Morality refers to traditions or beliefs that have evolved in societies concerning right and wrong conduct (see Babbie, 2014; Howe & Moses, 1999; Israel, 2014; Polonsky & Waller, 2010; Shamoo & Resnick, 2009).

5 Politics as presented in this chapter refers to political considerations in educational research that are subtle, ambiguous, and arguable. Such considerations involve the nature of various power relationships between researcher and researched, researcher and funding agency, researcher and policy makers, and how one may be antithetical to the other, working against opposing agendas and understandings (see Babbie, 2014; Emihovich, 1999; MacLean, 2006; Simons, 1995).

6 The terms 'mission creep', 'ethical fading', 'ethics drift', and 'ethical drift' connote a significant problem in educational research, and the broader category of social science research. The terms generally reflect when an individual or individuals do not follow an ethical path in decision making. For the purposes of this chapter, 'ethical drift' will be used throughout (see Sullivan, 2011; Kleinman, 2006; Moore & Gino, 2013; Sternberg, 2012a, 2012b for further discussion).

Chapter 5

# Play the game or get played?
## Researchers' strategies around R&D policies

*Sofia Viseu*

## 5.1 Introduction

This chapter focuses on the possible effects of current Research and Development (R&D) policies on educational research, exploring some of the dilemmas and critical issues they pose to researchers. More precisely, I will present a study centred in educational research in Portugal in the last 30 years[1] that will be taken as an example of the tensions featuring R&D policies and the work of researchers. I am driven by the search to understand how the new trends cross in the domain of science public policies (focused on accountability and with an interested, even calculating eye on the production of scientific knowledge), and the way educational researchers (whether contesting or not) relate to and reinvent these guidelines.

The starting point of this study is the note that, on a transnational scale, there is a traveling policy (Lawn & Grek, 2012), where R&D policies embrace performance-based research funding (PBRF) systems, such as the Research Excellence Framework in the UK, the Excellence in Research for Australia or the PBRF Exercise in New Zealand. And in Belgium, Denmark, Finland, Italy, Norway, Poland, Portugal, the Slovak Republic, Sweden, United States, Hong Kong and China, to name a few, there are growing approaches to PBRF (Hicks, 2012). Despite national specificities, PBRF stresses evaluation as the most powerful and significant instrument of science regulation: indirect financial provisions, evaluation based on bibliometric criteria and publishing in refereed journals are now central in scientific activity (Vincent-Lancrin, 2006). Worldwide, PBRF is often justified by the importance of knowledge in public policies or conceived as part of the new managerialism regime in public policies (Curtis, 2008). In this respect, Fitzgerald (2012) points out that

> in a relatively short period of time, academic work and academic identity has shifted from being largely autonomous, self-governing with particular privileges and public duties, to a profession that has been modernised, rationalised, re-organised and intensely scrutinised.
>
> (p. 2)

Described critically by Ozga, Seddon & Popkewitz (2006) as business aspects of research, PBRF measures call for a greater relevance of academic research, the need to obtain alternative sources of public funding and also the demand to disclose research results among peers, potential users and stakeholders. As a consequence, there is a growing global standardisation on research topics, agendas and methodologies (Amos et al., 2002) and the raising "of new kinds of 'research' knowledge" based on performativity (Ball, 2010, p. 124). In educational research these measures tend to emphasise its instrumental character; as Denzin (2009) states, "like an elephant in the living room, the evidence-based model is an intruder whose presence can no longer be ignored" (p. 139). In fact, transnational agencies, such as OECD (2003), recommend use-inspired basic research to solve contemporary educational issues.

Given the demands and constraints they put on researchers, these policies generate debates, controversy and contestation (Brown & Schubert, 2000). All over the world, researchers have expressed their disagreement on recent R&D policies signing, for instance, *The Slow Science Manifesto* or the *San Francisco Declaration on Research Assessment (DORA)*. We must note, however, that in most Western countries, public investment in science has grown in a sustained and continuous manner (Eurostat, 2013). A good example is Horizon 2020, which has a higher overall budget of over €77 billion for science and innovation until 2020. So it seems that this contestation is not so much about the lack of investment in science, but rather about the process of reconfiguration of scientific work.

With a view to understanding how researchers conceive and receive R&D policies, this chapter presents a study focused on the strategies developed by researchers regarding R&D policies: what kind of strategies do they develop? Do they play the game or do they get played by it? The study aims to be considered an example of what Waitere et al. (2011) called "choosing whether to resist or reinforce" R&D policies.

These questions rely on a conceptual framework that claims researchers as strategic actors (Crozier & Friedberg, 1977) with personal agendas and interests. In the same way, Reynaud (2003) refers to autonomous regulation to describe how social actors receive and (re)adjust to control mechanisms according to their interests, seeking to maintain or achieve margins of autonomy. The game is conceived as a political arena where researchers and R&D policy trends meet, following Lucas' (2006) proposal for the "research game" as the "specific stakes and terms (. . .) of university research" (p. 3). Researchers' strategies are perceived as political, considering that it is in the context of their practices that policy is interpreted and reinvented (Bowe, Ball, & Gold, 1992).

This chapter presents the results of a study that revealed a strategic calculation made by researchers concerning R&D policies, taking educational research in Portugal as an example. In the recent and accelerated growth of the research system in Portugal in the last 20 years,[2] public authorities have adopted new modes of science regulation inspired by PBRS. The shift that has taken place in a relatively short period of time, aiming for an accountable science, makes Portugal a potential breeding ground to study researchers' arising strategies.

In the next two sections, I will present the research methods followed in the study and the results which showed converging and divergent strategies of researchers with regard to R&D policies. In the final section, I discuss the coexistence of both strategies as a sign of the complexity of public policies (Lascoumes & Le Galès, 2007b).

## 5.2 Methods

The study followed a general qualitative approach (Huberman & Miles, 2002) and it started by gathering documental data about the main trends of R&D policies regarding educational research. For that, I chose two public agencies responsible for R&D and/or educational research: (a) the Foundation for Science and Technology (FCT), the public agency currently (since 1997) in charge of funding and evaluating the Portuguese scientific system in all scientific domains; and (b) the Institute for Educational Innovation (IEI), an agency which operated in the late 1980s and early 2000 under the supervision of the Ministry of Education in Portugal, and was created to coordinate and influence educational research, in particular by creating a framework oriented towards the production of useful knowledge for policy-making. This procedure allowed the major tendencies in R&D policies to be identified, namely public funding for science and science evaluation guidelines.

The next step was focused on understanding how educational researchers conceive and strategically reinvent these R&D policies. Initially, I interviewed two senior researchers, who were also coordinators of research centres (E1 and E2) and three former directors and managers of IEI (E3, E4 and E5). The prevailing criterion to choose these two researchers consisted in the inherent functions they performed as well as in the fact that, over the years, they have talked publicly about science policy. The interviews were open and exploratory (Cohen, Manion, & Keith, 2007) in order to allow the respondents to talk about their representation of educational research work and R&D policy trends. I also gathered research centres' activity reports, internal and external evaluation reports, including FCT evaluation reports.

After an exploratory reading, both documents and interviews were analysed in order to obtain emergent insights about conceptions and actions regarding educational research and R&D policies, thoroughly searching for researchers' strategies. This process allowed me to identify two categories that organised the present chapter: the convergent and the divergent strategies around R&D policies.

In order to understand these strategies more deeply and capture indicators about the ways researchers organise their work I studied co-authorship relations, since these are an established indicator for the analysis of relations between researchers (Molina, Muñoz, & Domenech, 2002). Considering scientific activity as a social process, peer relationships are an important issue (Rossoni & Graeml, 2009): researchers share ideas, use similar methods and techniques, influence one another, and one of the possible results of these collaborations is co-authoring (Moody, 2004).

The analysis focused on the publications mentioned in the scientific reports made by researchers for evaluation by FCT. These reports were directly requested from the 15 research centres and I received 13 in which I identified 690 authors and 832 publications. Using social network analysis guiding procedures (Scott, 2000) and through UCINET and NETDraw (Borgatti, Everett, & Freeman, 2002), the analysis of co-authoring relationships was developed to identify networks that revealed the ways researchers organise their work in their research centres, namely, with whom they write (department colleagues, other researchers, experts outside academia) and where they write (national or international publications).[3]

It is important to note that only parts of this data are presented in this chapter and that this procedure does not capture all the work dynamics of researchers nor does it exhaust the description of the full conditions of scientific production. What mattered was to capture autonomous regulation phenomena that covered scientific work strategies. I should also add that the more sociometric take on social networks is merely to provide methodological tools capable of describing the way researchers relate to each other.

## 5.3 Results: play the game or get played by it

Data showed that researchers develop several strategies concerning national R&D policies. As one of the interviewees sums up, "it is all about knowing how to play the game" (E2). In the next sections I will describe and illustrate convergent strategies around R&D policies, in which researchers comply with and support the orientations of public authorities, and divergent strategies, when researchers tend to question and contest those orientations.

### 5.3.1 Convergent strategies: "know how to play the game very well"

In convergent strategies towards R&D policies, researchers seek to adjust their scientific activity to the programs and initiatives of public authorities. Data revealed three main convergent strategies.

First, since 2000 there has been an increasing involvement of researchers in R&D policies. This phenomenon can be seen, for example, through the continuous growth of applications for competitive calls for funding of R&D projects in all scientific areas, as Figure 5.1 shows (FCT, 2015).

In this respect one can argue that there are no other options to obtain public funding and so, naturally, researchers play the game. However, it is still a signal of a convergent movement with the initiatives of the national authorities.

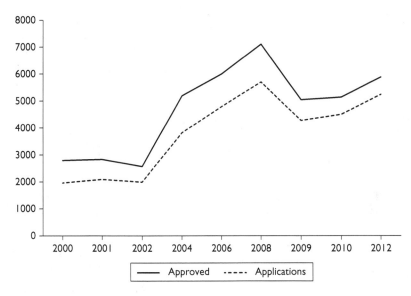

Figure 5.1 FCT applications and approved calls evolution in all scientific areas (2000–2012).

Second, researchers seek to adjust their scientific activity to the programmes and initiatives of public authorities, developing a kind of isomorphism with national policies. Regarding this point, interviewees reported the increasing adoption of the evaluation criteria used by public authorities as a guideline for research centres and researchers. One of the interviewees states:

> [We must] readjust the objectives of the research centre according to external evaluation ... We are forced to do it. It is not democratic, but it is a matter of survival.
>
> (E1)

The same interviewee described that his university research centre is now promoting calls for funding just like the ones that public authorities promote. This action was justified by three reasons: to coach researchers in applications and calls abroad; to encourage them to participate in competitive calls; and to stress the central role of research in researchers' agendas.

Third, in the same convergent pattern, another researcher justified that some research centres had higher ratings because they prepared themselves strategically and in advance for the evaluation model, stating that these researchers "know how to play the game very well" (E2). This interviewee mentioned the widespread practice of seeking to publish papers in peer review journals, namely the ones that are co-authored publications with doctoral students, as central in some research centres, signing up for a "cumulative model of science", as he describes in his own words. For him, there was a *before*, when researchers did not publish "to be cited" but rather to pursue a social value of the research work; and an *after*, when the researchers began publishing in light of the FCT assessment criteria. It seems that this action is looked upon as an obligation or, as Waitere et al. (2011) described in their study, as if researchers felt they are "forced ... by a government agency" to adopt these measures.

A good example of this phenomenon can be seen through the analysis of the publications mentioned in the scientific reports made by researchers for FCT evaluation. Using social network analysis procedures, it was possible to identify a unique and exclusive researchers' network, composed of the researchers of the only centres classified as "excellent" by FCT in its 2010 evaluation.

This network has a remarkable international brand: 48.7 per cent of the researchers are not Portuguese and their publications are published only in English and outside Portugal. It should be noted that 7.7 per cent of the authors of this network are technicians or consultants. This phenomenon illustrates the progressive expansion of the production of scientific work contexts, reflecting the emergence of new spaces and institutional contexts of knowledge production, such as offices of government agencies, consulting firms or supranational organisations (Schuller et al., 2006). In this case, research appears as a collective work that is predominantly international and legitimised not only by the university but also by other organisations. The appearance of these networks is, therefore, convergent with current R&D policies orientations.

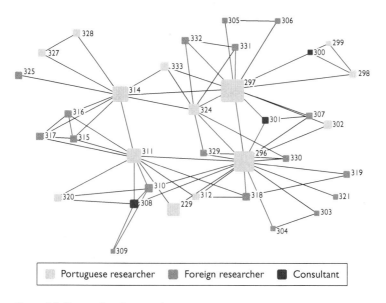

*Figure 5.2* Researchers' network.

### 5.3.2 Divergent strategies: against the new "Taylorism in science"

Simultaneously, researchers develop divergent strategies from R&D policy orientations. Recalling Bourdieu (2001), one of the interviewees claimed that national authorities are playing a "clear injunction" (E2) in scientific work, threatening the autonomy of science. For him, the growing evaluation and financing constraints brings an emergent "Taylorism in science" (E2), with much more control in scientific activity, both in topics and methods to be used as well as in the diffusion and publication of results. A first type of divergent strategy that emerged from the data includes actions of protest and contestation towards the public authorities. Two examples can be found.

First, the reaction of education research centres to the FCT evaluation back in 2010. Until then, educational research centres had obtained higher evaluation ratings than the national average of all scientific areas. However, in 2010 there was an increase in the evaluation results for research centres in all scientific areas and a decrease in education research centres, as illustrated by Figures 5.3 and 5.4.

Claiming a general downgrade in the evaluation results of education research centres, a group of 11 scientific coordinators got together and signed a protest addressed to FCT, requesting a review and a reopening of the evaluation process. As a result, a new evaluation process took place, with a new evaluation panel, and five of the research centres raised their ranking position (FCT, 2015). Besides collective reaction, it became more common to administratively contest results of the FCT evaluations regarding the R&D call for funding research projects when the decision is not to fund the project (even when the research project is rated as "excellent", there are some cases where, for lack of public funds, projects do not obtain funding).

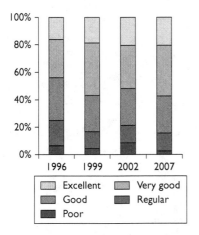

*Figure 5.3* Research centres' rating in all scientific areas (1996–2007).

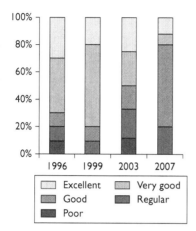

*Figure 5.4* Educational research centres' rating (1996–2007).

Another example of actions of protest and contestation is the creation of informal structures to pressure national authorities into playing a more relevant role in R&D policies. With respect to this point, interviewees described the attempt to create a lobby group composed of the scientific coordinators of education research centres, claiming "more public and transparent processes of research evaluation" (E1). This initiative led to the creation of a national council of education research centres in 2010, a "forum for debate on science policy, scientific and academic cooperation" (Declaration of Constitution of the Council of Education Research Centres, 2010). This council also sought to promote the acknowledgement of educational research among other social sciences and public authorities responsible for science policy.

The second kind of divergent strategy consists in the researchers' efforts to maintain a degree of autonomy regarding the orientations of public authorities. In this respect, data showed the researchers' attempts to align the criteria of financial provisions with their own personal agendas. Two of the former directors and managers of IEI, the national agency created to promote educational research, talked about the frustration they felt in trying to compel researchers to produce a more "practical" and "useful knowledge" (E5). Even with clear objectives in the calls for financial support for research, calling for certain themes or issues around the educational policy agenda, the interviewees affirm that

> [Researchers] do not meet the more objective criteria.
>
> (E4)

> We defined some selection criteria that would lead [research] . . . but it was not always possible.
>
> (E3)

One of the interviewees reported that to escape a merely reactive action to the national educational policy agenda, researchers also seek scientific international networks to access different funding sources.

To sum up, data showed that researchers develop convergent and divergent strategies around R&D policies. They converge by adhering to the calls and programmes of public authorities, by using FCT evaluation criteria for internal and self-evaluation or by pursuing more international, published and peer-reviewed research. Regarding this point, "researchers get played by the game", since they are caught up in the rules defined by public authorities. Simultaneously, researchers are also critical and contest the orientations of public authorities: they either manage to create pressure groups, questioning FCT evaluation results, or they try to maintain scientific autonomy regarding themes and methodologies. These divergent strategies are clear attempts to avoid or minimise PBRF trends in R&D policies by redefining and readjusting the game rules. However, what seems to be more interesting than the existence of these two kinds of strategies is the fact that they co-exist; I shall discuss this in the next and final section of this chapter.

## 5.4 Final remarks

Considering the scenario of educational research in Portugal in the last few years, this chapter presented some of the strategies of researchers concerning new regulation modes in R&D policies. The study and its findings call for three final remarks.

A first remark must emphasise the remarkably consistent results of this study with others that have increasingly shown that today's R&D policies, namely through PBRF systems, are at the root of changes in the means of scientific production and even in researchers' perceptions of their work (see, for instance Shore, 2010). In this sense, the case of Portugal is a good example of science public policy reconfiguration processes and of the dilemmas and tensions they cause in scientific work.

A second remark is related to the fact that data showed researchers play an active role in receiving and reinventing public policy orientations. They may or may not be convergent with public policies, and their strategies may be more or less visible, but they represent the way researchers deal with attempts to control scientific work. In that sense, the strategies researchers develop are a sign of autonomous regulation in science policy and place researchers as policy authors.

A final remark to be made refers to the overlapping and co-existence of convergent and divergent strategies of researchers around R&D policies. This co-existence is a clear sign of the complexity of public policies and a motive to avoid establishing linear relations between pressures from R&D policies and researchers' work.

To justify this observation, I start by recalling the review by Abramo et al. (2011), which demonstrates that while some studies reveal that researchers are adapting their work considering evaluation criteria, other studies show that there is no linear connection between funding science policies and changes in scientific work. However, these are not inconsistent results and this apparent contradiction needs to be reconceptualised because it tends "to ignore the importance of the context" (idem, p. 653) in which researchers are inserted and the complexity and unpredictable character of public policies.

In fact, despite the transnational dimension of the science public policies underway, and the dilemmas and tensions they pose to researchers, public policy studies have increasingly shown the importance of the social actors' reinterpretations and the contexts in which they operate as they define the course of the policies. The multiplicity of actors and the growing sources and tools of regulation give today's public policies a hybrid, fragmented character (Maroy, 2008). Public policies are complex, given the plurality of actors, with different intentions and interests, present in multiple scales and interdependencies which produce "forms of regulation of collective activity" (Commaille, 2006, p. 413). As a result, some rules and orientations are mutually cancelled out, thanks to the successive "adjustments and readjustments" made by actors according to their objectives and strategies (Barroso, 2005). Consequently, public policies also remain unpredictable because of the difficulty in establishing a causal link between normative production and the action of actors, given the strategic sense in public action (Jenkins-Smith & Sabatier, 1993). The apparent contradictory results and/or the presence of convergent and divergent researcher strategies around R&D public policies are a reflection of the presence of multiple regulatory sources that influence the course of public action, such as the state, the market, and the academic profession (Dill, 2014); management, organisational and cultural dynamics on scientific production (Edgar & Geare, 2013); or individual researchers' and policy-makers' objectives. As Ozga (2000) points out, this study showed that "there is no straightforward polarity of academic autonomy and state instrumentalism" (Ozga, 2000, p. 76), but a strategic game between social actors.

However, we must not ignore that PBRF and current R&D policies try and often succeed in "reshap[ing] institutional and disciplinary governance structures, policies, individual outputs, work practices and careers" (Bobis et al., 2013, p. 454). In fact, as this chapter has shown, there are already several effects on R&D policies on scientific work that were analysed as strategic actions. Even without the initial goal to draw implications for public policy and practice, two remarks must be made. First, regarding public policy, the study findings converge towards the lack of evidence that "research evaluation tool enhances research performance and scientific progress in general" (Moed, 2008, p. 160). On the contrary, some state that PBRF-inspired systems do not provide the necessary conditions for science. *The Slow Science Manifesto* is very clear in this respect:

> We do need time to think. We do need time to digest. We do need time to mis-understand each other, especially when fostering lost dialogue between humanities and natural sciences.

Second, regarding researchers' autonomy, as this study has also shown, despite all constraints and pressures on researchers' work, there is always a margin of action played by social actors. We must recall that, in the last centuries, scientific work has been marked by publications, collaborative work and international organisations (Charle, Schriewer, & Wagner, 2004). Thus, we are witnessing a conversion and appropriation by the public authorities of the researchers' activities: writing is now regarded as not necessarily having a mercantile nature, and whereas circulation of scientific forums was an affirmation of autonomy and scientific freedom, these are now emergent and powerful control mechanisms of scientific activity. But, as the study showed, whilst we cannot ignore the effects R&D policies have on researchers, we must not take them as completely determinant of scientific work (Nóvoa, 2015).

## Notes

1 The study was conducted as part of a broader investigation, supported by FCT (SFRH / BD / 60714/2009), that aimed to study educational research regulation modes in Portugal.
2 Some quantitative data show this evolution: "The number of researchers per thousand labor force, which was 2.4 FTE in 1995, reached a value of 11 FTE in 2012, above the EU and OECD averages; the number of international scientific publications (...) has grown almost ten-fold between 1995 and 2013 (...). R&D expenses for the Higher Education sector more than tripled between 1995 and 2011" (FCT, 2015).
3 For more detail, consult Viseu (2015).

Chapter 6

# On relevance and norms of science in times of restructuring
Educational research in Sweden

*Rita Foss Lindblad and Sverker Lindblad*

## 6.1 Introduction

This chapter addresses the nature and consequences of changes in public research policy towards increased competitiveness and strategic funding for educational research in Sweden. Motivated by the basic fact that state interference within the realms of educational research always relates to political interests in its social value, our focus will be on the transition of arrangements and conceptions of such ideas and their implications for critical and autonomous research, long considered to guarantee the production of high-quality research of societal importance.

The case we are analysing is Sweden – a Nordic welfare state in the process of rapid restructuring of higher education and research. We consider this a fruitful case with processes and practices that are common to other national and international settings, but with some specific characteristics in the ways in which research and higher education policy has operated in the social and intellectual organization of educational research. More precisely we put forward three characteristics: First, educational research was organized as a specific discipline (Pedagogik) as in continental Europe (e.g. the Nordic countries and Germany and Switzerland) and is now transformed into a field of educational sciences (pedagogik, psychology, political science, humanities, etc.) competing for recognition and resources. Second, educational research was previously to a large extent carried out outside teacher education colleges in specific university departments, but is now getting a more prominent position in teacher education, where, third, the previous organization of teacher colleges are being dissolved and instead organized into multi-disciplinary university departments. Thus, by means of these specific characteristics the Swedish case has the potential to further clarify the complex and intriguing political nature of research organization more generally.

As we hope to show, the pressures of the political on educational research works in tandem with the more general transformation of the Swedish higher education system, where previous lines between politics and research have been broken and new pathways for high-quality and relevant educational research has been outlined. To our understanding, the supposed existence of norms or a scientific ethos (Merton, 1942, 1968) has previously worked in order to protect academia and research from being eroded by non-scientific and ideological influences (important not least symbolically). But because of the changed relations between politics and research, we see it as urgent to re-address questions about their existence, nature and role in the transformation and re-organization of educational research into what supposedly is considered to be knowledge of increased social relevance.

Thus, we are dealing with a problem of science–society interaction that links to a large set of studies on higher education and research in societal contexts, such as Gieryn (1983), Nowotny et al. (2001), and Ziman (1994, 2002). Viewed from the perspective of global trends of strategic funding, marketization and increasing competition between researchers, research sectors and higher education institutions, such interplay has become urgent to analyse and to discuss in relation to our understanding of science and knowledge production in society (cf Whitley, 2000, and Furlong & Lawn, 2011). To us, the situation in the early 2000s reminds us of the state of affairs in the 1930s and 1940s considering debates on academic heteronomy and autonomy (cf Gustavsson, 1971), but the situation of increased external pressures put upon tertiary research is radically different and actualizes once again questions about what norms we can – and should – adhere to as educational scholars.

Given this framing we put forward the following research questions:

- How have demands of the social value of educational research been embedded in its organization, funding and governance – and what changes are occurring over time?
- What rationalities are inscribed in current ideas about the relevance of educational research and how, and with what consequences for an academic ethos, are they turned into action?

Our answers to these questions are used to discuss current preconditions and demands on educational research.

## 6.2 Norms of science: why and how they (still) matter for educational research

Before turning to our specific case, we will first and briefly clarify the linkages between scientific norms and how and why they matter to educational research. Such norms are, as we will argue, important for regulating relations between research and politics. They are important for keeping politics as well as commerce and stakeholders at a distance, while at the same time guaranteeing the research community the power of regulating its own business in the name of such things as science, truth, democracy and the welfare of citizens and society (Mulkay, 1976). This gives norms of science political significance, first on the conduct and evaluation of research and second, on the organization and governance of scientific knowledge (see Lamont, 2009). Both issues reveal the necessity of repeatedly reconstructing the foundations for the boundaries between science and politics (Brown & Malone, 2004, p. 114).[1]

Debates and studies that concern scientific norms are extensive. Most well known is Merton's *scientific ethos* (1942, 1968), whose norms of communism, universalism, dis-interestedness and organized scepticism (the so called CUDOS norms) express a defence of the autonomy and social value of science and, also, its dependence on particular types of social structure. Protecting science from external and ideological pressures by defending scientific autonomy could in his view not be upheld without a defence of liberal democracy in society as well as in academia.[2] It is important to note that the defence of autonomy and the addressed incompatibility between science and politics concerned totalitarianism, not science-society or science relations as such, and concerns as much the totalitarianism of Nazism as the influence from markets and markets ideologies (Kalleberg, 2007).

This openness for societal matters may also be a reason for the long interest in and reference to Merton's norms and a scientific ethos that serves the interests of both science and society. Even now references to the CUDOS norms are common in various professional ethics and codex where they have been translated into binding rules and regulations of research practices, usually set up on a contractual basis by state authorities and research councils.[3] But the supposed existence of norms is also essential and frequently referred to in reflexive discussions about changes in higher education and research, as well as society. Here, again, their political and symbolically powerful importance for the protection and maintenance of the relative autonomy of scientific knowledge production comes into focus.

The case of educational research in terms of autonomy and science-society relations is special. Being a science it should serve societal needs which means a dependence on discourses where these needs, and how they are scientifically answered, are authorized scientifically as well as politically. Thus, ideas about and pressures put upon educational research to fulfil social uses or relevance will discursively have to bend over ideas of science. Typically, this involves manifold processes of demarcations of an epistemological, as well as an organizational nature, which over time has given the social embedment of educational research some intellectual as well as institutional specificity. Needless to say, one characteristic outcome has been that its status as a science has frequently been questioned, as to some extent it has come to be viewed as a misfit according to standard views on science and existing internal hierarchies of disciplines and research traditions (Barnehouse Walters, Lareau & Ranis, 2009).[4]

This situation could, however, be viewed from different perspectives, where the struggles to set boundaries for its identity have involved a politics of knowledge that has engaged researchers as well as policy-makers and professionals such as teachers. Whatever route its development and internal differentiation has taken over time, it is, we will argue, best understood as a political struggle over identity and research objectives – over what educational research is and should be about. Norms of science have played a crucial role here; for defence of the routes taken, for the critique delivered or answered, and for the rhetoric that follows in the making of research objectives.

The next section briefly describes the contours of this situation and how the struggles over its identity and developments have been played out in the Swedish context. It will be sketched and described from a perspective where the social value and use of educational research has been transformed, from periods of time of status quo to those of greater conflict. From periods of time where its social value, use and relevance was more or less taken for granted, to the present time of discourse where relevance has come to mean limitations even in the freedom of researchers to define their research agendas. As we will show, competitive and strategic funding is today one important strategy used, out of which one possible outcome is that the *diversity* and therefore also the *robustness* of research can be said to be under threat (Jacob, 2014). If correct, this will mean one of two things. It will *either* mean changes and transformations in the norms that are thought to guide higher education institutions and its activities *or* the emergence of new counter-strategies where the supposed norms as we know them will be used in new ways.

## 6.3 Educational research in Sweden: trajectories of relevancing and funding

Our next step is to turn to the history of educational research in Sweden – the period of the early 20th century up to today. We focus on its establishment as a scientific discipline, "Pedagogik", and follow its transformation from the humanities to a social science (as sociology, psychology, etc.) and then its transition into the current construction as part of a field of study researching educational issues (together with, e.g. psychology, sociology and political science).[5]

This is a somewhat specific trajectory of research organization. In Continental Europe and the Nordic Countries a similar disciplinary road was taken in the 19th and early 20th century, in contrast to most Anglo-Saxon contexts, where intellectual organization was developed as a field of study consisting of different departments (e.g. in maths education, curriculum studies, educational psychology), which are connected to teacher education but also related to founding disciplines (see, e.g., Schriewer & Keiner, 1992; Hofstetter & Schneuwly, 2002).

Though this kind of organization was originally different from the Anglo-Saxon context, the organization and governance of educational research has turned to be convergent with other national contexts. For example, when comparing Australia and Sweden (Lindblad & Foss Lindblad, 2013; Besley, 2008). Added to such convergent tendencies, Swedish educational research is operating in – and is part of – globalizing tendencies, where transnational and supranational agents, such as the OECD or UNESCO, are at work. Important here is the European Union with the creation of a European Higher Education Area and the making of a European Research Space. Such tendencies are a part of educational research over the world and are assumed to have an innovating and standardizing impact on research, as well as radical changes in the norms of science (Ziman, 1994). This means the Swedish case today has several characteristics in common with other national cases in terms of an increasingly competitive academic culture of market-oriented norms, research agendas, international cooperation and pressures upon educational research.[6]

## 6.4 A periodization: from conquered trust to contested relevance for educational research

In order to identify translations and materializations of research relevance we present a periodization in the trajectory of educational research in Sweden.[7] In the first section we present our intent to put research relevance and production of educational knowledge in the context of research governance and organizational matters. Our point of departure is that changes in such contexts for educational research are working in tandem with the restructuring of its organization and identity as a science – and as a science of scientific as well as social value and use.

It is our ambition that the periodization will help to clarify the interplay between higher education and research policy, the social and intellectual organization of educational research and the preconditions for the production of educational knowledge and its scientific and political authority and legacies.

## 6.5 Institutionalization: aspiring academic relevance

In Sweden educational science was institutionalized as a discipline – "Pedagogik" – in the early 20th century. This achievement was preceded by inquiries and investigations – often internationally inspired – in education matters in the 19th century. Studies of education issues were mostly carried out in philosophy, see for instance Immanuel Kant's lectures "Über Pädagogik" (1803) or various analyses considering "Bildung" (Bruford, 1975) and of elites or of the population as a whole.[8] The strategy and necessity for making "educational research" a discipline fit well with ways of organizing scientific knowledge within higher education institutions (HEIs) at that time.

First, the proponents for Pedagogik argued that its institutionalization as a discipline would allow and guarantee a growth of knowledge that would make important contributions not only for Swedish society but also for universities, thus using the rhetoric of rational modernization built on science. The university should provide a scientific education of secondary school teachers in pedagogical matters such as philosophical rationales for goal-setting and the psychology of student learning, and through that reinforce the position of science in society.[9]

Second, opponents put forward some obstacles for accepting Pedagogik. Such an aspiring discipline was needed to demonstrate recognized academic qualities to be trusted as an entry into academia with its dominating scientific ideals and with room for different tasks. Arguments considering the importance of Pedagogik in the education of teachers were countered by statements that teaching is not a scientific endeavor but a craft, and that Pedagogik as part of teacher education would lessen the time for other – and more important – disciplines in the education of secondary school teachers. The proponents for Pedagogik had to struggle inside as well as outside academia. Their arguments were a combination of different kinds of rationalities – that Pedagogik was part of recognized philosophical inquiries in combination with pragmatic issues that it would be an improvement in making science matter in the education of teachers compared to the traditional craft exercised by school masters.[10] We note here intense political struggles in the universities to formulate and give contours of its specificity and identity as an autonomous discipline, as well as to counteract its inclusion. However, in these discourses pragmatic arguments about its societal relevance became successful. In 1907 the Swedish parliament decided to give resources for Pedagogik as a university discipline. At Uppsala University a chair in Pedagogik was installed in 1912 (with some hesitation) and at Lund University an initial refusal to install a chair turned into acceptance when it was realized that students would lack important merits if they did not have Pedagogik courses in their portfolios.[11]

In sum, the institutionalization of Pedagogik as a scientific discipline was to a large extent based on political decisions and needs. However, when the position of being a discipline was conquered, Pedagogik was recognized as a trusted member of academia.

## 6.6 Expansion: taking advantage of given academic relevance

During the following decades Pedagogik performed as a minor institution in the Swedish system of higher education and research, mostly dealing with the education of upper secondary education teachers and civil servants.[12] However, this changed with the progress of the education sector in the welfare state, such as the comprehensive school system with compulsory secondary education, and later in the making of higher education reforms.

The relevance of Pedagogik for education of teachers and civil servants had been proven in previous discourses. After World War 2 the given legitimacy and authority of Pedagogik as a scientific discipline was heavily exploited in policy discourses and public debates. Inquiries and statements based on educational research were in many ways assumed to guide policy decisions and to evaluate how well such decisions functioned. In a way prominent educational researchers achieved the position of state intellectuals in the making of welfare state education.[13] Antagonists to the reform policy did not question the results and conclusions based on educational research, but put forward more demands for educational research in order to analyze the preconditions and consequences of ongoing reforms. In sum, Pedagogik was trusted in producing policy-relevant research given its scientific qualities, while there was less trust in school-based innovations and teachers' development work at that time.[14]

The trust given to the scientific value of Pedagogik as relevant for social uses was taken advantage of by the research community as well as administrators and policy-makers of different kinds. It was assumed that educational research could serve the purposes of presenting conclusions about educational problems in an authoritative way, such as presenting solutions to political or administrative problems. Seen in retrospect it is obvious that this given trust would erode due to the problematic and high expectations put upon Pedagogik as a science.

This period of expansion was significantly captured by the evaluation of Swedish educational research carried out in the middle of the 1990s, initiated by educational researchers in the research council commission of Pedagogik. The vast majority of research in education was actually carried out within the discipline of Pedagogik and was regarded by international evaluators as being successful (Rosengren & Öhngren, 1997). However, the evaluators pointed to a blind spot in Swedish Pedagogik – that the researchers did not see or reflect on its intimate connection to political and administrative powers in education. Furthermore, the expansion made it possible to develop research specialties in Pedagogik without confronting the research community – there was little need to fight for resources for research. This was also commented on in the evaluation report, which pointed to opportunities for research cooperation and integration – opportunities that were not, to our understanding, considered in the expansion period.

To sum up the expansion period: it was founded on trust given to Pedagogik as an academic discipline serving societal and political needs. How to use these qualities was discussed in different ways and became somewhat of a problem in terms of scientific status. However, the distinction between theoretical and applied research and the making of sectorial research programs, such as at the national Board of Education and the Board of Higher Education, came to guarantee its expansion. We note here different ways of nuancing the accuracy of the relevance in directions and outcomes of current research and in the establishment of alternative routes, such as teacher research or multi-disciplinary approaches.

## 6.7 Contraction: competing in a period of contested relevance

The expansion period ended with the millennium. At that time the disciplinary organization in terms of Pedagogik was transformed into "Educational Research" as a field of study – multi-disciplinary or trans-disciplinary – by research policy decision-making. Two issues are important for capturing the relevance of Pedagogik: first, the finalization of sectorial research was regarded as being too politically informed and lacking scientific quality. Second, the transfer of resources for educational research into the research councils that dealt with education as a multi-disciplinary field of study. Added to this was a general restructuring of the system of higher education and research with little direct state funding and more external funding by means of competition.

This transformation meant increasing competition for research funds both within Pedagogik and within the field of educational research. Thus, the hey-day of Pedagogik having a privileged position in access to educational research funds was over.[15] In sum, the relevance previously attributed to educational research was translated into contested relevance based on assessments of social relevance and academic qualities by research councils that organized in a multi-disciplinary way.

This transformation was combined with the movement of teacher education from specific departments or teacher colleges to an all-encompassing issue for all parts of HEIs. Teacher education at a university is organized by a constellation of departments and faculties, what Calandar (2004) coined as a transition from a Ptolemaic to a Network organization of teacher education within a shared economy. This is a transition from a given relevance to a contested relevance in education programs. In the period of contraction the Swedish case turns out not to be Swedish at all, given the strong restructuring of the system of higher education and research in Sweden and the introduction of new public management strategies to govern the system and to make it more effective.

During this period the autonomy of educational research was questioned. Issues of political and social relevance increased and also has the prescription for researchers to use specific research approaches and methodologies, such as to do research on international comparisons in order to improve Swedish schools.[16]

## 6.8 Different periods – different organizations, relevancing and research positions

We have now made a short journey into educational research over time in Sweden. In Table 6.1 this journey is summarized in terms of organization, relevance and significant research positions for the respective periods.

The contents in the table have been introduced in previous sections. What we are now presenting is a set of ideal types of research positions in different circumstances.

First, we note that the preconditions for educational research have changed radically – from a disciplinary organization with given relevance, to a field of study with contested relevance. Indications of this are displayed in the transitions in the significant positions of educational research during the different periods. These positions are regarded as ideal types with different characteristics and strategies. By means of this typology we will discuss demands put on an academic ethos for educational research.

Table 6.1 Summary of periods in relevance and position of educational research in Sweden 1900–2015.

| Period | Organisation | Relevance | Research Position |
| --- | --- | --- | --- |
| Institutionalizing | Disciplinary | Given | Academy aspirant |
| Expanding | Disciplinary | Given and applied | State intellectual |
| Contracting | Field of study | Contested | Entrepreneur |

### 6.8.1 The institutionalizing period

Educational research had turned into an academic discipline of importance for providing a scientific education of secondary school teachers. The position was that of an aspirant that has to adjust to the manner of the academy demanded by a discipline. However, in this position we also find connections to other actors and kinds of knowledge, in terms of the knowledge and expertise that teachers are displaying at work or at teacher seminars that fall outside academia. Thus, Pedagogik had to bridge traditional boundaries between academic knowledge and practical professional knowledge. Adherence to academic values mattered to both sides.

### 6.8.2 The expanding period

This is what many consider as the golden age of Swedish Pedagogik, starting slowly in the 1940s but speeding up in the 1960s and 1970s. The expansion was based on a conjunction of the given academic relevance and the making of large school reforms in the Swedish welfare state. The specific position of educational research was privileged in terms of its recognized social value and access to economic resources. There was less need for boundary work, and notions of academic ethos in terms of academic freedom and autonomy were seldom referred to and seemed, from the position of a state intellectual, to be of no value. However, during this period, and especially at its end, the predominant position was questioned inside academia (the positivism battle for instance), by teacher education, and among teachers' professional organizations. Times were, indeed, changing.

### 6.8.3 The contracting period

At the turn of the millennium preconditions for higher education and research altered in a profound way. The HEIs became more autonomous from state interference, and in the spirit of new public management collegiality was put aside and the disciplinary structures weakened (and to some extent broken). To this was added a governance built more on competition and performance indicators. In the beginning of this period the previous trust or assumed relevance of Pedagogik was lost and its researchers were forced to navigate in a multi-disciplinary landscape, among researchers from different faculties and disciplines, all competing over scarce resources and measured by different performance indicators. During these circumstances the researchers had to operate as entrepreneurs – trying to build strong research programs highly valued by the research councils, or searching for research money wherever it was available. What matters most seems not primarily to be scientific endeavors for new and robust knowledge about educational problems and possibilities, but research that can follow political agendas and thereby obtain and maximize research funds.

What we see today is a disorganized field of educational research. There is a lack of cooperation and little defense of an academic ethos of liberal democracy and academic values. There are more struggles within a highly fragmented field. We do not know what will happen in the future, but as far as we can see the situation for Pedagogik as a discipline and for educational research as a field of study is not very promising and we find the need for an academic ethos of freedom and relative autonomy of research urgent.

## 6.9 Concluding comments on educational research in an era of contraction

One obvious argument in this chapter is that educational research during its whole history has been thought of as serving societal needs and values – be it demands of pedagogical training within universities or needs originating from challenges in the education of a population as defined by education policies. However, such expectations of educational research have been expressed in different ways – as relevance given by the scientific qualities of research carried out inside academia, or as contested by competition and politically predefined research challenges and agendas.

A second point put forward is the universal need for educational research to deal with expectations consistent with institutional imperatives for research – what are often called norms of science. The importance of this is pointed out by Novoa (2015), stating that academic freedom is everything. In this chapter we have dealt with such issues under the title of academic ethos in the way Merton (1942) conceptualized it as a defense of science in a troubled time. We are now in another troubled time, emphasizing demands of defending academic communality, disinterestedness as well as organized scepticism. In the history of educational research this is not new – we can identify it in the way Pedagogik aspired to be a discipline in higher education institutions, as well as in the expansion of educational research and the questioning of its relevance in different ways. However, as has been shown by Ziman (1994, 2002) the situation is different in higher education and research today – as presented by the distinction between mode 1 and mode 2 knowledge (Gibbons et al., 1994). This is a very good example of the predicament that educational research is in. First, we note that the traditional and symbolically important boundaries between science and society are weakened and demands for accountability hold researchers within all fields responsible to politicians, stakeholders and professionals – and this in a period of increased competition for scarce research funds and intellectual fragmentation (Weingart, 2008). This leads to two problems: one is that the agenda for educational research is formulated by other agents, the other is that demands for certain kinds of research methodologies are put forward for more or less strategic reasons – to develop instruments for educational control or betterment in educational systems and practices rather than for producing new knowledge. In this situation we can – or must – believe in the possibility of making choices that include the obligation to challenge existing knowledge in the search for new knowledge, and with respect given to science and society, their interrelations as well as their differences.

## Notes

1 See Nóvoa (2015) on the vital importance of academic freedom in educational research.
2 Liberal democracy in academia means that argument, not position, should matter.
3 The combination of ethical codices and academic ethos and practices to deal with such issues are present at the Swedish Research Council. See http://www.vr.se/inenglish/ethics.
4 This text is in a way written as a constructive response to such questioning.
5 Our data has mostly been policy documents (e.g. parliamentary commissions and white papers, plus information from previous analyses of educational science organisation and policy.
6 However, it must be kept in mind that while many nations have increased their dependency on private funding, Sweden is known for its low amount of private funding and for spending as much as half of its total higher education expenditures on research. Furthermore, Swedish universities were constructed as research universities with the ambition to be of equal value in terms of education and research.
7 The periodization is similar to Lindberg (2006). However, we are focusing on the expansion and contraction of educational research and are putting the year spans a bit differently.
8 Bruford, W. H. (1975). *The German tradition of self-cultivation: Bildung from Humboldt to Thomas Mann*. Cambridge University Press.
9 See here Fransson & Lundgren (2003) for different intellectual traditions in the construction of Pedagogik as a discipline.
10 These arguments take another form in Durkheim's lectures on the evolution of educational thought and distinctions between science, ideology and craft. Durkheim, E. (1971). Pedagogy and sociology. *School and Society*, 91–95.
11 Lund and Uppsala universities are old and prestigious HEIs in Sweden.
12 Dahllöf (1989).
13 Hunter (1994) names the Swedish professor Torsten Husén as an example of such state intellectuals.
14 During this period trust in teachers' professional knowledge was decreasing, indicated by the way teachers' comments and advice on reform design and evaluation were treated by the authorities. A more teacher-centered approach was created in the 1960s and worked for more than a decade with support from the Swedish National Board of Education after a research based evaluation. See Lindblad (1984).
15 During the period 2005–2010 Pedagogik and Didaktik got a total of 56 percent of funds for educational research. The social sciences got 25 percent and the Humanities 18 percent according to the Swedish Research Council (Broady, Börjesson, Dalberg, Krigh & Lidegran, 2011).
16 See e.g. the Swedish Research Council (2015). *Forskningskvalitet för framtiden*. (Research quality for the future). Stockholm: Vetenskapsrådet.

Chapter 7

# Is the Emperor naked?

## Experiencing the 'PISA hysteria', branding and education export in Finnish academia

*Fred Dervin*

### 7.1 Introduction

> The work of an intellectual is (...), through the analyses he does in his own domains, to bring assumptions and things taken for granted again into question, to shake habits, ways of acting and thinking, to dispel the familiarity of the accepted (...).
>
> (Foucault, in Gordon [2000, p. xxxiv])

In 2012 I started working at a department of teacher education in the capital city of Finland. Before that, I had a position in the humanities in a less influential university. The shift between fields occurred easily as part of my research in the other Finnish university had involved work on language and intercultural education. However the major difference was related to the emphasis on promoting and selling Finnish education that my new position entailed and which brought to mind the words of Foucault (in Gordon, 2000, p. xxxiv) above. I became intrigued by the mantra of "the best education system in the world", and the visits of hundreds of "pedagogical tourists" in search of the "miracle of Finnish education" (Niemi, Toom & Kallioniemi, 2012) in my new department. But what was most surprising was the omnipresent use of the expression "Finnish education export" to which the department contributed actively.

According to Egginger (2013) the current interest in Finnish education is not new if one looks back in history. As such, during the World Fairs of 1889/1900, Finland, which was a Grand Duchy of Russia before its independence in 1917, was already presented as some sort of "miracle". A Finnish school had been set up in Paris with a teacher and Finnish pupils involved in reading activities (Egginger, ibid.). Finnish education was already said to be *efficient, modern,* and *equalitarian* at the time.

4.12.2001 marks an important date for Finland. This is when the results of the first Programme for International Student Assessment (PISA) of the OECD were released. Finland came first, which put the small Nordic country of 5 million inhabitants on the map for many years to come and earned the country the status of "educational utopia". According to the "global ambassador and guru of Finnish education", Pasi Sahlberg:

> This [was] a very new situation for Finns. 10 years ago before 2002 we were very rarely asked to go anywhere so now if somebody wants to hear stories from Finland we... you know I wanna go... because I also understand that this is not gonna last forever that at some point we will be taken over by somebody else then all these things will be a nice memory.
> (Pasi Sahlberg, *Stanford Center for Opportunity Policy in Education*, March 2012, my transcription)

The triennial international survey aims to evaluate education systems worldwide by testing the skills and knowledge in reading, mathematics and science of 15-year-old students. Around 510,000 students from 65 countries participate in the assessment. PISA has managed to establish an increasingly strong and mediatised "comparative turn" amongst educational systems around the world, where top systems attract attention and become models for others (Grek, 2009). The most recent published results are from 2012. Finland's performance was less impressive in the last study as the country ranked number 12. However, the flow of visitors (especially from America) has not decreased, neither has the amount of requests from international media.

As we shall see in this chapter the promotion and export of Finnish education to certain parts of the world have been part of the current national branding and commercial strategies. These derive directly from the PISA fame and have led to what I shall refer to as the 'PISA hysteria'. The reputation of Finland abroad has thus been very important over the last decade and conscious efforts have been made by decision-makers and scholars, up to a point, to protect this reputation. But in September 2015 attacks on arriving asylum seekers to the country dented Finland's reputation. For instance anti-refugee protesters hurled rocks at an employee of the Finnish Red Cross, journalists and security guards and shot fireworks at a bus carrying refugees. One protester was also wearing a robe and hood, inspired by the Ku Klux Klan. Interestingly the influential evening press (*Iltasanomat/Iltalehti*) shared the worries of Finnish decision-makers and businessmen about this having a negative impact on the country's ailing economy and reputation on their ubiquitous covers all over the country – instead of condemning the attacks (28.9.2015).

In this chapter I am interested in describing how I have experienced the positioning of Finland as a utopia and the consequences it has had on scholarly work. I argue that, especially in relation to its famous education, *The Emperor is naked* when one has an insider insight. This is a reference to Hans Christian Andersen's short story *The Emperor's New Clothes* (*Kejserens nye klæder* in Danish, 1837) about two swindlers who made an Emperor believe that they could weave the most magnificent clothes for him. They also claimed that the clothes – which they pretended to weave but were in fact imaginary – could help him to identify anyone unfit for his office by becoming invisible. The Emperor decided to wear the "imaginary" clothes in a parade before his people. People started flattering him – even though he was not wearing any clothes – until a child said that the Emperor had nothing on, the "Emperor is naked." As in the story, I often have the impression that one thinks one sees a miraculous system of education in Finland, but the Emperor may not be wearing the clothes that one believes one sees. Finnish academia, especially teacher education, can appear to have acted, in a sense, like the weavers in the story.

In order to justify this claim, I am problematizing the influence of country branding, education export and the "PISA hysteria" on academic work through my own experience. I review the main actors, related to the academic world, that contribute to these phenomena. I shall refer to these elements as being *paratexts*, a term used in literary interpretation to refer to material surrounding the main text (for example: a blurb on the back of a book or the illustration on the cover). Paratexts usually have a meaning and add to that of the text (e.g. a novel) (Åström, 2014). They are nested within the main text like Russian dolls. In order to do so I use the somewhat uncomfortable approach of autoethnography to describe my position in relation to these phenomena, as a critical researcher and thinker but also as an outsider (I was not born in Finland). According to Ellis, Adams & Bochner (2010, n. p.) autoethnography is an approach that "seeks to describe and systematically analyze personal experience in order to understand cultural experience." This approach treats research as political and socially-just (ibid.). Autoethnography thus represents a combination of autobiography and ethnography, using hindsight (Freeman, 2004). According to Kiesinger (2002), autoethnography may be therapeutic for the researcher as s/he tries to make sense of themselves and their experiences, in my case the influence of the political marketization and branding on my work as a scholar. By using autoethnography I am aware of the current criticisms addressed to this perspective as being too emotional and biased, insufficiently rigorous and analytical (Hooks, 1994). Yet I do believe that the combination of the 'emotional' and the 'scientific' can help me to find answers to the following question: As a specialist on intercultural education who is critical of ethnocentrism, essentialism and culturalism (Dervin, 2015), how do I negotiate my identities in a societal and academic context like Finland? How unearthing and being aware of the mechanisms hidden behind marketization and branding can empower other scholars in other contexts – these phenomena being "universal" today? This quote from Slaughter also guides my thinking here: "Like all academics, in our heart of hearts, we believe that knowledge is power, and understanding what is happening will enable us to change it" (Slaughter, 2014, p. x).

## 7.2 Marketization, branding and the "PISA hysteria" in Finnish higher education

For Cantwell and Kauppinen (2014, p. 3), it is important to understand the complex ways in which today's universities are integrated into local, national and global political economies. They write: "nearly all aspects of higher education (e.g. student recruitment and learning, governance, organizational administration and strategy, public policy, and the academic profession) are embedded in the political economy with links to the marker, non-profit and non-governmental organisations, and the state" (ibid.). The marketization of education is a reality in Finland and is imbricated, especially, in higher education despite claims that it is not (e.g. Sahlberg, 2015). Over the last 10 years, since the semi-privatization of Finnish universities, there has been "a move from the public good knowledge/learning regime to the academic capitalist knowledge/learning regime" (Slaughter, 2014: p. vii). Teacher education being part of universities in Finland has especially triggered many business-like ventures. The economization of Finnish higher education is evident today through, for example, an increase in activities related to education export (sale of made-to-order training, knowledge, services and consultancy to other countries, see Cai & Kivistö, 2010); these represented about 100 million euros in 2013 – against, for example, 22 billion euros for the UK (Team Finland, 2014). According to the Finnish Ministry of Education and Culture (2010: p. 13), "Higher education institutions will be encouraged to be active and assume a major role as education export operators."

More importantly, institutions producing international league tables of school performance like the OECD – responsible for PISA studies – or the World Trade Organization, have played an important role in stimulating marketization and branding in Finland. They constitute what Spring (2015, p.1) calls a "global education superstructure" that "directly and indirectly influences national school systems along with multinational education corporations and schools." These also increase the influence of educational research conducted by economists and judging educational outcomes in economic terms (e.g. rankings). Scott, Posner, Martin & Guzman (2015, p. 65) claim, for instance, that the OECD "simultaneously acts as a diagnostician, judge, and policy advisor" for member states and others. These superstructures tend to continue working from a methodological nationalistic approach which is nation-based and thus, (in-)directly contribute to some sort of neo-nationalism, especially when the best performers advertise or sell their education to others. However Dale (2005) argues that our world can no longer be apprehended as local entities separated from each other in our accelerated global world, even in education where discourses and practices circulate.

Since the "PISA hysteria" started in the 2000s, imaginaries about Finnish education have blossomed: *Finland is one of the most equal countries in the world; Finnish people are hard-working and honest; Finnish children do not need to work hard at school even if they perform excellently in PISA studies,* etc. (Dervin, 2013; Sahlberg, 2015). Decision-makers', country branders', practitioners' and even researchers' voices (see e.g. Sahlberg, 2011) from Finland have contributed to spreading this common sense, supported by international media, politically engaged scholars and foreign politicians in need of inspiration. Critics of PISA have noted many methodological concerns about the conduct, analysis and interpretation of its results (Goldstein, 2004). For instance, I have been personally very critical of interpretations such as the following, concerning Finnish pupils' excellent results at reading:

> This is due to both educational and socio-cultural reasons: teaching children to read in school is based on individual development and pace rather than standardised instruction and frequent testing; Finnish parents read a lot themselves and also to their children; books and newspapers are easily available through a dense library network; and children watch subtitled TV programmes from early on.
>
> (Sahlberg, 2011, p. 25)

Although Sahlberg's arguments include larger societal aspects such as TV and reading outside schools, it seems to me that too much emphasis is laid on the positive influence of parents and teachers. I believe that looking into the specificities of the Finnish language, which has regular spelling, compared to, for example, speakers of English, should retain our attention. While in Finnish every single letter is pronounced, English pronunciation is quite challenging as the way words are written rarely correspond to how they are read aloud. Take for example the words *Leicestershire* ['lestəʃə(r)] and *Marimekko* in Finnish. Ignoring this aspect can rhetorically serve the purpose of showing the "superiority" of Finnish education and society (teachers are excellent; parents caring, etc.). Again as a linguist and interculturalist I have often felt very uncomfortable with this uncritical claim.

Such imaginaries about Finnish education often construct Finland as a different place that has very little in common with other countries – especially in terms of education (Sahlberg, 2015). The insistence on dissimilarities makes the Nordic country both an "exotic" place and a "better" place. Finland has somewhat understood the value of these aspects in advertising and selling its educational system. Adopting an ambiguous form of *bovarysm* (Gaultier, 1902), through which Finland is constructing herself as better than she is, those who sell implicitly or explicitly her education often lessen the value of others by othering them and representing them as "bad examples" to follow (the case of China) or as being ruthless and even "primitive" forms of education (Schatz, Popovic & Dervin, 2015). Falling into these traps of "apparent neutrality of description" (Holliday, 2010) represents a danger for those who get compared. Chung's (2015, p. 476) warning about comparing Finland's education system with other systems argues for a different approach to comparison:

> While I have argued thus far that Finland provides a good example of education policy, especially in terms of teacher education and political consensus, there is the underlying and tempting risk of viewing Finnish education uncritically, as a "silver bullet" for all educational pitfalls and problems.

This leads me to the idea of nation branding, which, in the case of Finland, has clearly had an influence on the phenomena described above. Over the last 10 years this phenomenon has spread in certain fields of research in Finland – such as teacher education – and contributed to uncritical claims about Finnish education. The concept of country branding has been introduced by, for example, Aronczyk (2013) and Anholt (2009). Aronczyk defines country branding as:

> Using the tools, techniques and expertise of commercial branding is believed to help nations articulate a more coherent and cohesive identity, attract foreign capital, and maintain citizen loyalty. In short, the goal of nation branding is to make the nation *matter* in a world where borders and boundaries appear increasingly obsolete.
>
> (ibid., p. 12)

In the document entitled *Mission for Finland* published in 2010, the Finnish authorities place education at the centre of the nation branding strategy. The document also justifies the need for nation branding in the following terms:

> 1) Increasing the appreciation of the fruits of Finnish labor, that is, promoting the export of Finnish products and services, 2) Promoting international investments in Finland, 3) Promoting inbound tourism to Finland, 4) Promoting the international status of the Finnish State, 5) Promoting the appeal of Finland among international professionals, 6) Raising the national self-esteem of Finns.
>
> (CBR, 2010, p. 23)

Interestingly nation branding represents, in a sense, a "renationalization" of Finland, a new phase in defining Finnish people's identity and appeal to the world through the forces of the market. Of course, Finland was not the first nation to explicitly brand itself in 2010. As a "smaller power" in the world Finland needs to legitimize its very existence and nation branding represents a powerful way to do so (Lehti, 2011), especially as Finland has had a good reputation in most international rankings. Reinikainen (2012, p. 17) notes that:

> Newsweek (2010) ranked Finland as a best country in the world using factors related to health, economic dynamism (. . .), education, political environment, and quality of life. Another, so-called Legatum Institute's Prosperity Index (2010) ranking of 110 countries covering 90% of the World's population ranked Finland also among the happiest countries.

Anholt's Good Country Index placed Finland number 2 after Ireland (http://www.goodcountry.org/overall) in 2014. The controversial idea of the Index is to measure what countries contribute to the common good of humanity and what they take away.

As major actors in education export and in branding Finland abroad, Finnish institutions of higher education have taken part (ex-/implicitly) in the common branding strategies that have been defined by the last governments.

## 7.3 Marketization and branding in practice: actors, (hidden) agendas and impact

In the summer of 2015 I organized a summer school course entitled "Understanding Finnish education: Myths and Realities". My motivation was to contribute to deconstructing the "miracle of Finnish education" with students from around the world. During three weeks, the students attended "critical" lectures and visited schools. In order to be selected into the course the students had to write a motivation letter. It is interesting to see that most letters contained references to "actors" that had passed onto them knowledge about Finnish education. Let me share some examples:

> As an educator who has been teaching and has future research goals, Finnish education has been a growing interest of mine. **I have read articles and watched videos of faculty discussing and telling** the core principles and success stories of education in Finland.

> One of the reasons for the international top position that Finland holds, concerning education, would be the quality of teachers. (...) **Pasi Sahlberg**, a **Finnish education expert**, once said that the quality of the teacher is crucial but that demanding a higher degree is not a recipe for better education. According to him the Dutch policymakers make a mistake in their thinking. **Sahlberg** says that you should not develop education policy to become the best, but because you want to achieve something with your education.

> I follow Finnish transformation in education for many years, through online news as well as books like **Pasi Sahlberg's FINNISH LESSONS 2.0** (and the earlier version), Amanda Ripley's *The Smartest Kids in the World*, as well as Andy Hargreaves and Michael Fullan's *Professional Capital: Transforming Teaching in Every School*.

> The starting point that I am interested in Finland's education is the book *Finnish Lessons: What Can the World Learn from the Educational Change in Finland*, written by **Parsi** *(sic)* **Sahlberg**. I was so impressed by the education system in Finland.

It is fair to say that the aforementioned actors have an influence on how these students perceive Finnish education and the reasons behind its "miraculous" system of education. The students mention a scholar (Sahlberg) but also the media, which tend to blend in to create certain images of Finnish education.

As asserted earlier, an institution like a university does not stand on its own, but is dependent on other forces (Cantwell & Kauppinen, 2014). My interest in what follows is to discuss the multifaceted actors who have contributed to Finnish education beyond its borders and in relation to my own university. While I am doing this I am also sharing my uncomfortable feelings about these aspects of branding Finnish education. While "digging", one finds that there are very obvious influencers but also, and often more importantly, invisible actors. What agendas do they serve and what is their potential impact on the work and definition of a researcher?

In terms of direct influencers, many individuals who are active in English on social media contribute to "advertise" for Finnish education and are somewhat interrelated by the multimodality of these media (i.e. they tend to interact with each other). Let me mention a few (selected) examples. Pasi Sahlberg,[1] who was visiting professor at Harvard University at the time of writing, is very active on Twitter where he often "advertises" for Finnish education. In the view of this author, his (few) critiques of Finnish education can sometimes appear to be somewhat selective and his discourses about it somewhat unstable (depending on the language he writes in). For instance at the Stanford Centre for Opportunity Policy in Education in March 2012, Sahlberg was unable to respond to criticisms from a colleague of his hostess, Linda Darling-Hammond, Charles E. Ducommun Professor of Education:

- You don't include that you have the most expensive early childhood education, you don't include that they start at 2 years old.
- Your PISA scores went down between 2003 and 2009 in literacy. Why?
- If you don't include that stuff, if you don't include the social welfare, you're really not telling the whole story.

(my transcription)

Darling-Hammond quickly silenced her colleague (*I was just asking if you had a question, I do want to get other folks in*) while Sahlberg was unable to respond to these essential questions.

Sahlberg is the author of the best seller *Finnish Lessons: What Can the World Learn from Educational Change in Finland?* (2011) and *Finnish Lessons 2.0* (2015). He has travelled the world and given hundreds of talks on Finnish education, hence his unofficial title of "Ambassador of Finnish education". He also consults with many governments around the world and is on the board of the University of Oulu in the North of Finland. Many pedagogical tourists who visit Finland mention his book as the "bible" about Finnish education. Interestingly, in an article published in 2015, which contained a disclosure statement, one could read that "Pasi Sahlberg does not work for, consult, own shares in or receive funding from any company or organization that would benefit from this article, and has disclosed no relevant affiliations beyond the academic appointment above [Harvard University]." It is important to note, however, that he is an adjunct professor at the University of Helsinki (and uses a Helsinki.fi e-mail address) and that he often cooperates with, for example, the Finnish Embassy in the US and contributes thus to Finnish nation branding. The global influence of this "guru" on discourses about Finland and his political claims about education can be felt in the everyday experiences of scholars involved in Finnish teacher education. His influence is so important that it is often difficult to question his views and assumptions which circulate amongst, for example, pedagogical tourists and international students who visit Finland. Recently, while discussing potential examiners for one of my doctoral students' work on intercultural education, one of my colleagues who co-supervised my student suggested that Sahlberg should be included in the reviewing panel arguing that "(he) could be a good contact for the student to have." I vehemently disagreed, explaining that intercultural and linguistic matters were not amongst his research interests . . . In my opinion, as one of the only Finnish scholars to have reached global stardom, I believe it is easy to see through this example how Sahlberg can tend to be used as a way of boosting other people's potential place in his "spotlight".

Another influencer on the reputation of Finnish education is of course the "father" of the official Finnish country branding, who was former Prime Minister at the time of writing, Alexander Stubb. He has been extensively involved in advertising for Finnish education around the world. In 2015 an American teacher who worked in Finland also contributed actively to advertise for Finland through his writings in online American magazines. The teacher, called Tim Walker,[2] used to be a Grade 5 classroom teacher at a Helsinki public school before moving to a smaller town in Finland. From my critical intercultural perspective, his writings on Finnish education can sometimes appear to exaggerate its positive side. Interestingly, the national newspaper Helsingin Sanomat ran a piece in September 2015 asserting that he had left his job because he was tired of the traditional and "boring" teaching methods in Finland. But according to Walker: "This morning I received a phone call from the Finnish newspaper Helsingin Sanomat, apologizing for their article's misleading title, which said that I left my Helsinki school because I was 'bored' with Finnish teaching methods. Now they've changed the title of the article" (Facebook). He is often referred to on Sahlberg's Twitter. Most interesting for me is the fact that Walker is registered as a doctoral student at my own department at the University of Helsinki, and, at the time of writing, was writing a book about Finnish education. One other very important voice for Finland's country branding is the company behind the mobile game *Angry Birds*, Rovio. The company's Chief Marketing Director, Peter Vesterbacka, is probably one of the best promoters of Finnish education, especially since his company has decided to join forces with the University of Helsinki to develop gaming and learning spaces. According to the company, Rovio aims at combining two top brands, Finnish Learning and Angry Birds. The Department of Teacher Education and Rovio have together set up an "inspiring physical environment combined with the creative educational program [to] make learning a fun experience". Angry Birds Playground has been sold to China. A VP and Head Teacher of a Chinese kindergarten explains that, "We can together introduce the world-class Finnish education to children in China with Angry Birds Playground and the learn through playing concept – this will evolutionalise the way Chinese parents and children view early-years education". Rovio's marketing prospectuses include pictures of many of the influencers mentioned earlier at events such as signing agreements with important foreign partners.

Another direct influencer, whose clear role is to advertise for Finland, is called Team Finland[3] – an organization which is attached directly to the Prime Minister's Office. Team Finland is described as follows:

> The Team Finland network promotes Finland and its interests abroad: Finland's external economic relations, the internationalization of Finnish enterprises, investments in Finland and the country brand. The Team Finland operating model brings together key actors in these fields both at home and abroad. The actors are guided by shared goals annually approved by the Government. The aim of cooperation is to create a clear, flexible and customer-oriented operating model where projects falling under the scope of Team Finland activities are carried out in cooperation between state and private actors.[4]

The University of Helsinki, like most institutions of Higher Education in Finland, works closely with Team Finland. According to a document published by Team Finland key actors in Finland's national branding should share similar messages about Finland and Finns – universities included. In their Strategy Update of 2015 Team Finland explains that the aim of country image communications is: "to ensure that a consistent country image is built and relayed through all channels; to keep the shared message clear; to offer support and tools to produce new communications materials supporting the country image".[5] They thus propose to promote Finland and Finns as follows:

- We are solution-focused, straightforward – and cool: Messages about Finland and Finns.
- We export our creativity and expertise to the world: Culture and education are our soft power.

(Team Finland, 2015)

Team Finland has an extensive network of local teams around the world. Embassies and cultural centers are their partners and most continents are covered. Documentation has been produced for these partners as well as for other key actors to help them spread the message about Finland. Four key areas have been highlighted as selling points: *1. Cleanliness, 2. Education, 3. Design and 4. Competence.* On top of these, Finland has been packaged as "the most functional country in the world" ("we educate problem solvers") and a long list of competences shared by Finns has been decided upon: *natural competence, authenticity, problem-solving ability, quality and top products, reliability, language skills*, etc. The following elements are contained in the Finland country image communications workbook (n. d.):

### Fluency

Finns have a direct, no-nonsense attitude. Finns do not dwell on things but solve them. In Finland, systems – education, social support, political, transport, infrastructure, etc. – work. Problems are anticipated and solved when they are encountered. The authorities can be trusted. Simple solutions are found to complex problems.

### Sincerity and authenticity

Finnishness is specificity, particularity, creativity and positive difference. Finns are partly children of nature and partly engineers. Finland is a humane country of smart international people.[6]

These are, I think, idealised, essentialistic, ethnocentric discourses on Finns and Finland.

Team Finland also suggests to its partners and key actors to represent Finland and Finns in certain ways: "the image of Finland highlights active people solving problems, there is something going on inside their brains all the time, the image of Finland is vibrant and full of rhythm." Examples of pictures are also included: a young man jumping on his bike, a young person moving through a library, a young lady writing in a notebook, etc. Out of curiosity I checked the images included on the website of the University of Helsinki[7] and found striking similarities: there is a picture of a woman measuring a man's eyesight with a machine; a beautiful lady thinking surrounded by the words *society, interest groups, vision to the top* and *out to the society, objectives, feedback*; an Asian lady smiling and looking at a mug that says *Think* in three languages (Finnish, Swedish and English) and finally someone who looks like a professor standing in front of a blackboard full of mathematical formulas with a piece of chalk in his hand, smiling happily. The three criteria set up by Team Finland seemed to be met: active people solving problems, there is something going on inside their brains, the image is vibrant and full of life.

Team Finland also has a certain number of ready-made presentations about Finland available on its website. These can be used free of charge and include: *Finland – keeping the world on the move; Finnish game industry; Finland in brief*, and also *Education in Finland*. Team Finland explains that the presentations "can be tailored for your own needs and made suitable for your own target group. The key message of all presentations is the same: there is demand for Finnish competence and problem-solving capability abroad." All the presentations are available only in English. One of the presentations claims that: "Finns are among the happiest people in the world" (a discourse that is often shared with pedagogical tourists or international media, without problematizing what happiness actually means); "Finland is a world pioneer of gender equity. The first women to receive full voting powers in the world, i.e. to elect and be elected, were Finnish. As early as 1906, Finnish women occupied seats in the national parliament. In recent years, women have held, on two occasions, the positions of President and Prime Minister at the same time," and, "At the heart of Finnish ingenuity is that things should work. Form and function must find each other in a seamless process towards a novel yet simple display of inventive genius". Interestingly, the point about gender equality fails to mention that women have not been equal to men in Finnish politics. The example of a female president and prime minister is given, but Team Finland does not explain that the Finnish president is more of a symbol than a real powerful figure – the Prime Minister is – and that the female prime minister in question rapidly left office because she made a mistake – which is never the case for male prime ministers in the country. Also, in order to illustrate Finnish ingenuity, a reference to the Rovio game is made: "The Angry Birds highly original game has taken over the world with its basically simple puzzle logic and mechanics that have easily become second nature for its tens of millions of regular players." This demonstrates that the actors that we have reviewed do intersect, in one way or another.

Team Finland has also created a specific organization for China called *Pure Finland* (纯净芬兰)[8] in order to raise Finland's profile in China. On its website the project says: "Pure Finland will prove that Finland is one of the most innovative countries in the world and that its innovations can greatly contribute to the development in China and around the globe." The project has many business partners, such as national carrier Finnair, Nokia and Kone. Interestingly, the University of Helsinki is one of the Gold Partners of the project and is advertised on the Pure Finland website. In November 2014 Pure Finland (and thus Team Finland) mediated an event between the University of Helsinki and Peking University called "Science in Dialogue". The event poster shows two women wearing stereotypical headsets, representing both Finland and China. Different specialists from both universities were invited to share ideas and representatives of Rovio Learning were also present (Peter Vesterbacka tweeted about the event). One session was offered on Master's Programmes at Helsinki:

> Come and discover the comprehensive selection of multidisciplinary two-year International Master's Programmes at the University of Helsinki, meet students and staff, and learn how to apply. Admission Services, University of Helsinki.

Thus the event served as advertising for the University too.

Since the liberalization of Finnish higher education, all universities are actively involved in education export and are partners in companies that provide education export such as Future learning Finland, Finland University, Education Export at the University of Helsinki (which welcomes its visitors with "*We welcome you to visit the experts behind the PISA success*") and EduCluster Finland. These companies organize study visits (eduvisits), educational consultancy abroad, education system development, etc.

The company called EduCluster Finland Ltd was the most successful organizations in 2015. Part of the University of Jyväskylä group and owned by University of Jyväskylä, Jyväskylä University of Applied Sciences and Jyväskylä Educational Consortium, EduCluster is described on its website as: "an expert organization creating educational excellence. Tailored solutions are designed and implemented in collaboration with partners and Finnish experts to enable competence building." Their values consist of creativity, reliability and quality. Interestingly, the company has been involved mostly with countries in the Middle East, such as Saudi Arabia, Qatar and the UAE. As a company, they are of course very protective of Finnish education. In April 2015 one of EduCluster's lead experts, who describes himself as "an author, analyst and project manager", wrote a harsh review of the book *Real Finnish Lessons: The True Story of an Education Superpower* (2015), written by Swede Gabriel Sahlgren from the right-wing think tank, the Centre for Policy Studies based in the UK. The book argues that PISA tests failed to reveal the real, traditional education system in Finland. EduCluster, as a company selling Finnish education, reacted by posting a response by their lead expert. He calls the work an "opinionated monograph" which makes claims that "are far from fact and reality". Interestingly, the expert finishes his review with the following sentence: "This monograph is not about education. It is about politics and industry". As someone being paid by a company to sell Finnish education to the world – and sometimes to countries which have a track record of serious human rights problems and injustice – I am of the view that this last sentence sounds quite paradoxical.

The final direct influencer is, of course, my own department which was involved in education export until recently – when the university announced large cuts. This is how the activities of the department are described:

> Department of Teacher Education staff members have been active in organising various teacher education programmes and courses, developing whole programmes for the Bachelor, Masters and PhD levels and consulting on the development of programmes in many countries all over the world. Our staff members have also evaluated programmes, courses and national level projects in various countries.

The department also provides:

- training programmes abroad:
    - Graduate Diploma in Early Childhood Education Studies in Singapore and Beijing
    - improving teachers' in-service training in Higher Education in Peru

- development of teacher education programmes abroad:
    - a new bachelor and masters level teacher education programme in Eritrea
    - masters level subject teacher education programmes in Serbia
    - a new masters level teacher education programme in Norway
    - a teacher training school for the University of Johannesburg
- consulting programmes abroad:
    - consulting on new language curricula in Sweden
    - consulting on the development of teacher education programmes in Spain, Malta, Mauritius, Jordan, Greece, Taiwan, etc.
- evaluation of national programmes/strategies/recent research.

Let me now mention a few indirect influencers on Finnish education marketization and export. The first indirect influence on Finland's country branding and the marketization of higher education is the results that the country has received for the Programme for International Student Assessment (PISA), a triennial international survey which aims to evaluate education systems worldwide, organised by the OECD. The programme is mentioned every time Finnish education is in focus (see e.g. Sahlberg, 2015). Many international students confess having decided to study in Finland based on this factor. Here are some randomly chosen typical examples of students' discourses on Finnish education and PISA: "One of the reasons I turned to Finland as a possible place to live and study was its constant presence in the media as a shining example of education services and social policy"; "The Finnish educational system is held up as the system to emulate." Thanks to PISA most departments of teacher education in Finnish universities have welcomed hundreds of guests from abroad who have been interested in getting to know about Finnish teacher education while Finnish scholars and decision-makers are invited abroad to tell all about the "miracle".

Another indirect influencer is the Finnish national media in both English and international media, especially when reporting about the "wonders" of Finnish education. For example, on 31.10.2014 Yahoo published an item of news entitled "Finnish educational company opens online training center in Vietnam", explaining that the country was exporting its excellent system of education to the "developing world"; on 19.11.2014 *The Arab Times Kuwait English Daily* published a piece called "May Finland be our education model". There are hundreds of such articles in the international press. Many Finnish scholars have spoken to journalists around the world and explained what they see as the *miracle of Finnish education*.

Cultural institutions around the world have also contributed to creating a positive image of Finland. For example the Museum of Modern Art (MoMA) in New York proposed that its visitors eat "Finnish school lunch" in October 2012. The MoMA website says, "This special lunch program gives guests an opportunity to savour Finnish school lunch favourites such as salmon soup and macaroni casserole." The text continues: "Finland is consistently recognised for excelling in all aspects of public education. A factor, which may be often unrecognised, is the importance of nutritious school lunches. Finland was the first country in the world to serve free, regulated school meals to children on a large scale, beginning in 1948." This aspect of Finnish education has also been advertised on the website of the Faculty of Behavioural Sciences of the University of Helsinki English, in relation to a visit of Chinese journalists having lunch during their visit to the Viikki Teacher Training School, which is attached to the university[9].

## 7.4 Discussion and conclusion

This chapter, based on an autoethnography of political marketization and branding of Finnish education and close contact with its main actors, aimed at describing and problematizing the enmeshment between these phenomena and the reputation of Finnish education, especially thanks to PISA studies. All the actors described in this chapter have been involved with promoting and selling, in one way or another, our system of education. Of course when one starts to sell a system to the rest of the world, one needs to create, in a sense, a marketing narrative around it and to silence potential critical voices in oneself and in others. As a passive actor in this "game", I have observed how people can lose their criticality and reflexivity when they talk about Finnish education (both "salesmen" and "buyers"). Academics are no exception to this rule. On one occasion I organised a seminar for visitors from another European country, who had been forced to come to Finland by their Ministry of Education to learn to become "real teachers". They had read Sahlberg's book and were overly enthusiastic about Finnish education. I had invited a certain number of colleagues to make presentations for them and had to intervene a few times to question some of the "white lies" and ready-made narratives that I heard from time to time (*there are no social classes in Finland; everybody is equal; pupils don't have any homework,* etc.). The school we visited was not the usual "teaching training school" attached to the university (where teachers have the minimum of a licentiate and are actively involved in research) but a school which is rarely entered by our "pedagogical tourists". Although the teachers were trying their best to be professional, the vast majority of the students were off-task, the teaching activities were "useless" and behaviour problems were constant. My guests left Finland reassured somewhat that they might not be such bad teachers, after all.

For a period of six months in 2015 the Finnish innovation fund Sitra, an organization that "promotes Finland's competitiveness and the well-being of the Finnish people" (http://www.sitra.fi/en/well-being), set up a New Education Forum involving many specialists who came together to discuss the future of Finnish education. One of the participants, who was the Head of the Teacher Education Department at the University of Jyväskylä, said during one of the meetings:

> We have long ridden the wave of PISA hysteria, telling ourselves that our schools are good. And they are excellent – by yesterday's standards. Our schools do not meet current or future needs.
>
> (Sitra, 2015)

This is quite different from the usual narrative of excellence that the actors reviewed in this chapter present and sell to the world.

It does take courage to question this narrative in Finnish academia and to show that the *Emperor may be more naked than we think,* as suggested at the beginning of this chapter. If universities are involved in contributing to the "mirage" and "white lies" about Finnish education, being a disruptive voice can be problematic as it means that by speaking and writing about this in a critical way *we'll be losing customers*. In times of economic woes this is important. Yet going back to Foucault, in Gordon (2000), quoted at the beginning of this chapter, I personally prefer to question assumptions, things taken for granted and to shake habits rather than play the political game of marketization and branding of my discourses and research. Criticality in Finnish academia sometimes appears to be in dire need of reassessment. The mixing of research, teaching and social involvement (with the latter sometimes taking over the others through the use, overuse and abuse of social networks) sometimes contributes too easily to neo-nationalism, feelings of superiority and a clear lack of criticality. As a specialist in critical interculturality and an outsider myself, I worry about the potential consequences. Let me finish with an example to illustrate this: When the Finnish Prime Minister (Centre party) announced in September 2015 that he would lend one of his homes (he is a millionaire) to refugees coming to Finland, many Finnish scholars spread the news via social networks. The hidden message was probably: *Look how wonderful we are. Even our Prime Minister is lending his house to the needy.* Interestingly, on the same day, the same scholars forgot to mention that the government slashed its development assistance funds and its annual contribution to the UN Environment Programme by millions of euros . . . *Undressing the Emperor* should be the main objective of scholars and thinkers in our world of marketization and branding . . .

> *So off went the Emperor in procession under his splendid canopy. Everyone in the streets and the windows said, "Oh, how fine are the Emperor's new clothes! Don't they fit him to perfection? . . . "But he hasn't got anything on," a little child said.*
>
> (Hans Christian Andersen, The Emperor's New Clothes, 1837)

## Notes

1 https://twitter.com/pasi_sahlberg
2 http://www.taughtbyfinland.com
3 http://team.finland.fi/public/default.aspx?culture=en-US&contentlan=2
4 http://team.finland.fi/public/default.aspx?culture=en-US&contentlan=2
5 http://vnk.fi/documents/10616/1098657/J0714_Team+Finland+Strategy+2015.pdf/19ff0f61-1f74-4003-8b7b-8b029ba00d8e
6 http://team.finland.fi/public/download.aspx?ID=127539&GUID=%7BFEAB1518-AF20-43FC-AE69-4CDD8004D93B%7D
7 http://www.helsinki.fi/university/
8 http://purefinland.cn
9 https://university.helsinki.fi/sv/node/2199

Chapter 8

# Making an impact

## Politics and persuasions in 21st-century higher education

*Joanne Doyle and Lisa McDonald*

### 8.1 Introduction

The contemporary focus on research impact, beyond contributions to academia, is changing the way research is being approached and undertaken by higher education institutions. The 'impact agenda' is having its own impact, by changing the practices and behaviours of researchers and research funders across the globe (Chandler, 2014, p. 3). The impact agenda refers to the assessment and monetisation of research undertaken in higher education institutions beyond the traditional peer-review process (Rogers, Bear, Hunt, Mills, & Sandover, 2014).

The global higher education sector is being influenced by political agendas and public persuasions. Researchers, research funders and community groups are favouring applied research that addresses identified priorities and delivers tangible benefits for society. Many funding programs have started to favour research projects that deliver clear and immediate impact, rather than research that is less applied (Winckler & Fieder, 2012). Governments are demanding research that 'earns its keep' (Phillips, 2010) and there is an increasing focus on 'real-world' research that responds to the 'real and tangible everyday needs' of societies (O'Leary, 2004, p. 5). A useful way to conceptualise the real world is presented in the theoretical separation between knowing and doing where, in the real world, knowledge is 'situated' in terms of activity, context and culture (Brown, Collins, & Duguid, 1989).

As the boundaries between 'traditional' and 'real-world' research continue to blur and expose inherent tensions between differing modes of knowledge production (Gunasekara, 2006), there remains a need to further explore what constitutes 'impact'. There is limited understanding of research impact as a concept, and variations in the way impact terminology is used across the higher education sector (Penfield, Baker, Scoble, & Wykes, 2013). Tensions between 'traditional' and 'real-world' research are 'characterised by the integration of supply and demand factors' as a result of the 'economic and social development imperatives of the state and industry', and carry with them the expectations of diverse communities (Gunasekara, 2006, pp. 329–330). Dispersed throughout society, such factors render complex the relationship between higher education research and 'real-world' impact as it seeks recognition at both national and local levels (Gunasekara, 2006).

This chapter seeks to outline the nature and influence of impact in contemporary higher education research.

## 8.2 Understanding impact

The quest for impact is certainly not new. In the United Kingdom, as far back as 1965, there are references to 'dissemination of knowledge' so that publicly funded science can provide benefit (Payne-Gifford, 2013, p. 14). Since the early 2000s, the way impact is conceptualised has changed the nature and purpose of research (Chandler, 2014). It is widely believed that publicly funded researchers have an obligation to return something of value to society (Martin, 2011). Such perspectives in Australia have emerged through a British genealogy which links impact assessment to monetisation, reflecting greater emphasis on adopting business models for research endeavours.

### 8.2.1 United Kingdom

In the UK, the first higher education Research Assessment Exercise (RAE) was conducted in 1986 (Bence & Oppenheim, 2005) and its main purpose was to enable higher education funding bodies to distribute public research funds on the basis of quality (Research Assessment Exercise, 2002). The RAE has since been replaced by the Research Excellence Framework (REF). The REF is a peer assessment of the quality of research in UK universities across all disciplines (Research Excellence Framework, 2013). The outcomes of the REF are significant for institutions as results are used to determine how much research funding each institution will receive.

In an attempt to recognise the broader contribution of research, the 2014 REF accepted case study submissions as evidence of research impact (Higher Education Funding Council of England, 2014a). Assessments of impact will contribute 20 per cent to each university's research quality profile, with research outputs and research environment contributing 65 per cent and 15 per cent respectively. REF results were made publicly available on 18 December 2014.

The REF is administered by the Higher Education Funding Council for England (HEFCE) that defines research impact as 'an effect on, change or benefit to the economy, society, culture, public policy or services, health, the environment or quality of life, beyond academia' (Research Excellence Framework, 2011). The 2014 REF reviewed a total of 1,911 submissions made by 154 universities in 36 sub-based units of assessment (Higher Education Funding Council of England, 2014a). The overall quality of the submissions was derived from three key elements of outputs, impact and environment.

In terms of research outputs, 72 per cent were deemed to be world-leading or internationally significant. This was an increase of 21 per cent on the results achieved in the previous assessment exercise conducted in 2008. In the case of impact, assessments were made on the basis of 'reach and significance'. On average across all submissions, 84 per cent were judged to be either outstanding or very considerable impacts reflecting 'productive engagements with a very wide range of public, private and third sector organisations, and engagement directly with the public' (Higher Education Funding Council of England, 2014b, p. 2). The final element, environment, was assessed on the basis of strategy, resources and infrastructure, with 85 per cent of submissions receiving a ranking of world-leading or internationally excellent.

The REF process has been criticised for the time and effort required by institutions to prepare REF submissions. It has even been suggested that calculating H-indices for a particular department may be equally effective in predicting research assessment results (Jump, 2014). However, the REF has been praised for encouraging researchers to consider 'real connections with users of the research' (Marginson, 2014).

### *8.2.2 Australia*

While the impact agenda has been driven by the review of research excellence in the United Kingdom, many other countries, including Australia and New Zealand, are entering into discussions about research impact (Rogers et al., 2014). Inspired by the work undertaken in the United Kingdom, the Australian impact assessment model is tied to an understanding of impact in which research excellence dictates the allocation of research funding (Watermeyer, 2014). The Australian Research Council (ARC), for example, manages public-sector investment in research and development and provides advice to the Australian Government on research matters, including impact. The ARC defines research impact as 'the demonstrable contribution that research makes to the economy, society, culture, national security, public policy or services, health, the environment, or quality of life, beyond contributions to academia' (Australian Research Council, 2014).

In 2011, the Australian Government undertook a review to determine the quality and value of its investment in publicly funded research. One of the review recommendations was that the Government explore 'research impact assessment mechanisms' to evaluate the broader benefits of publicly funded research (Department of Innovation Industry Science and Research, 2011). Two years later, the Australian Government released a discussion paper entitled 'Assessing the wider benefits arising from university-based research' (Commonwealth of Australia & Department of Industry Innovation Climate Change Science Research and Tertiary Education, 2013). The paper sought public comment on a concept to assess the wider benefits of university-based research by using submitted case studies to demonstrate non-academic research impact, in addition to research-reporting metrics such as publications, patents, grants, and so on. The final report has not been released at the time of writing.

## 8.3 Research to 'make a difference'

A good degree of research has been undertaken in the attempt to understand how research findings are operationalised. Societies are seeking to understand the 'relevance' of academic research (Phillips, 2010) and researchers themselves want their research to have a positive impact (Buxton, 2011) by making a difference (Meagher, Lyall, & Nutley, 2008).

Research has many different purposes, however. Research generates knowledge, shapes public opinion (Kuruvilla, Mays, & Walt, 2007), informs policy and guides practice (Cleaver & Franks, 2008; Smith, 2007). Research impact literature suggests that findings from research must be adapted to policy or practice contexts in order to be useful (Walter, Nutley, & Davies, 2003) yet the transfer of research findings to policy and practice is a complex process (Bastow, Dunleavy, & Tinkler, 2014). It is often difficult to measure the long term impact of research on policy or professional practice (Marginson, 2014). In some cases, impact is serendipitous, so tracing results back to specific research activities may be equally accidental, or indeed, even unlikely (Meagher et al., 2008). Other impacts may be cumulative, suggesting that to attribute impact to one particular research activity is not possible (Spaapen & van Drooge, 2011; Timmer, 2004; Wolf, Lindenthal, Szerencsits, Holbrook, & Heß, 2013). In a further complication, policy impacts practice (Adelle, Jordan, & Turnpenny, 2012), and practice impacts policy (McLaughlin, 2005). Given these complexities, which modes of impact assessment might be feasible?

In the case of assessing the impact of research on policy or practice, for example, there are two recognised approaches – forward tracking and backward tracking. Forward tracking traces impacts from research to policy or practice, whereas backward tracking follows policy or practice back to research (Boaz, Fitzpatrick, & Shaw, 2008; Boaz, Grayson, Levitt, & Solesbury, 2008; Morton, 2015). Whilst a combination of these approaches is sometimes used (Morton, 2015), forward tracking tends to be a more common approach than backward tracking (Hilderbrand, Simon, & Hyder, 2000).

Complications in assessing research impact may also arise where, despite the combination of approaches into a non-linear and simultaneous forward-and-backward tracking method, research is co-designed and produced with, for example, external partners (Morris, 2006). Such circumstances can introduce a greater degree of risk between research parameters which are, in other circumstances, set entirely by researchers, and the input of research partners whose specific experiences are brought to bear on the research process. Not uncommonly, then, collaborative research can produce unanticipated outcomes which extend beyond those stated at the outset of a project, and can substantially add unexpected value to the needs of both researchers and external partners (Leisey, Holton, & Davey, 2012). It can therefore be asked whether a forward tracking approach alone can adequately account for the unforeseen in collaborative research practice. Equally, should it be considered if the experimental act of collaborative research practice is itself a viable model for future research production?

## 8.4 Assessment not evaluation

Assessing research impact is, therefore, challenging. Valuing the work of universities can be difficult and controversial due to conceptual, definitional, methodological and data challenges (Kelly & McNicoll, 2011). Any assessment of research incorporates the perspectives of research stakeholders (Group of Eight, 2011; Kristjanson, Place, Franzel, & Thornton, 2002) and is ultimately based on the notion of value (Kelly & McNicoll, 2011). In contrast to research outputs that are measurable, research impact is a value judgement based upon benefit to users (Brewer, 2011).

The assessment of academic research endeavours is different to program evaluation. Assessment and evaluation are used for different purposes with different methodologies for each. The aim of assessment is to achieve improvements in the level of quality, whereas the aim of evaluation is to determine or judge the level of quality (Baehr, 2005). Assessment is process-oriented whereas evaluation is product-oriented (Angelo & Cross, 1993). In the case of higher education research, publications and citations are outputs of academic endeavour appropriate for evaluation. Evaluation relies upon clearly specified goals and objectives that provide specific and measurable criteria for assessing performance, and goals and objectives should be determined as bases for program development prior to initiating the program. In the case of research impact, then, determining the non-academic 'real-world' influence of research in society is an assessment of process rather than an evaluation of performance. Regardless of terminology, 'all evaluation mechanisms distort the processes they purport to evaluate' (Roberts, 2003). Assessing research impact should not be confused with assessing research value (Davies, Nutley, & Walter, 2005).

## 8.5 The complexity of research impact

Ensuring that research delivers impact is a complicated process which is influenced by both the establishment of enduring academic scholarship and the often short-term nature of research appointments (Kwok, 2013). A focus on impact has immense implications for the nature of research and the future of research whereby the 'doing, thinking and delivering' of research becomes an epic 'socio-spatial journey' to impact (Conlon, Gill, Tyler, & Oeppen, 2014). Yet, as Pickerill (2014, p. 26) notes, 'ideas and knowledge take time to develop'. Academics are under increasing pressure to produce 'quick impact at a broader scale' to satisfy funding agency requirements and ensure impressive researcher CVs, which are essential for academic survival (Pickerill, 2014, p. 25). There are three main issues with the 'quick impact' approach.

First, impact is not a one-way process but a participatory, collaborative process where knowledge is co-produced between academics and the broader community (Pain, Kesby, & Askins, 2011, p. 8). To expand, the UK model is aligned with a producer/consumer business model that aims to 'impact' the knowledge and activities of research users. This does not achieve positive social change in partnership with non-academics (Pain et al., 2011, p. 7). Concerns have therefore been raised with this approach and situate the impact agenda within a power/knowledge differential that reinforces the disassociation of academic research from wider society (Pain et al., 2011, p. 12).

Second, impact may be unpredictable and serendipitous (Molas-Gallart, Salter, Patel, Scott, & Duran, 2002). The influence of impact can extend well beyond individual-level impact into the values and behaviours of organisations and society (Pope, Bond, Morrison-Saunders, & Retief, 2013). There is a well-recognised gap between research findings and their uptake in policy and practice (Brownson & Jones, 2009), and a range of literature laments the 'research–practice gap.' The delayed, haphazard or non-existent uptake of research findings produces situations where recourse to research is not evident (Squires et al., 2011). In the case of medical research, this gap has been named the 'valley of death' (Butler, 2008) where 'promising scientific discoveries linger and die' (Roberts, Fischhoff, Sakowski, & Feldman, 2012). As we have noted above, the fact that impact does not always occur in a direct or easily identifiable manner complicates impact assessment activities (Rogers et al., 2014). The complication may also, however, be evidence of the 'real-world' influence of research which can be said to necessarily privilege process over performance, reflecting the distinction between assessment and evaluation.

Third, a researcher's enthusiasm to demonstrate impact quickly may influence the type of research being undertaken or encourage undeveloped research to be disseminated. This may adversely influence policy and decision-making (Rogers et al., 2014), but conversely, the effect of decelerating research also raises the significant issue of how curiosity and experimentation can be effectively cultivated and sustained (Phillips, 2010). As Phillips (2010) and others have noted, universities should be 'spaces of adventure' where the development of 'curiosity driven research has led to major scientific and cultural advances' (Hunt, 2009). Concerns have, therefore, been raised that the current impact agenda re-frames the science–society relationship by restricting researcher autonomy while simultaneously supporting a degree of disciplinary freedom. Correlatively, it has also been thought that embedding impact considerations in researcher behaviour may enhance autonomy through reflexive practice, through a degree of interaction between one's own self-monitoring and expected outcomes (Smith, Ward, & House, 2011). Other concerns that the impact agenda puts accountancy before accountability have also been raised (Rogers et al., 2014).

## 8.6 Communicating and translating research

Concerning the external exposure of research, unease about the relationship between knowledge production for 'its own sake' and the interpretation and utility of that production to the 'end user' has developed in the humanities (Ang, 2006). The concept of an 'outsider' to the academy having access to the intellectual capital that academics produce in 'real' or tangible ways has remained as central to the assessment of research impact here as it has in fields which have perhaps been perceived as more closely aligned with the solving of research 'problems' than their critique. Indeed, and as Ang (2006, p. 186) suggests, 'increasing importance is now placed on "commercialisation," on collaborative partnerships with "industry", and so on – all in the context of governmental schemes to put academic research in the service of the emergent "knowledge economy"'. While such an economy can be said to be a product of 'neoliberal developments and their consequences' (Ang, 2006, p. 186), Ang equally notes that to resist these kinds of developments would not be productive. Rather, and pointing specifically to the humanities, resistance may make peripheral the strengths of material production at a time which requires greater complexity of approach in the application of research to address 'real-world' problems (Ang, 2006; see also Morris, 2006).

In addition, there has been criticism of universities for being disconnected from the real world and failing to consider the needs of ordinary people (Rowe & Brass, 2008). Here, accessibility of research results is key to end-user consideration and potential adoption (Chan et al., 2014). Translating research findings to policy or practice is largely dependent upon effective dissemination practices. The differing perspectives of academics and practitioners may contribute to the delayed or non-existent uptake of research. In some fields, academics seek to convey abstract understandings with greater degrees of generalisability whereas practitioners seek more specific answers to discrete problems (Steffens, Weeks, Davidsson, & Isaak, 2014).

It is thought, for example, that scholarly writing should be accessible, transparent and easily understood (Sampson, 2014). Academic language that is 'obscurantist, theoretically impenetrable and jargon-laden' will further encourage criticism of universities as being disconnected from the real world (Rowe & Brass, 2008) and render real-world impact more difficult to achieve and assess. The open sharing of academic outputs is considered good 'corporate citizenship' which enables potential benefit to a wide range of individuals and interests (Mannay, 2014). Broadbent (2014) has also suggested that researchers should incorporate effective dissemination strategies as a part of research design activities.

Knowledge translation (Walsh et al., 2012), research utilisation (Estabrooks, Floyd, Scott-Findlay, O'Leary, & Gushta, 2003) and translational research (Homer-Vanniasinkam & Tsui, 2012) are other terms used to denote the utilisation of research findings in real-world applications. The growing field of implementation research focuses on users of research rather than production of knowledge (Peters, Adam, Alonge, Agyepong, & Tran, 2014), even though context is thought particularly important in the implementation of research as researchers seek to understand and work with real-world settings and populations (Peters et al., 2014). Further exploring the conceptualisation of research, the chapter by Hung–Chang Chen explains how political pressures influence the commission and conduct of research.

Academic researchers in the social sciences have more readily embraced the culture of impact and tend to consider impact at the outset of their research, yet this can be more challenging for those in pure science fields (Chubb, 2014). Further, the impact of research varies across disciplines. In the case of health research, there are several discipline-specific impact assessment frameworks that have proven useful in identifying the real-world impacts of research (Buxton & Hanney, 1994; Buykx et al., 2012; Kuruvilla et al., 2007). On the other hand, business research has been criticised for its irrelevance to business practice (Bennis & O'Toole, 2005; Dostaler & Tomberlin, 2013) and its failure to generate commercial value (Hitt & Greer, 2011).

## 8.7 The future of research

The higher education research environment is changing. There is increased emphasis on collaborative research (van den Besselaar, Hemlin, & van der Weijden, 2012), yet at the same time less collegiality and greater competition due to what has been termed academic 'game-playing' (Butler & Spoelstra, 2015). There has also been an overall decrease in the total research funding pool and an increase in the number of research applications (Research Excellence Framework, 2013). The rise of the evidence-based practice movement in the 1980s and 1990s that prioritises applied research has created further challenges for the 'status and value of academic research' (Hammersley, 2013, p. 10).

The current focus on impact is changing research expectations, practices and relationships (Rogers et al., 2014) to re-define the future of higher education research. In the contemporary research environment, it is thought that the findings from high-quality research must guide real-world activities (Munro & Savel, 2014) and demonstrate societal merit (Staeheli & Mitchell, 2005). More frequently, researchers are being required to describe the impact of their work in grant proposals, project reports, press releases and research assessment exercises (Kuruvilla, Mays, Pleasant, & Walt, 2006). Public-sector funders are seeking evidence of impact as a way of justifying research expenditure and allocating future funding. As a result, many funding agencies have started to embed impact within funding guidelines, and applications for funding must seek to deliver 'positive and substantial impact' (Office for Learning and

Teaching, 2014, p. 12). The Australian Research Council has well-developed Impact Measurement Principles and invites evidence of impact from funding applicants as part of their Research Opportunity and Performance Evidence (ROPE) Statement (Australian Research Council, 2014). The National Health and Medical Research Council (2014) no longer requests Journal Impact Factors as a part of funding applications in recognition of the fact that 'impact cannot be inferred from a simple list of publications'.

The way in which research knowledge is created, published and scrutinised is changing (Cronin, 2005). The peer-review process, for instance, is recognised as the assessment mechanism for research quality, but is also resource-intensive and has been criticised for its lack of reliability (Satyanarayana, 2013). While ensuring the quality of research for use in and by the broader society should not be compromised, making research findings available to wider audiences also situates research as being available to a range of readings and uses. In that sense, research can be thought an 'open work', (Eco, 1989), available to multiple interpretations and applications, and therefore a site of inherent and pluralistic complexity (Morris, 2006). The issue of how public policy impacts researcher behaviour is explored in another chapter by Sofia Viseu who explains how scientific activity is adjusted to suit public programs and policies.

The embedding of impact can be seen to place greater pressure on the production of rigorous, independent and ethical research which must be seen to respond to funding imperatives rather than lead innovation and discovery. The relevance of research is being determined by the users of the research and the extent to which scholarly knowledge is used or not used (Staeheli & Mitchell, 2005). Australia performs well in the area of international excellence as it relates to research impact, however, it has also been proposed that there is a need to improve interactions between research and industry and better articulate Australia's research priorities in the national interest (Garrett-Jones, 2000).

Contemporary researchers are faced with a series of questions. For example, are researchers pressured to reshape research objectives to suit funding priorities? Does research reporting for funding agencies tend toward the reporting of 'palatable' outcomes which align with program objectives rather than ameliorate the topic or issue at hand? What do these questions imply about the structure, nature and worth of research today?

## 8.8 Conclusions

Across the globe, researchers, research institutions, funding agencies and societies are increasingly focused on the real-world or non-academic impact of research. The imperative to demonstrate societal value afforded by public expenditure on research (Rogers et al., 2014) and deliver impact beyond the academy (Pickerill, 2014) is changing the future of academic research.

Identifying research impacts beyond contributions to academia is becoming increasingly necessary to help articulate the benefits of research and justify its public expenditure. Impact is no longer the 'serendipitous outcome of research', but rather, a requirement of research audits (Kelly, 2014) and funding investment (Chandler, 2014, p. 6). For this reason, there is a concern that impact-led research may compromise basic or 'blue-skies' research, and a focus on 'promised product' may reduce opportunities for discovering unexpected phenomena (Stipp, 2010, p. 140).

In all fields, the generation of knowledge requires understanding, and research energies should not be compromised by focusing on usefulness alone (Boulton & Lucas, 2011). Complications arise when researchers and research institutions are pressured to demonstrate research impact at the expense of research quality. Between this awkward tension can be seen the inherent difference between citational frequency as a measure of apparent impact and the actual dispersive nature of quality dissemination or knowledge exchange.

We begin to see, then, that achieving impact from research is reliant upon wide dissemination processes to ensure that research findings are made available to audiences outside academia, even though these effects can be difficult to measure. It is therefore important for dissemination methods to be appropriately contextualised so that research integrity is maintained, whether for funding agencies or members of the wider community. While it is argued that reducing the 'research–practice gap' should be a primary concern for contemporary researchers, it can be equally argued that research impact depends on a volatile and creative economy of experimentation. Such a higher education economy, one built on risk and ethical exchange (Barcan, 2014), may be precisely what extends research practice into viable research impact. Yet, it is clear that debates which focus singularly on a measure of research impact as either good or bad for the future of academic research will continue (Lakey, Rodgers, & Scoble, 2013).

Chapter 9

# The impact of managerial performance frameworks on research activities among Australian early career researchers

*Eva Bendix Petersen*[1]

## 9.1 Introduction

The emergence of the corporate university has involved a formalisation of performance expectations in regard to academic work including research activity (Hicks, 2012; Thornton, 2008; Guthrie & Neumann, 2007; Taylor & Taylor, 2003; Taylor, 2001; Otley, 1999). From the more elusive dictate to 'publish or perish' academics are now subject to much more specific and weighty measurement frameworks. In many places in Australia, and elsewhere, research performance expectations are broken down into a yearly count of publications, PhD completions and amount of research income obtained via external grants. Such performance measures can be considered political in the sense that they are the direct result of contemporary research policies and figure as an externally determined form of calculation that (1) is at odds with traditional ways of enabling and assessing research and (2) has little regard for the individual academic's circumstances, strengths, or investments. Contemporary policy dictates, among other things, that academics' work needs to be managed and measured 'more effectively' and new managerial forms, such as performance management, is seen as the answer – although it is important to remember that it is not the only possible answer. While performance frameworks may be an externally determined form of calculation, managers and academics themselves have taken these tools up as their own (Davies & Petersen, 2005; Davies & Bansel, 2010). Therefore, it is not entirely meaningful to think in terms of an 'external', 'political' outside to the 'opposed', 'academic' inside. Rather, we must pay attention to how and with what effect the new discourses with their new practices intersect with other discursive practices and capture the hearts and minds of those who inhabit universities.

Drawing on poststructural narrative theory (Bansel, 2015; Petersen, 2014; Davies, 2000), which I will explain below, this chapter explores the lived experience of the new managerial research performance frameworks among Australian early career researchers (ECRs) from different disciplines including the professional disciplines of Teacher Education and Social Work (which in the Australian system are university degrees). It seeks to make a contribution to our understanding of the transformation of the university under neoliberal governmental rationalities (Brown, 2003) and the impact they have on academic work, identities and subjectivities. Performance frameworks are being used in other systems including the United Kingdom (Deem & Brehony, 2005), North America (Sidhu, 2006) and New Zealand (Middleton, 2005), and the study I present here may aid analyses of academic practices in these and other contexts, although as Carney (2009), amongst others, reminds us, it is important to consider carefully how global neoliberal policies are rolled out and taken up in various locales. Neoliberalism, to put it very briefly, is here understood to be a form of governmental rationality which, among other things, configures everything 'from the quotidian experience of buying and selling commodities from the market, which is then extended across other social spaces' (Read, 2009, p. 26). One effect of this, among many, is that the subject is reconfigured as an individual 'entrepreneur', who has to create and capitalise on her/his opportunities, and has to consider himself/herself as a product to be constantly optimised and marketed (Read, 2009). I argue that while we know that corporatisation and marketisation of universities has been taking place for well over 25 years (Gunter, 2012; Shore, 2010) there is still work to be done in carefully mapping its effects both in order to better understand what contemporary academic work is and to enable a critical assessment of the tools and values that come with corporatisation and their effects. In particular, the impact that enhanced forms of competition, corporate-speak and accountability measures have had on research practices and research imaginations among the new generation of researchers remain under-explored.

## 9.2 The larger study

The article draws on data from a larger study, where I undertook qualitative interviews with 20 ECRs across three different Australian universities: an old research-intensive 'sandstone', a younger one with research intensity in particular areas, and a 'new' (post-Dawkins) university with an emerging research profile. The idea was to gain a spread in perspectives and to allow for an exploration of the extent to which different research environments seemed to have an impact on the lived experience of academic work among the study participants.[2] While the term 'early career researcher' can take different meanings (Bazeley, 2003), it was defined in the study as an academic working in an ongoing teaching and research position, whose doctorate was less than five years old. This definition allowed for a focus on a group of potentially very productive academics. Because they had completed their doctorates they were already potentially active in publishing, applying for research grants, and supervising postgraduate research students. Their status as ongoing members of academic staff also meant that many of them had taken up various service or leadership roles, and because they all had teaching responsibilities, they were familiar with the full gamut of academic work life. In a highly competitive job market, which relies on extensive use of casual and contract staff (Ryan et al., 2013; Kimber, 2003), these academics had been successful in securing an ongoing position. In other words, this particular group is arguably the cohort that will be required to take up significant positions of academic and research leadership over the next decade.

Participant recruitment occurred through general calls for expression of interest on the universities' digital message boards as well as some snow-balling. As it was a poststructuralist qualitative study (Lather, 2012) the aim was never to obtain a representative sample, but to allow for in-depth exploration of the meanings co-produced in the space of the interview (Koro-Ljungberg, 2008). The final sample included interviews with ECRs from all the major disciplinary groups, although there was markedly stronger interest in participation amongst ECRs in the humanities, social sciences and the professional programmes. Individual semi-structured interviews conducted by the author of up to 2.5 hours' duration were held and transcribed in full. The one-on-one interview method was chosen to allow the participant to reflect at length and perhaps share thoughts and feelings that would be difficult to express in a group (Fontana and Frey, 2005). The data set also included detailed work logs that each ECR had kept for two weeks prior to the interview. The objective of the logs was to gain a sense of the composition and flow of work, and what activities participants undertook in the two-week period, how much time they spent on these activities, and so on. Of course, the logs are not necessarily representative of 'normal' time, as some were undertaken during teaching-free periods and a few of them even during marking time. Nevertheless, the data that the logs yield give interesting insight into everyday academic work.

As mentioned, this study is conceptually and analytically couched in narrative theory, which asserts that narratives are central to human meaning making and are constitutive of our sense of self, our feelings, thoughts and actions (Riessman, 2008; Polkinghorne, 1988). Narratives are the stories we live by (McAdams, Josselson and Leiblich, 2006; Goodson, 2006). Poststructuralist theory entails the additional assumption that there is nothing behind the narratives, so to speak, that narratives are all we have through which to understand human experience (Davies, 2000). In effect that means that it is not meaningful to look for the truth behind the more or less accurate accounts participants may give, but to consider what the effects of the given narratives are.

Specifically, the ECRs were prompted to give a narrative account of their current work life and why they chose an academic career. The objective of the study was to canvass ECRs' work narratives generally, to understand their conditions and aspirations, so the stories around research activities were told in that context. The stories that interviewees tell are circumscribed by the context in which they are told, in that the interview format comes with its own set of scripts, which are negotiated by the agents involved (Koro-Ljungberg, 2008). Many other available storylines and positionings (Harré and van Langenhove, 1998) play out in that space, for example, conventions around how academics talk to each other or how social categories are variously embodied and come to matter. In other words, the narratives that interviewees tell are both personal and shared; they are embodied situated negotiations of available and culturally intelligible stories and subject positions. This matters in relation to the question of whether the results of a study such as this are generalisable. While narrative researchers do not work with statistical notions of representativeness nor can make grand claims about generalisability, we would nevertheless argue that what goes on in the interview is never strictly idiosyncratic. The stories that our participants tell us are available and possible in the cultural context and in that way significant.

Narrative analysis can take many forms. For the analysis presented in this chapter an exploratory thematic approach has been chosen. The data set was read through several times and I identified a number of possible narrative themes to pursue for more detailed analysis. For the purposes of this chapter, I chose to focus on two common concerns around research performance, which figured strongly across the participants' narratives. In the following I will first present these two themes and subsequently I will discuss some of the implications of these narratives for academic work and for the future of university research.

## 9.3 Theme 1: objectionable research practices

Most of the ECRs in the study expressed a strong desire to undertake research and expressed palpable frustration with not having enough time to do it. Teaching and administration filled their days and many of them felt they had to fight hard to carve out time to research, and during some periods of the year had to give up altogether. Some expressed that if this situation continued they would consider leaving and a number of them considered on a regular basis to leave academia altogether (Petersen, 2011). Most of them said that research, and the promise of being able to pursue their research interests, was the main reason why they chose an academic career path, albeit that the notions of what research involves differed among the participants. They also believed that the reason why they had been successful in obtaining an ongoing position was because of their proven capacity as researchers, which contributed to the frustration not to be able to get to it all the more.

Concurrently, they also accounted for the pressure to get 'runs on the board', that is, to publish journal articles and chapters or to obtain research grants. As an ECR in the social sciences expressed,

> There's a ridiculous pressure to publish. I think we have to publish at least two things a year and they have to be in top international journals. It's now November and I've only been able to get one paper finished, actually submitted – apart from two conference papers – and I'm feeling really stressed out. Every time I think about it I feel my heart rate goes up, like a really stressed out scary feeling.

The ECR here narrates her experience in terms of stress and expresses that the stress manifests physically. The stress comes from what is here constituted as an external pressure, that is, an institutional expectation to deliver a set number of publications. The term 'I think' suggests that the participant may not know the number for certain but it is the number that she has come to believe she must meet. Further, she indicates that the two conference papers do not count in terms of the calculations of her workplace. She seems to have learned to count in the same way (you can mention a conference paper but you cannot add it to the official tally), and she believes and feels that she does not currently measure up. As Winefield et al. (2002) and others (Davies & Bansel, 2005) demonstrate, Australian university academics have been found to be highly stressed, and more so than other comparable groups.

From other participants' narratives it seems that part of the stress they experience is linked to the fear of being deemed 'research inactive'. They account how within their institutions there are frameworks for determining who is research active and who is not. If you publish a certain number of articles, see to completion a number of doctoral students, and obtain a certain amount of external research income you will be deemed research active, which in some places translates into yearly research quota on your workload. If you, on the other hand, are deemed research inactive this quota, or other 'privileges' such as support for participation on writing retreats, will be withdrawn, and consequently, make returning to research active status even more challenging. Given that the ECRs in my study had all completed doctorates and constituted themselves as researchers or scholars, the threat of experiencing additional difficulty in getting to do research was significant. Furthermore, the fear of being recognised and pigeon-holed as research inactive constituted a serious threat to their sense of self and purpose.

In response to these pressures, some of the ECRs told stories about how they had had to 'learn to be smart', as one of them articulated it. It was evident that sharing these stories was riddled with various forms of strong emotion, sometimes with anxiety, sometimes with a strong form of sarcasm, but usually couched in particular terms. As one participant said,

> You are probably going to think that I am a really terrible person, you know, this is not so cool, I know, but, uhm, it's just a survival strategy, not something I'm proud of or that I would talk about if it wasn't in complete confidence. But, you know, we learn to cheat a little, to produce, you know, we have to take short cuts sometimes.

While not all the participants who spoke of 'cheating' and 'taking short cuts' used the word 'survival strategy', this was the common storyline (see also Hughes and Bennett, 2013). They conveyed that they had to do something that was not entirely 'cool', proud-making or above board, in order to get 'runs on the board'. In other words, according to this narrative, these things were not something they would have done or chosen to do had it not been for the specific circumstances. Among these surreptitious objectionable practices was putting pressure on their PhD students to co-publish with them, to use data that PhD or Masters students had collected for their own studies, to re-publish very similar articles under new titles in different journals, to not read sources carefully and deeply, etc. One participant stated,

> I've come to call it 'do a dirty'. Like just last week I wrote an article in about 8 or 9 hours. It wasn't very good, I admit that. I copy and pasted a bit from other things I've written, I added some new references that I found on Google Scholar that I'd never read and never will read. I referenced some articles on the same topic from the same journal, and so on; you know, really quick work, not very good. Then I submitted it thinking now I can say that something's in the works, and if they accept it then all good. It won't be my finest piece that's for sure, but nobody cares about that, it's an output.

'Doing a dirty' then is about completing a piece of writing quickly and submitting something that you yourself do not feel is entirely up to standard. Again, it is not a piece of work that you feel proud of, where you feel you have stretched or exerted yourself. Rather than feeling clean/virtuous perhaps, this process and product is dirty, makes you feel unclean/immoral. The objective is simply to be able to say that you have submitted an article, regardless of the quality. The participant conveys that his experience is that 'nobody', perhaps meaning his institution generally, his manager, his colleagues or even the rest of the community, cares about the quality of the work. The only thing that counts is that there is something to count and a box can be ticked.

It is not so that all the participants would agree that either 'doing a dirty' or the other 'objectionable' practices are objectionable or that they 'objectively' are. For example, some thought that recycling the same argument or analysis in different places was entirely appropriate. What is significant is that particular participants narrate them into existence that way. *They* constitute them as objectionable, as immoral, as it were, and in that sense confess to having sinned in relation to a higher norm. In these accounts they renounce responsibility by constituting these actions as something they *have* to do to survive, perhaps meaning to keep their employment, keep their status as research active, and so on.

In relation to objectionable practices some of the ECRs worried very much about their effects on their CVs or even as one ECR said, his 'legacy'. Some of the ECRs accounted how they had co-published papers with colleagues they really did not want to be associated with or on topics they really knew very little about or had co-published papers using methods they thought were flawed or even 'ridiculous'. Yet the opportunity to get a run on the board, despite its effect on the crafting of a particular scholarly profile through a publication list, overrode those concerns. One of the ECRs went so far as to call himself a 'prostitute' – meaning that he was willing to do almost anything for an output.

## 9.4 Theme 2: the grant game

The second theme that ran across in the narratives in various ways had to do with gaining research income. As mentioned at the outset many current research performance calculations also stipulate that each academic must attract a certain amount of external research funding per year. It is understood that a grant may not be obtained every year, but that over a three-year period it averages out to the set amount. The amount differs according to the level at which you work. While the expectation to attract external grants may not be as acute for ECRs than for more senior academics, the ECRs in this study all talked about it as an expectation – either in terms of having to be actively involved in applying for them or to work specifically towards getting oneself in a position where one could be competitive in the grant game (called 'building a track record'). Several participants in this study said that they believed that obtaining external research funding without a doubt was 'the main game' if they wanted to go for promotion and even that publishing articles was really all about making oneself look productive and 'fundable'. One said,

> It is my distinct impression that you only matter here if you obtain either category 1 grants [prestigious competitive grants like Research Council grants] or very large category 2 grants [partnership grants with industry]. The dean literally doesn't know you unless you do. I was quite surprised to see how he seemed to have learned my name after we were successful with the [mentions an industry partner] grant, coming up to me and shaking my hand like we were old mates. The week before he wouldn't have known me from Adam.

In this participant's experience obtaining grants is a condition for becoming visible, it decides whether you are seen as someone of worth and value in his workplace. Other participants told similar stories about who and what was valued in their workplace, conveying how this became visible in faculty newsletters, in Christmas lunch speeches, and so on. One even said that she had received a personal letter of thank you from the Vice Chancellor after she had been successful in obtaining a prestigious grant, whereas other accomplishments go entirely unnoticed. This, of course, is a direct consequence of the government's research funding policies, where in the calculation of block funding the ability to attract non-government or competitive government funding weighs in more than, for example, publication rates. In a sense the policy stipulates that attracting money is more important than sharing findings and insights, which is acutely and viscerally felt 'on the floor'.

Several of the participants had experiences with applying for external research funding. A few of them had done so by themselves, aiming for schemes targeting ECRs, and others had been members of a team led by more senior colleagues. One of the participants who had applied for an Australian Research Council ECR grant, said the following

> When I was preparing my application I talked to a lot of people about it, my head of school, and also my old supervisor, and some colleagues here. I have no experience with this sort of thing so I just wanted to get as much advice as I could. I ran my drafts by a few people and so on. The feedback I kept getting was that I didn't sell my project hard enough but also that qualitative methods were not going to cut it. People kept saying I should do mixed methods, that mixed methods sell, and that it's the way to get stats [statistics] assessors on board. So that's what I did, even though I thought that qualitative would have done the job just fine.

The objective here is to submit a grant proposal which will be successful in attracting funds. To work out the parameters of a good bid this ECR seeks advice from more experienced colleagues. Their advice, which she takes, is to change the research design, the research methods, that she proposes to use. In other words, word on the street has it that this is more likely to 'sell'. With the help of others more experienced than she, she tries to read the unwritten criteria for success and despite thinking that from a methodological point of view that certain methods would be adequate, the reading has an effect on the kind of scientific endeavour she proposes. The criteria are 'unwritten' in the sense that the funding scheme in question nowhere stipulated that qualitative methods would not be accepted. The notions of what sells and what doesn't are constructed and exchanged among academics in various fields based on personal experience or observation, and intelligence in regard to how assessors with predilection for statistics are likely to operate or in regard to who is on the assessors' panel, etc. In other words, the grant game entails reading and learning the written and unwritten rules, and learning how to participate in the exchange of know-how and the readings of what is likely and what is fundable. It also entails learning not only how to translate the advice one gets about one's applications, but also how to position oneself in relation to this advice (as an ECR who listens to the sage advice of senior colleagues despite her own view).

Again the question here is not whether the advice that this ECR received was sound. Readers may know of several successful qualitative research grant proposals, for example. The point is that this is the narrative landscape that this particular ECR lives in and that it matters to how she ended up constructing her study. A potential effect of this is that her decision contributes to a further valorisation of mixed methods designs, perhaps helping to make a self-fulfilling prophecy out of her colleagues' 'predictions'. The fewer applications that advance arguments for exclusively qualitative research designs the more unconventional they become.

Another participant, who had been the more junior member of a team of several senior colleagues, told the following story about his experience,

> I was part of this group of people who went for a Linkage [Australian research council partnership grant] – my old supervisor invited me on

board, which was nice. I was there at some of those meetings in the beginning and just listened. I was really a little bit shocked to be honest . . . about how some of the senior people talked and stuff. They were like, let's map from the issues that are hot at the moment and then shape our application so we make sure that we tick all the boxes, like sustainability, tick, community engagement, tick, employability, tick, and so on. I could see it was the smart way to go, but to be honest it felt a little too strategic for my liking . . . Funny enough, I sort of did the same thing with a small grant application I went for with two other people a little while ago, found myself doing something like that . . . but I figured there's nothing wrong with being smart about it, right?

The notion of 'being strategic' is interesting. As in the above story where the ECR made a 'strategic' decision to change from qualitative methods to mixed methods, the story here is also about constructing a fundable research proposal based on reading, what the ECR calls, 'the issues that are hot at the moment'. He narrates it as a box-ticking exercise, where a research project in large part was created by backwards-mapping from 'timely' questions and concepts. He positions himself as a bit shocked, as an outsider looking in with surprise and some alarm. He did not initiate this nor was he responsible for this, he merely observed. The assumed moral position here seems to be a research project that arises without a care about what sells, in other words a non-strategic project. Interestingly, he goes on to construct a difference between being 'smart' and being 'too strategic'. Being smart is something other, he seems to suggest, than being occupied with ticking boxes. It is, perhaps, not nearly as calculated, but we do not get enough information here to be able to say precisely how he constructs the binary and what 'being smart about it' entails. Suffice to say that he speaks himself into existence as slightly more moral in a potentially immoral game.

## 9.5 Discussion

So, we have now canvassed two themes that run through Australian ECRs' narratives about research work in contemporary universities. At this point it needs to be stated that no patterns in terms of institutional affiliation could be made except perhaps that ECRs from the research-intensive universities tended to be more articulate about research expectations in performance management terms. The study does not include any data that could support or refute a claim that current ECRs to a greater extent than earlier use objectionable research practices or have become more strategic in their grant seeking. It is plausible that none of these practices are entirely new to the academy. Furthermore, we cannot from this study determine whether ECRs' activities and accounts of their activities are different from those of their senior colleagues. Nevertheless it is worth considering whether contemporary policy formations, and their associated effects 'on the ground', are likely to intensify, encourage and legitimise these behaviours. Essentially they are behaviours that suppress scientific, disciplinary, intellectual and methodological agendas for more 'strategic' ones. They are practices that give precedence to output, the quantity of output and funding, rather than intellectual and scientific substance.

As Biesta (2009) argues in a related discussion, the rise of the measurement performativity culture in education has had a profound impact on educational practice. A culture of performativity is a culture in which 'means become ends in themselves so that targets and indicators of quality become mistaken for quality itself' (p. 35). It becomes a culture in which a *demonstration* of activity becomes the focus rather than the activity itself. Others have found how the age of measurement in research in various ways corrupts scientific practices (Calver and Beattie, 2015). For example Østerud (2015) argues how researchers' focus has moved from scientific curiosity towards marketing, which we see reverberated in the ECRs' narratives around 'sell-ability' and 'fundability' of ideas and projects. Bølstad (2014) argues that we live in the time of fast research, where the speed with which results and outputs come out is more important than the quality of the work. Again, the notion of 'doing a dirty' in the study at hand echoes this. As such senior researchers seem to agree that research activity is changing profoundly as a result of the new performance frameworks. Politically determined ways of funding and measuring research are enacted in everyday decisions about what to prioritise and what to do. For example, as many of the ECRs observed, their workplaces seemed almost exclusively to provide support for obtaining external money, for example by offering ample professional development seminars and workshops on how to attract grants, whilst reducing opportunities to actually undertake research (e.g. writing retreats or funding of fieldwork) and grow stimulating intellectual environments.

The ECRs in the study at hand have not experienced working under different conditions and expectations, 'the golden age' as it is sometimes called, which refers to a time where academics were left alone and given sufficient time to pursue their research and teaching. Nevertheless most of the ECRs expressed astonishment in regard to the extent of the pressure placed upon them once they commenced ongoing positions – they had no idea it was going to be *that* bad, as one of them expressed it. Their stories are stories about daily struggles to navigate and negotiate the pressure to deliver outputs with the desire to do good work, both in their teaching, research and administration. In this highly pressurised environment it becomes difficult to develop and maintain agendas that compete with neoliberal performance agendas. Many of them said, for example, that they had become so worried about student evaluations of their teaching (i.e. the neoliberal positioning of the student as consumer or customer) that they were more concerned with making sure to *not* get bad evaluations than make the difficult demands that, in their view, would promote student learning. Similarly with their research they talked about giving up on topics, questions, theoretical frameworks and so on that they themselves deemed worthwhile and important because they could sense that they would 'go nowhere', meaning would not produce a lot of output or attract external funding.

It is important to note that two out of the 20 participants expressed frustration with workloads but did not account for a struggle between their own desires and agendas with those of their workplace in terms of their research. These particular ECRs found the clear and set performance expectations preferable to more tacit ones and expressed no concern with the marketability of their research topics and methodologies. They both worked on research topics for which there was relatively easy funding (one worked in engineering, the other in health promotion). They were quite comfortable with the language of the performance frameworks and said they thrived on the competitive environment and felt both seen and rewarded. They both made the point that it was in everyone's interest to get rid of those colleagues who did not 'pull their weight', as one of them expressed it, in terms of obtaining external grants. In this way the narrative of struggle and alienation is not universal; for some there is meaning and pleasure to be found in the performance regime.

## 9.6 Conclusion

In this exploratory narrative study we saw how 20 Australian early career researchers respond to the current research performance frameworks. Two major themes were identified, one that illuminated how the pressures to perform entailed taking up practices that the ECRs considered objectionable in research terms, and a second that showed how the pressures to obtain external research funding invited the ECRs to allow 'strategic' concerns to supersede scientific or scholarly ones. As Biesta (2009) reminds us, despite the oft-heard claim that neoliberal performance frameworks are value-neutral, in that they merely are meant to address the form and pace but not the *content* of academic work, values are always at work. One of the key values lodged in many if not all Australian research performance frameworks is one of productivity, which is about quantity regardless of recent policy interest in quality. In relation to that it was worrying that the ECRs who struggled with the performance frameworks also in many cases struggled to articulate the value and worth of their work outside the productivity discourse. In some cases, in the midst of insurmountable workloads and high expectations, it seemed that they were close to losing sight of the purpose of their research other than to get runs on the board. Yet, what this study also begins to shed some light on is that the claim that performance frameworks only order the pace and form of the work does not hold up. The content of the work changes too. In many ways research work becomes all 'strategic' – what is likely to get published quickly, what is likely to get funded. In that light it is reasonable to assert that in the age of neoliberal performance management, research activity is in danger of becoming circumscribed to a question of output and of accruing revenue for one's university and department and for furthering one's personal career. In a scenario where a researcher is trained to become focussed on output and placed in a situation where they feel compelled to adopt compromised and strategic practices over other ones, researchers are vulnerable to becoming responsive to others' agendas, rather than be scientific and intellectual agenda-setters (see also Thornton, 2008). In other words, they and the substance of their work become easier to control. Whether one constitutes this as a concern or as progress depends on the values one lives by.

## Notes

1 The data for this chapter was collected whilst the author still worked in Australia.
2 It must be noted that the distinctions between universities have been made for the purpose of the study, but also that it was not assumed that because the universities by themselves and others were spoken into existence in hierarchical ways that these distinctions are *a priori* meaningful or capture anything specific about everyday work conditions.

# Part II

# Case studies from the field

# Chapter 10

# Ethical dilemmas in program evaluation

*Carina Calzoni*

## 10.1 Introduction

Evaluation involves the process of determining the merit, worth or significance of something (Scriven, 1996). As this definition implies, the primary aim of evaluation is to formulate value judgments or draw evaluative conclusions using information collected through the evaluation process. In contrast, the aim of social research traditionally is to produce empirical and generalisable knowledge, not to deduce value conclusions (Vestman & Conner, 2006). This is one of the key differences given between research and evaluation.

Another distinction is that in a democratic society the act of evaluation operates in a social-political environment in which there are power structures, sets of rules and choices about resources (Simons, 2006). Chelimsky (2008) argues that "evaluators practising in the public domain can never escape the world of politics". As such, the process of evaluation involves navigating complex social interactions with various vested interests, whilst balancing the need to be independent.

## 10.2 Ethical dilemmas in evaluation

There are many inherent dilemmas that arise through the unique role of evaluation that the evaluator needs to attend to throughout the entire process. However, there is a relative dearth of published literature or professional debates on ethical issues encountered in the practice of evaluation. It seems that evaluators tend to avoid ethical discussions. This was shown in a study of evaluators' views on ethical issues in their everyday practice. The study of over 450 evaluators found that approximately 35 percent felt that they had never encountered ethical problems to which they had to respond (Morris, 1999). Although this research was undertaken 15 years ago, there is still relative silence on ethics in the evaluation literature that exists today. It seems that there is a tendency for evaluators to feel that by adhering to professional ethical principles and structured methodologies, they can tick the "ethics box" and move on to "more important things".

However, ethical dilemmas are not rare, whether realised or not, they are pervasive in every evaluation exercise and across the whole evaluation process. With over 15 years' experience working in the evaluation space as a commissioner of evaluation within government and later as an evaluation practitioner, I have found that ethical dilemmas arise through the demand for transparency, the need to manage competing interests and existing power structure, together with the expectation to deliver a useful evaluation that is responsive to the client's needs. Dilemmas surface through the trade-offs that are made when choosing what to evaluate, how to evaluate and who has a say in these decisions.

## 10.3 Case study: evaluation of a mental health court program

Several years ago, I was involved in a team commissioned to undertake an evaluation of the effectiveness of a mental health court diversion pilot program. Mental health courts are relatively new innovations that are focused on providing diversionary options for offenders who are suffering from a persistent and severe mental illness. Research has found that "people with mental illness comprise a disproportionate number of the people who are arrested, who come before the courts and who are imprisoned" (Senate Select Committee on Mental Health, 2006).

It is also well documented that there is inadequate treatment provided to offenders who are experiencing mental illness and there is a need for court interventions that can offer suitable alternatives to sentencing. As such, the Australian Parliament Senate Select Committee on Mental Health recommended a significant expansion of mental health courts and diversion programs focused on "keeping people with mental illness out of prison and supporting them with health, housing and employment services that will reduce offending behaviour and assist with recovery" (Senate Select Committee on Mental Health, 2006).

The court diversion program being evaluated was a solution-focused and recovery-orientated court dedicated to identifying and responding to the underlying causes of offending behaviour and promoting participant accountability for their actions and rehabilitation. It was based on therapeutic jurisprudence principles, meaning that the mental health court "seeks to facilitate the integration of treatment and support services for mentally impaired offenders which are optimally conducive in promoting individual wellbeing" (Zafirakis, 2010).

The program was voluntary and provided clinical services and community support to offenders with mental illness who were assessed as suitable for the program. Not all of those assessed were deemed suitable for the program for reasons such as the person was acutely unwell and/or may not have been able to engage safely in the program; another program was found to be more suitable; or the original charges were withdrawn. The program was focused on serving the needs of vulnerable people in a crisis situation and was aimed at supporting the justice system to be more responsive to the complex situations of people with mental illness.

The evaluation was conducted two years into the program implementation. The evaluation period was six months and the methodology included focus groups with the various agencies and community support services involved in implementing the program, qualitative interviews with program participants, families and key stakeholders; a structured survey of current program participants and families; an analysis of program data; and a literature review.

It is now well understood that consumers of mental health services directly impacted by the quality and effectiveness of mental health care provide a unique experience and understanding that is valuable in the evaluation of mental health practices and priorities (National Consumer and Carer Forum, 2004). The empowerment of consumers in mental health services represents a paradigm shift in service delivery with a strong ethos of recovery-oriented practice[1] and a person-centred approach (Phillips, 2006).

## 10.4 Ethical considerations around involving mental health consumers in evaluations

In this case study, the consumers were "offenders with a mental illness" and the importance of their involvement in the evaluation was recognised by the specialist clinical mental health team implementing the program. However, the team found consumer involvement principles more difficult to attain in practice. Mentally impaired offenders are a particularly vulnerable group and the mental well-being of these people was the primary consideration for the team implementing the program. As such, the clinical team were concerned that the privacy of offenders would be compromised if their contact details were given to the evaluators, without seeking their prior consent. The clinical team were also concerned for the well-being of those involved in the evaluation and wanted to ensure that participants would not be harmed by their involvement.

This led to in-depth ethical discussions between the evaluators and program deliverers on how to manage the involvement of offenders in the evaluation in a way that gave the greatest opportunity for involvement whilst minimising the potential for any harm caused to the well-being of offenders. After careful consideration it was decided that participants in the evaluation would be selected by the implementation team, even though this could be seen as somewhat inconsistent with the principles of recovery-oriented practice. The selected participants were either currently in the program or had completed the program and the implementing team held their current contact details. Once selected, potential participants had their mental health status assessed, and if deemed mentally well, were asked if they would agree to be contacted for an interview. It was at this stage, that the evaluators were provided with their contact details.

In addition, for privacy and practical reasons, contact details for many past program participants were not available and they could not be contacted by the implementation team. This was particularly the case for those who had prematurely exited the program or had finished the program early in its implementation. Furthermore the contact details for those who did not access the program were not kept. As there was no way of contacting these offenders, their voices were naturally excluded from the evaluation.

## 10.5 The ethical trade-offs in selecting evaluation participants

For the evaluators, the trade-offs inherent in the selection of the participants raised a number of ethical dilemmas because it meant that ultimately some voices would be privileged over others in the evaluation. In particular, this dilemma raises ethical questions such as:

- Should the evaluation only include the voices of those who are in the program and who have been assessed as being well and suitable for an interview?
- Those participants who are assessed as "well" may have a different experience to those who assessed as "unwell". Is it therefore appropriate to exclude the voices of those who are unwell at the time of the evaluation?
- Time-constrained evaluation often results in excluding some participants. Should there be more flexibility in evaluation timelines to ensure greater opportunity for inclusion of mental health consumer voices?
- Equally, can the effectiveness of the program be assessed without including the views of those who were excluded from the program, as well as those who have exited the program and are no longer in contact with the clinical team?
- Finally, could the selection of interview participants by the clinical team influence the outcomes of the evaluation? Would the views of participants be different if recruited independently by the evaluators?

## 10.6 The limitation of accepted ethical principles

In the course of deciding which path is the most ethical or least unethical to take in this situation, the evaluators' first reference point is to apply the accepted principles that guide the practice of evaluation, written in professional ethical standards and codes of conduct. These principles have been developed and revised over time based on the experiences of numerous academics and practitioners. They address the common ethical matters faced in evaluating social programs. The AES Guidelines for the Ethical Conduct of Evaluations (Australasian Evaluation Society, 2014), for instance, includes ethical principles around the commissioning of evaluation, reciprocity (i.e. giving back useful evaluation outputs to evaluation participants), making sound and informed judgments, fair and balanced reporting and reporting to multiple audiences.

However, no set of ethical principles are inclusive of all cases or are free from contradictions. Often the evaluator is faced with having to make decisions about the application of these principles and weighing up their options. For example, an AES ethical principles states that as part of obtaining informed consent, participants should be told about any likely risks and benefits arising from their participation in the evaluation. If the evaluation is likely to lead to a decision on whether or not to continue funding a program, the biggest risk to those benefiting would be to lose access to the program. However, having this knowledge is likely to influence a more favourable response from program participants, which will in turn limit the extent to which the evaluation can present a true and accurate account of program effectiveness.

## 10.7 Applying evaluation theoretical approaches to these ethical dilemmas

It is debatable whether guidelines, codes and principles can ever go far enough because of the diversity of evaluation approaches, the diversity of social programs, the diversity of interested and affected stakeholders and the political nature of the evaluation. What is required is the application of higher-order moral reasoning and for this, evaluators can turn to evaluation theorists for guidance. In this instance, there are a number of different evaluation approaches with the associated ethical theories that could be considered to guide the ethical choices raised in the case study.

For example, Scriven (1996) is an evaluation scholar who advocates that the role of the evaluator is to make independent judgments. The evaluator should minimise the effects of stakeholder influence and rely on rigorous evaluation designs using preset standards. In applying Scriven's approach to the dilemmas raised in the case study, the evaluator would advocate for a rigorous design with minimal stakeholder influence. This could lead the evaluator to apply consequential ethical principles and demand methodological rigor for the evaluation which would prevent the clinician in the program from selecting the individuals in favour of an independent clinical assessment and selection process.

Alternatively Patton (2012) advocates focusing on ways to increase the likelihood that the evaluation is used and this often involves adjusting the evaluation design to accommodate stakeholder concerns. "Utilisation focused evaluation begins with the promise that evaluation should be judged by [its] utility and actual use" (Patton, 2012, p. 4). Under this approach, the role of the evaluator varies depending on the purpose of the evaluation, the context of the program, the needs of the decision-makers and the evaluator's own sense of what is ethical. The list of roles that the evaluator may play could include advisor, trainer, group facilitator, external expert and methodologist.

Applying a utilisation-focused evaluation lens to the case study might lead the evaluator to work with the clients of the evaluation to understand their moral standing and design the selection and recruitment process accordingly.

In this case, the evaluator might operate from a stance that ensures the evaluation applies established principles of ethical conduct, in particular attempting to do no harm by not including those individuals not well enough to participate.

Fetterman is known for his developments on empowerment evaluation. This involves the use of evaluation concepts, techniques and findings to foster improvement and self-determination (Fetterman, 2013). Through the use of empowerment evaluation approaches, Fetterman advocates for community empowerment, inclusivity, democratic participation and social justice. The role of the evaluator is not to make judgments but to guide and coach participants to perform their own evaluation. Through an empowerment approach, the evaluator would involve the wider community in the evaluation. Under this approach the evaluator could adopt a social justice standing and consider involving mental health services consumer groups in the evaluation process, including seeking their input in designing appropriate methods for data collection, recruiting service consumers to be part of the data collection process and involving consumers in reviewing the findings of the evaluation and development of recommendations.

Mertens lifework is reflected in the development of the transformative paradigm which explicitly places value on the pursuit of social justice and the furtherance of human rights (Mertens, 2013). Mertens advises that the evaluator has a moral obligation to be aware that discrimination and oppression are pervasive and she argues that the evaluator has a moral responsibility to challenge the status quo (Mertens, 2009). Through a transformative lens, the evaluator might ask themselves, in terms of this mental health program, what are the cultural norms that are supportive of or deleterious to the pursuit of social justice? It might be that the protectionist view of clinicians is seen as a paternalistic cultural norm that is detrimental to the pursuit of social justice for this group of people. The evaluator might consider this view as violating the rights to fairness and justice of a vulnerable subgroup of people and might decide not to be involved in the evaluation because it is viewed as supporting the status quo.

## 10.8 Conclusion: the need for more open discussion on ethical dilemmas in evaluation

Ethical dilemmas in evaluation require choices to be made between competing opinions and values. Choices are made about which way to proceed in the evaluation and how the evaluator should behave with respect to the individuals involved in the evaluation. Relying solely on ethical principles included in codes of practice and professional standards are limited because each evaluation exercise is unique and faced with its own set of ethical choices.

In addressing ethical dilemmas, it is helpful for the evaluator to go beyond the professional practice codes, to more fully appreciate the theoretical grounding of different evaluation approaches and to consider the ethical choices associated with them. It is clear from the options for ethical practice that could be applied in the case study that the choices available to an evaluator are extensive and there is a wide range of evaluation approaches that can facilitate these decisions. This is a useful framework for evaluators to explore real-world ethical dilemmas.

It is also clear there is no agreement among the theorists on the right and ethical way to conduct an evaluation and there are many contradictions. For example, is an evaluator's independent judgment of merit or worth any more worthy than that of a group of informed stakeholders, and in answering this question, whose values are privileged? The fact that there are divergent views on this is why it is so important for the evaluator to be cognisant of the moral underpinnings of evaluation and why we need to discuss the ethical dilemmas with clients and amongst peers.

As pointed out by Simons (2006) it is through the consideration of the ethical issues surrounding the process of evaluation that the moral standing of the practice can be judged. It is through more open, reflexive practice, where evaluators and commissioners talk about ethical issues throughout the evaluation process, that we can truly judge the ethical rigor of an evaluation.

There are always trade-offs between ethical principles when choosing what to evaluate, how to evaluate and who to involve in the evaluation. By facilitating discussions on ethical dilemmas between those with vested interests in the evaluation outcome and the evaluator, there can be greater transparency and legitimacy given to those decisions. As demonstrated in the case study, although not completely consistent with recovery-oriented practice, program clinicians selected the participants suitable for the evaluation in order to protect their mental well-being. Discussions on the "right way to proceed" between the evaluators and program implementers ensured there was accountability for decisions made around the ethical trade-offs associated with excluding some voices from the evaluation.

In addition, much can be learned from a broader professional-wide dialogue on the ethical dilemmas and choices faced in evaluation and what ultimate decisions were made. It is important for the professionalism of a growing and important discipline that those working in the evaluation space, as either evaluators or commissioners, are encouraged to share their experience and speak frankly about their ethical concerns. Through the discussions of the ethical dilemmas in this chapter, I hope that I have been able to contribute, even in a small way to this dialogue.

## Note

1 Recovery-oriented practice is defined as "gaining and retaining hope, understanding of one's abilities and disabilities, engagement in an active life, personal autonomy, social identity, meaning and purpose in life, and a positive sense of self" (*National Standards for Mental Health Services*, Australian Government, 2010).

# Chapter 11

# Surfacing the implicit

*Kevin Gaitskell*

## 11.1 Introduction

The momentum to evaluate boards has impacted across the three sectors of private, government and not-for-profit. This chapter draws on the author's experience in all three, however the weight of experience is in the private sector.

Periodic evaluations of board performance are an indication of good corporate governance. Corporate boards are increasingly searching for external validation and insight into opportunities to improve through evaluations. Drivers of this search are individual boards' own desires to improve their practice and their response to substantially increased scrutiny externally.

The very nature of these bodies causes evaluations to be centered on the exercise of power. Corporate boards are at the top of the organisational tree – their impact is felt intensely by the management and stakeholders of organisations. Board power is manifest in its impact but elusive in its application. Bringing power to the surface ensures the board can most effectively govern both itself and the affected organisation.

The potent but latent nature of board power creates a range of "moments of truth" for the evaluator. These moments are best navigated by modeling good governance at every step in the evaluation.

The author has over three decades' experience as an executive and director. His roles in boards have included director, chair, advisor and evaluator. He has been engaged in over 30 evaluations of corporate boards.

Because of the nature of boards, evaluations conducted by the author involve first bringing to the surface and then leveraging board power.

## 11.2 The paradox of boards

Boards are beset by paradoxes. Understanding and responding to these paradoxes is critical to successful board evaluation.

Boards are responsible for overall company performance. Functions of boards include: setting company direction (including establishing policy settings), making available resources, monitoring company performance, ensuring company compliance, ensuring risks are managed and communicating progress to a range of stakeholders.

Whilst often appointed by and accountable to shareholders, a board's duties are owed to the more ambiguous "company". Directors are required to act in good faith in the best interests of the *company* – both as it currently stands and as they aspire it to be. This substantial responsibility is reinforced by significant and increasing levels of civil and criminal compliance requirements and scrutiny.

The threat of exposure is a driver to *conformance* (the past and present orientation) by individual directors and the board collectively, at the expense of company *performance* or future positioning. Drivers reinforcing conformance at the expense of performance orientations is one paradox presenting for the board and its member directors.

Most boards operate part time, despite their onerous role and responsibilities. By contrast, company management (including Chief Executive Officers) are engaged full-time in the pursuit of smaller scoped roles, delivering against parameters set by the board. The board occupies a manifestly more powerful and significant role, including holding management to account. A paradox exists where management is relatively information rich and required to share this resource with the part-time entity holding it to account. This creates information asymmetry – another paradox which the board must confront.

Theoretically, boards operate on the basis of democratic process. Generally, each director's view has equal weight with the chair being *primus inter pares* or "the first among equals". Respect, collegiality, confidentiality and trust are keys that bond this social system. In any group these attributes take time to establish. The ability of a board to become a sound social system is limited by their part-time status. In corporate boards social cohesion tends to come via enacting their role rather than deliberative investment in group reflection and feedback. In contrast, management has more distinctive roles and more time, information and levers to reward membership behaviour and cement its own social system.

This paradox of role and availability between boards and management extends to:

1 the simultaneous application of interdependence (for example in the use of information) *and* independence (for example in decision-making, such as CEO appraisals) between boards and management; and
2 the contrasting board roles to be a mentor/partner/collaborator *as well as* monitor/controller/reviewer of management.

Boards are expected to exercise their "wisdom" of experience. An additional paradox surrounds the application of this quality.

Management texts and professional bodies are increasingly exploring concepts of emotional intelligence and empathy (i.e. putting oneself in another's shoes).

The proposition is that emotional intelligence and empathy are more important in the acquisition and exercise of power than classical authority mechanisms, such as force and control.

Empathic responses may be limited in boards in three key ways.

Empathy is enhanced through relating. The first limitation involves the lack of physical contact with management (and also as previously outlined *within* the board) due to finite director time and the perceived imperative for boards to invest in traditional and often more pressing agendas.

The second limitation is the more pervasive aspect of this paradox.

Levels of empathy can reduce the higher the rank. This phenomenon is not new and is reflected in Lord Acton's nineteenth-century quote: *'Power tends to corrupt and absolute power corrupts absolutely'*. Once people assume positions of power they may be less likely to be empathic to those below in organisational structures. Although directors tend to be senior in experience there is a risk that the lessons learnt in getting to the boardroom may not be willingly shared due to a reduction in empathy arising from relative positions.

The final limitation relates to the availability of wisdom.

Diversity of experience is an important ingredient in complex decision-making such as that undertaken by boards. In contrast to the scope for choosing managers, the market for directors is narrow. This market is frequently perceived as an exclusive "club". Pathways to join are greatly influenced by existing members. A possible example of this phenomenon is peak governance associations resisting attempts to broaden representation by campaigning against mandating an increase in women sitting on boards.

The smaller the market the smaller the "gene pool" of expertise and therefore the depth and breadth of "wisdom" available to the board.

Interlocking directorates are a manifestation of this restricted market. These are the linkage among corporations created when individuals sit on two or more boards. Interlocking can be used as a cartel-like device whereby individuals and organisations expand their power. Interlocking affects the quality of experience and the exercise of power and influence *within* boards. Legal structures, including significant penalties for non-compliance, are designed to limit these "conflicts of interest". Directors may be required, in compliance with regulatory expectations, to absent themselves from associated discussions and decisions when a potential conflict has been identified. Boards may exclude a director on similar grounds. Therefore, in managing a conflict of interest, a diligent director/board may be required to exclude the director(s) who is be best equipped to inform decisions.

The real or manufactured restrictions on the market for talent and the existence of interlocking directorates limits both the extent of a board's wisdom *and* its application. A final paradox.

## 11.3 Evaluating boards

Sensitivity to the above paradoxes, combined with the author's broader experience and industry good practice form the basis of his board evaluations.

Although substantially iterative and dynamic, evaluations conducted by the author centre around five phases. These phases are broadly applied by many other evaluators in this market. They can however vary significantly between engagements and on the basis of the evaluators approach. Drivers for variation are discussed in the following sections.

### 11.3.1 Phase 1: engagement

The exclusivity surrounding boards (discussed above) works in favour of some evaluators in the selection process.

Invitations to present methodology and personnel directly to boards dominates over open tendering processes. These invitations are often predicated on previous director experience with the evaluator and/or the evaluator's reputation within the industry. To an extent this prior knowledge of the evaluator is an element of board 'wisdom'. But it can also present the paradox of 'conflict of interest' discussed earlier. Whilst trust in the relationship between board and evaluator is paramount, any pre-existing associations between directors and evaluator requires careful management. The evaluator may have their own 'conflict of interest' due to prior relationships with directors. These 'conflicts' need be managed with the same standards of good governance in the industry (i.e. an example of modelling good governance in the conduct of evaluations). This includes the evaluator ensuring the awareness and response of all parties of the underlying nature of the relationship, as personally uncomfortable as that may be.

Motivations for initiating evaluation are varied. In the early stages of this engagement phase motivations are essentially implicit. They may change and tend to become more explicit through well-moderated board discussions and the engagement processes underpinning effective evaluations. Initial board motivations may include:

- modelling to management;
- modelling to the board market (including peak bodies and colleagues);
- modelling to other external stakeholders such as regulators;
- self (board) continuous improvement; and
- dealing with specific issues of performance.

For the evaluator there are early moments of truth.

Stamping the independence of the role of the evaluator is critical as part of the broader process to explicitly model good governance. Such modelling includes ensuring directors will receive equal opportunity to both input and access findings and ensuring the board *as a body* will be responsible for resolving issues surfaced by the evaluation. Early demonstration of this independence mitigates accusations of evaluator bias. Importantly, this behaviour establishes the evaluator's position in relation to both the prevailing *and* emerging power dynamics within the board.

A second 'moment' comes from the engagement phase.

Boards often establish their evaluation budget prior to first contact with an evaluator. The budget is frequently based on the experience of individual directors with previous evaluations and established through board discussion. Thereafter, it may be revised following the evaluator's presentation. In the author's experience, typically the budget proposed by the evaluator is accepted. Acceptance is due to trust based on prior director association with the evaluator, directors' experiences with evaluations, and socialisation/advocacy within the board.

On occasion the author has been asked to reduce scope to meet the budget and/or director time limitations. Such 'corner cutting' can render the evaluation perfunctory, thereby creating risks to both the evaluation process and the evaluator's brand. A willingness to decline an offer to evaluate a board, whilst difficult, is necessary in these circumstances. Any refusal should be accompanied with an open explanation, including the articulation of risks to the board.

### *11.3.2 Phase 2: design*

Sensitivity to respective roles, authority and pressures of time in board evaluations requires two design considerations.

The first consideration relates to project management.

To meet expectations for quality and deliverables, a board subcommittee is often necessary to consider and resolve project management issues. Addressing the make-up of the subcommittee and its mandate are essential to good governance and include protecting individuals against any conflicts of interest. It is essential that the charter for this subcommittee is complementary to and not competing with that of the board. The subcommittee should be supported by a clear delegation from the board, generated in the engagement phase. The subcommittee make-up may vary between just the board chair to the chair and a couple of directors. The board chair's role of setting the tone and agenda for the board is reinforced by leadership of the subcommittee and by preparing for key deliverables and the implementation of agreed actions. In not a single evaluation conducted by the author has the CEO been involved in this group, unless he/she is a managing director or executive chair of the board. The subcommittee assists with managing the risks of information asymmetry and potentially divergent interests between board and management by ensuring management is appropriately engaged.

The second design consideration involves data management.

Similar to the first consideration, parameters are established in the engagement phase. These parameters should include: (1) the iterative nature of the process; (2) modelling good governance, especially through defined director roles and involvement; and (3) the explicit intention to bring to the surface issues of board performance.

Typically data collection and analysis involves:

- evaluator observations from first contact;
- written surveys of directors and agreed stakeholders;
- observation of board meetings;
- desk-top review of documents;
- interviews (of the board and identified stakeholders);
- presentation/board workshop;
- report drafting and presentation.

There are a number of evaluator moments of truth in this phase.

Chairs can request exclusive briefings ahead of the board, including feedback on individual responses. There can be significant pressure on the evaluator to comply, given the power of the chair's role, the force of the personality of the individual (as indicated earlier, directors are often senior industry figures) and the evaluator's own desire to partner with the chair to navigate the process. Respect and reference back to agreed parameters can be necessary. Issues of confidentiality need to be clarified from the outset to establish these reference points.

Written surveys of the board and identified stakeholders are a key component of evaluations. Survey results provide an important filter to more focused investigation, particularly through interview. In this phase a drop-down menu of possible survey questions is presented to the subcommittee. Dimensions of survey questions include:

1. roles and responsibilities;
2. board structure and accountability;
3. strategic focus;
4. risk management;
5. control systems and accountability;
6. culture of decision-making; and
7. board effectiveness.

Selecting questions is a key subcommittee decision on behalf of the board. Success involves getting the right balance for each dimension by accommodating what may be already known and explicit within the board, whilst remaining open to the unknown, avoided and/or implied. The evaluator has to be alert to the avoidance of issues. Frequently, one of these is the chair's own performance. The credibility of the evaluator, through both their experience and standing and the agreed approach, are critical to ensure balance both within and across the dimensions is established.

A final area of evaluator pressure can include identifying the range of respondents.

Generally the target audience is clear at the outset. Often this is exclusively the board. Less clear are the stakeholders to be included, particularly at interview.

In one case pressure was applied to the author by the board to exclude the CEO from interview on the basis that 'this was board business and not the province of management'. In response the author successfully proposed that being a key respondent to the board, the CEO had an important window into their performance. The CEO's views were included in the data. Subsequently the issue of distrust between the CEO and board was brought to the surface within the evaluation (at the workshop). Out of the evaluation the board agreed to take explicit action on this issue. Ultimately the board leveraged their power and assisted the CEO to leave the company. An issue with the board/CEO relationship was identified, clarified and resolved.

### 11.3.3 Phase 3: data collection

Board performance evaluations are skewed towards qualitative data. Quantitative dimensions are usually limited to a check of compliance obligations. The skill of the evaluator to access, analyse and present qualitative data at board level is critical to success.

In this phase, interviews are where most evaluator moments of truth occur.

Interviews reinforce equal access and contribution as well as garnering buy-in. Interviews should be introduced by an outline of standard protocols related to purpose and confidentiality. In interviews, the author also includes a reiteration of broader agreed evaluation protocols, such as surfacing the issues and ensuring the board as a body responds.

Interviews open up performance issues for the board, some reiterated, others articulated for the first time. In almost all circumstances directors relish the opportunity at interview to both comment upon *and* influence board performance. Interviews often involve an expression of individual director power. The author believes the willingness to engage is related to: the director's previous limited time to do so, the previously limited opportunities to do so and the frustration of not being able to do so within the prevailing business of the board.

Interviews provide considerable opportunity for moments of truth for the evaluator. Two examples are provided.

At one interview, an experienced director declared his exasperation with the performance of the chair and demanded the evaluator resolve this concern – 'you're the expert, fix it'. The evaluator reiterated the broader protocols and the intent to surface issues for the board as a body to agree and resolve. The evaluator also explained that the survey revealed only this director had identified issues with the chair's performance. This explanation, however, only marginally assuaged the director.

Given the director's vehemence, balanced against his isolation from other respondents, the evaluator proposed to provide a platform for the director to raise the issue at the board workshop. Scenarios for doing so were explored at interview. Ultimately, the director decided against the option. Subsequently, within the workshop, the questionnaire data on chair performance was presented and the evaluator issued an open invitation for any director to comment on this performance. This director did not take up this offer. Within months the director resigned his position.

The second example parallels the first. On this occasion it was the chair expressing concern with the CEO. Similarity lies in: the isolation of this position from the views expressed by the rest of the board, requests for the evaluator to deal with the concern and the evaluator's response. The relationship breakdown between the chair and CEO was identified at multiple points during the data-collection phase and surfaced in the board workshop. Through the leveraging of the board's collective power and individual professional reflection, the chair decided to resign.

### 11.3.4 Phase 4: surfacing – the board workshop

Armed with a range of data points the evaluator's role turns to analysis, synthesis and framing the board conversation(s). This entails surfacing the issues for all directors and navigating to a collective response.

It is customary for boards to deal with a wide range of highly complex information. Because of limitations of time and the decision-making pressures associated with their role, boards can be very demanding on how information is provided. In a further example of modelling good governance discussed in this paper, pre-workshop evaluation reports need to be sound, clear, accessible, compelling and directional. These reports assist in framing the board conversation. The whole of the board-workshops phase is an opportunity to engage the wisdom of the board in determining priority performance issues and to agree their resolution. The emphasis is upon engaging the collective wisdom.

These workshops can be controversial, confrontational and are frequently uncomfortable. This is an experience shared by all directors, the chair and the evaluator.

Best results flow from following the approach outlined, including: engaging the subcommittee in preparation; assisting the chair to both frame the conversation and demonstrate ownership of the results; confirming rules of play, such as equal input and a drive to consensus-based decision-making; providing and confirming a handful of issues rather than long lists; and judicious use and valuing of directors' time.

There are a number of moments of truth for the evaluator in such a politically charged environment.

Discomfort with the subject matter can be manifest through dissatisfaction with the process and the evaluator. When encountered, the author navigates this pressure through adherence to the approach discussed above and, importantly, by not personalising or overreacting.

A related moment involves the use of the authority of role in 'deep diving' into issues.

'Deep dives' involve boards selecting an issue and through focused and active challenge, getting to the bottom of management's response. These inquiry dives are an important tool for boards to make sense of management's response, hold them to account and change behaviour. They are a demonstration of both board skill and power.

The author has experienced the use of deep dive approaches for avoidance and obfuscation by boards when addressing issues of their *own* performance. As outlined above, not overreacting to when this presents is key. Allowing directors to reflect and self-govern by the evaluator pausing and/or naming this behaviour can be required. This approach is also necessary in other areas, such as director dominance, director passivity, the board too readily agreeing the issues presented and the 'seduction' of the evaluator through hollow flattery.

An example demonstrating the politically charged nature of board workshops involves the frequently coupled issues of information and performance as discussed in the section on paradox.

In this example a strong consensus of concern about the information provided by management was identified in the survey. Through interview this issue extended to broader dissatisfaction with management. Dissatisfaction included management's failure to value and appreciate the board's role and its use of the company's resources. During interview and through the workshop the board's accountability was first explored as to why it had not debated this issue earlier and provided feedback to management on its expectations and requirements.

Ownership of this accountability was agreed in the workshop. Furthermore, the issue was reframed and extended from one just related to information. The board swiftly agreed to provide clear feedback on *both* their information expectations and their prevailing dissatisfaction with management's performance. The CEO ultimately left the organisation.

Generally, more time is required in confirming the issues for attention than agreeing recommendations for action. Boards are in the business of accountability and usually move relatively quickly to agree actions, responsibilities, dependencies, timelines and resources.

Failure to adequately surface the issues increases the risk of boards responding only to presenting problems and challenges within their prevailing customs, practices and perspectives. This failure perpetuates the status quo. Challenging the status quo involves surfacing the underlying issues. Surfacing these issues involves significant moments of truth for the evaluator.

### *11.3.5 Phase 5: report*

Report writing for board evaluations cascades from the process outlined. Phase 4 is the most fraught and critical to success. Nonetheless a report is more than symbolic of the work undertaken. The final report is a document the board can integrate into their work programme and use to check progress, including holding each other and others to account.

In modelling good governance the report should centre on key issues and agreed actions. Comprehensive commentary on the approach is superfluous to future performance. Evaluator moments of truth are less frequent and impacting in this final phase. Dissemination of the report is often clear at the outset and confirmed through the process. In some circumstances the chair, sensitive to external scrutiny, has requested careful identification and definition of issues in the report.

Following an evaluation the author offers follow-up assistance in implementation. In most circumstances these offers are not accepted. Board feedback on the level of take-up of this offer includes: the levels of board ownership built through the process; limitations in time and budget; and, burdened board cycles of activity.

Many boards are adopting a two-year evaluation cycle; in every second year engaging independent evaluators. Evaluations in alternate years are often undertaken in-house (within the board), principally through surveys. Re-engagement of an evaluator occurs frequently. In these circumstances protocols established in Phase 1: engagement need to be re-affirmed.

Awareness of individual boards and being a 'trusted player' cannot compromise independence of the evaluator in identifying performance issues and assisting their resolution.

## 11.4 Conclusion

The author has observed the confluence between drivers, influences, roles and the formal authority of corporate boards. This confluence is more paradoxical than sequential and/or necessarily rational. It is through the exercise of their considerable political power that boards navigate these paradoxes.

Through a board's legal status, conventions, organisational positioning, composition and modus operandi, the exercise of board power is both inferential *and* implicit.

Evaluations of board performance are essentially a study of their power. Successful evaluations have at their heart an awareness of this power, surfacing how it is manifested and leveraging it to enhance performance.

Board evaluations bring a number of challenging moments of truth for the evaluator.

Whereas boards navigate paradoxes inherent in their role through the use of power, the successful evaluator navigates their own 'moments' by effective process involving modelling good governance. In so doing board evaluations involve direct engagement with all aspects of board power.

# Chapter 12

# Balancing relationships and intellectual rigour in research for government agencies

*Graeme Gower and Gary Partington*

## 12.1 Introduction

The drive to justify programs in the public sector has resulted in a growing desire by many organisations involved in education, social services, health and welfare to seek evidence of the outcomes that result from these programs. Pressure from governments for accountability of expenditure in these areas grew as the available resources to pay for them came under pressure in recent decades (Perry & McWilliam, 2007; Staley, 2008; Mundine, 2014; Department of the Prime Minister and Cabinet, 2014).

This search for quality can be due to a desire for information on the effectiveness of an innovation, including the identification of effective practices or practices that need improvement, but perhaps also to ensure there is clarity and consensus regarding the purpose of a program or to prove a program is of value to bodies funding it (Strengthening Non-profits, 2015). In all these cases, measurement of the outcomes of projects provides the data on which decisions can be made – whether it is to acknowledge success, revise for future practice, to terminate or to justify expenditure. For the writers of this chapter, outcomes-based decision-making was central to their research.

During the period that several major research projects involving the authors were conducted, outcomes-based decision-making was a core element of government agency program development. As a consequence, funding for projects was forthcoming for researchers who had a track record of effective research with industry partners. Following approximately ten years of partnership research with government departments, we were invited to conduct studies of specific projects that required analysis of outcomes to support decision-making.

The government department motivations for the studies included the desire for improved outcomes and confirmation of the effectiveness of programs, but also personal ambition and a desire to secure their position. External pressures for justification of programs drove all these motivations. For example, a demand for justification of expenditure could be met by providing evidence of superior outcomes due to the operation of the project; a threat to the continued operation of a program or department might stimulate a study to demonstrate the extent of the success.

When researchers accept a contract to carry out work for a government department, they enter into a relationship that has the potential to function smoothly or be challenging in various degrees (LSE GV13 Group, 2014).

For some projects, the industry partner is a silent partner, agreeing at the start to the research proposal, attending meetings at which progress is reported and celebrating the outcomes of the project when it is concluded. The LSE GV13 Group identified this relationship as "collegial" (Manzi & Smith-Bowers, cited in LSE GV13 Group, 2014). Other projects are subject to much greater surveillance and intervention. Manzi and Smith-Bowers identified three alternative relationships, all of which were evident, or at least potential, in the research described in this paper:

1. A servant/master relationship, in which strong control is exercised by the contracting body and the researcher, possibly because it has a vested interest in a certain outcome or the research topic involves complex and sensitive issues that could be embarrassing to the provider if outcomes are not as expected.
2. A docile relationship "intuitively oriented to producing satisfied funders" (LSE GV13 Group, 2014, p. 226).
3. A resistant relationship, whereby the researcher resists the pressure of the funding body to secure compliance.

A government department's approach to a research study might change during its lifetime as a consequence of the following:

- Personnel change: the replacement of one officer by another – at any level – can influence the direction and success of a research project, but in particular the senior manager responsible for the project within the government authority has considerable power (Lincoln & Guba, 2000).
- Departmental policy changes also influence research processes, especially when they affect the conduct of the research, as when officers appointed to participate in a project are impeded from fulfilling their role due to policy changes.
- Research outcomes are identified as threatening to the organisation or to individuals with influence in the organisation.

Problems also occur when the partner government department expects the participation of other departments in projects but does not anticipate the researchers' lack of a relationship with the department. There is substantial literature on the importance of such relationships and the processes by which they are developed, (Australia Department of Finance, 2015; O'Flynn, 2008; Pope & Jolly, 2008; VicHealth, 2011) yet for researchers involved in complex projects, liaison with other government departments can be for short-term, task specific purposes. However, the lack of a relationship can create difficulties.

The purpose of this paper is to outline the pitfalls of conducting research for government departments when there are unexpected changes in the direction of the research or hidden agendas emerge that influence the course of the study. These changes can invoke pressures on the researchers to add data that are not part of the study, delete data that may damage agendas promoted by the government department, or draw conclusions that do not represent the findings from the data. Consequences can also include the failure to provide financial, organisational or personnel support that have been negotiated for the research, as well as refusing to publish study reports.

The issues that researchers experience when working with governments can emerge during the planning stage, referred to as "commissioning" by The LSE GV13 Group, the management stage (when the government provides "advice and guidance in maintaining the policy focus of the research concerned and providing data and support in gathering evidence" (LSE GV13 Group, 2014, p. 226) and the writing-up stage, when an effort may be made to make the conclusions of the research more positive. During the course of the various projects described here, pressure was experienced at these stages.

Researchers experienced in research with funding partners would be aware of potential problems. This chapter is therefore directed at researchers embarking on partnerships with the bodies most likely to finance their research.

A body of published and unpublished research papers underlie the experiences reported in the chapter. It is unfortunate that we are unable to identify these reports to ensure the anonymity of the funding bodies who, advertently or inadvertently, were the cause of considerable anguish over the years. To publish this information would be to perish as researchers.

## 12.2 The student wellbeing study

The student wellbeing strategy exemplified the "servant/master" relationship between researcher and provider. It was originally initiated in a number of metropolitan schools with funding from the state health authority and then taken up by the state education provider. It was designed to enhance the social–emotional wellbeing of students – and especially Indigenous students – who were at risk on a number of measures. Two highly motivated and charismatic originators of the strategy were located in one of the schools and convinced the education provider and university researchers to carry out research to establish its effectiveness. The university researchers obtained a grant from a national research funding body to measure its effectiveness in achieving the outcomes that were predicted and to determine whether it could be implemented in other sites.

For schools commencing the strategy from scratch, this was an innovation that needed a considerable change in approach in working with students. Students chosen for the program were likely to possess behavioural problems but during the program were given considerable responsibility to develop social skills, decision-making skills and leadership skills. This required coordinators and other teachers to approach the strategy with new skills on their part. As a consequence, considerable skill development was needed. Mentoring by people already engaged in the strategy in the metropolitan area was a feature of the approach. For success, implementation required mentoring to change strategies that were known to bring about success (Hargreaves, 2003; Hargreaves & Fullan, 2000; Bitan-Friedlander, Dreyfus & Milgrom, 2004).

A study was initiated to track the project in the original metropolitan schools and to implement it in a group of schools in a regional town approximately 600km from the city so that the process of implementation of a new project from scratch could be studied. The research was carried out in partnership with the state education provider. To reflect the reality of school change, the provider was to be responsible for implementation and the researchers for analysis.

Four schools initiated the project in the regional town, and the original four metropolitan schools continued the project (another metropolitan school entered the project in the second year of operation) during the three years that the researchers studied the project.

Funds were allocated to pay part of the salary of a departmental officer to coordinate the project at the two sites. The originator of the strategy was appointed to the role to mentor the teachers. This would involve travel to the regional town as well as involvement with the metropolitan schools. The originator of the project was the first state coordinator and so had a detailed knowledge of the project and was its enthusiastic promoter. Unfortunately, for personal reasons she had to take leave from her position and was replaced in the role by another person who also was a program coordinator. Such a change in management in government departments is not unusual (LSE GV13 Group, 2014) but in the present study, the consequences were damaging to the conduct of research.

From information obtained by the research team, it quickly became apparent that the regional schools were not implementing the principal goals of the project with fidelity. The teachers involved with the project did not understand its underlying assumptions or the purpose of the main activities. They were unsure of the criteria for student selection and what activities to employ. There was an expectation on the part of the researchers that the coordinator would closely monitor the program in the different schools and mentor the teachers. When this was discussed with the education provider, the researchers were informed that policy had changed from directly working with teachers at the workface to operating at a policy level and informing schools of appropriate policy in relation to their activities. Policy change can have a significant effect on the conduct and outcome of research (LSE GV13 Group, 2014). The result for the research project was that there was to be no mentoring, no practical advice on what to do and no feedback on the effectiveness of what they were doing. This was despite the research project providing funding for the state coordinator to carry out the task of coordination.

In the cluster of metropolitan schools the school coordinators regularly met and exchanged ideas and strategies in order to enhance the project. The remaining coordinator in the originating school provided oversight on activities and was regarded as a leader by the group of schools. As a deputy principal, he had the status to support his expert knowledge and the enthusiasm to influence other teachers. The researchers, desperate to retrieve the failing situation in the regional schools, proposed sending him to the town to promote the goals and strategies of the project.

When the state coordinator became aware of this impending act, she complained to the director of the branch who called a meeting with the research team. We were warned that under the rules of this education provider, it was illegal for the deputy to visit the regional town. We didn't believe this and when we persisted with our intention, we were informed that the education provider would withdraw from the project if we proceeded to send the school coordinator.

It was clear that the researchers were caught in a servant/master relationship. They had no option in the matter and were forced to drop the plan to send the school coordinator. In the absence of the state coordinator, the task of mentoring the regional schools fell to the research team and, while this was beneficial, it did not have the intellectual authority of having a practitioner in the project and a fellow teacher embedded in the reality of school practice. For the researchers, the change in direction at organisational level from direct support to schools to remote policy development resulted in a less than desirable process of implementation. Teachers did not get the support necessary for effective change, nor did they receive mentoring from a colleague who had direct experience of the innovation. The key elements of support and trust were absent, and in the absence of departmental participation, the importance of the project would have diminished (Borko, Davinroy, Bliem & Cumbo, 2000).

The difficulty of mentoring these schools as a result of the policy change seriously affected the quality of the research. Results showed that the regional schools achieved significantly poorer outcomes than the metropolitan schools on all measures of social–emotional wellbeing, school achievement and program fidelity.

The partnership with the education provider was clearly beneficial for the researchers in obtaining a grant for a significant project. However, the researchers' lack of control over a major component of the study during the management phase of research frustrated the planned implementation process.

## 12.3 The attendance book

For the researchers involved in the studies described in this chapter, some research with the departmental directorate concerned were relatively free of efforts to influence the outcomes. However, as the LSE GV13 Group (2014) observed in previous research studies, political pressure can be applied at different stages of the research process, and this was the case when a group of researchers proposed that they write a text on Indigenous student attendance for distribution to teachers. The Indigenous education section of the education authority was very supportive: the researchers would write the text without payment (although funds were provided for expenses) and the directorate would foot the cost of publication and produce the book in departmental format. A budget was allocated and the lead author arranged for preparation of the text.

The text was designed to outline the current policies related to Indigenous student attendance at school and incorporate strategies for securing regular attendance. The authors liaised regularly with the provider and produced a text that was succinct, current and easily accessible by teachers. After revisions, a final proof copy was prepared for the authority: in effect, this was a report on prior research and it was at this stage that intervention occurred. However, this intervention was not by the directorate managing the grant, but by another directorate, and they were not in a position to seek a more positive report, as the LSE GV314 Group found in their studies.

The directorate responsible for school attendance requested a copy of the text on the grounds that they needed to ensure the contents conformed to the provider's policy on attendance.

After a period of two weeks, the director of the Indigenous education section informed us that we were not to proceed with the publication of the book. He was vague about the reasons for this about-turn, stating that the executive of the authority had decided it could not go ahead. We were led to believe that, when the attendance section staff read the draft, they implemented changes to policy to address the matters raised in the text, then reported to the executive that the book was dated and should not be published.

It is the authors view that, in their haste to ensure no failings could be attributed to their performance, the attendance directorate inflicted damage on the department overall by preventing any benefits accruing from the use of the book (Menon, Jaworski & Kohli, 1997). In effect, the authors were the victims of a power play between the two sections of the authority and the reality of their status as servants to a master (LSE GV314 Group, 2014) that controlled the outcome became painfully obvious. In hindsight, they should have examined the landscape of decision-making within the department to identify key groups with a vested interest in the outcome. By ensuring these groups were party to the initiative, it may have been possible to produce a text that accommodated all their needs. However, this could have had the consequence of compromising the integrity of the researchers (LSE GV13 Group, 2014).

## 12.4 Interdepartmental cooperation?

In this next project, the relationship with the partner was much more complex than a simple client–researcher experience because of the involvement of a number of agencies in the health field. It is this element of the research during the management phase that is the focus of this section.

In 2000, the Australian Government released the *Report of the MCEETYA Task Force on Indigenous Education* (Ministerial Council on Education Employment Training and Youth Affairs, 2000), that outlined possible solutions to the problems besetting Indigenous people – health, education, employment, longevity and justice. A principal vehicle for solving these issues was seen to be a cross-government approach so that multiple disadvantages were tackled simultaneously through cooperation among departments. The report recommended,

> Effective co-ordination in policy development, planning, management, provisions of services to Aboriginal peoples and Torres Strait Islanders will achieve more effective and efficient delivery of services, remove unnecessary duplication and will allow more effective use of resources.
> (MCEETYA, 2000, p. 54)

Commentary in the report on the proposal suggested that work would be needed to achieve this cooperation, but its implementation would enhance Indigenous people's outcomes from government intervention (MCEETYA, 2000), and recommended its circulation to the Health and Community Services Ministerial Councils with a view to their support for it. Interdepartmental cooperation is an enduring issue for governments (Kaarbo & Gruenfeld, 1998; O'Flynn, 2008; Australia Department of Finance, 2015).

Shortly after, the Australian Government initiated the National Indigenous Education Literacy and Numeracy strategy (Department of Education, Training and Youth Affairs, 2000) with a view to improving Indigenous students' literacy and numeracy skills (Watson, 2003). Different states were authorised to implement different initiatives to fulfil promises of improved outcomes. One project involved developing strategies for combating the negative impact of conductive hearing loss (CHL) on Indigenous students' literacy development. Conductive hearing loss, or otitis media, is a debilitating infection of the middle ear in children that results in transitory to long-term deafness. Caused by a range of bacteria, it is readily treated with antibiotics, but if treatment does not occur, or if effective follow-up management of the child's environment does not occur, reinfection is common.

The authors were engaged to carry out the study, which required considerable liaison with health providers in the state. The research team included members with education research backgrounds as well as others with a health background.

Given the recent publication of the MCEETYA report that promoted interagency cooperation and advice from the education provider, the researchers naively believed that cooperation would be forthcoming. However, it soon became clear that the health agencies had not read the report. Cooperation was sadly absent during the research.

The first step of obtaining agreement to participate and ethics clearance from the intended health industry partners was difficult: approving bodies included regional and local health authorities and there was no single body authorised to approve research for the whole state, and no hierarchy of approval, so multiple approaches had to be made in the several districts where the research was to happen. Consent was refused initially in a number of districts, awaiting approval from other organisations; decisions by regional medical boards were delegated to medical practitioners who were very slow to respond; correspondence was lost – twice by one general practitioner to whom the decision was delegated; meetings at which approval could be granted were cancelled or delayed. The project had to be delayed for a year as this process took three weeks short of a year to accomplish.

Today, ethics approval is a simpler process since the National Health and Medical Research Council ethics approval process minimises the number of ethics approvals required (National Health and Medical Research Council, 2007).

The problems didn't cease there. One of the requirements for the study was information on students' current hearing and their history of infection. This was expected to be supplied by the health professionals, either through school health nurses, who were very cooperative, or state government health agencies. The delays caused by this latter group were probably unintentional but were extremely frustrating for the researchers. Each time we approached one government health agency, there was a new administrator in the role, and each one was sceptical of our authority to conduct research on a health issue, even one involving school children. Each time, we were required to submit a statement of the research project and the ethics clearances provided by the university and health authorities before we could get access to any data.

The execution of a well-integrated interagency research study in an area that demanded such cooperation was never going to work in the existing environment of distrust and protection of turf. However, a subsequent project involving some of the same health professionals achieved much better cooperation, probably due to their growth of trust in the researchers and familiarity in working with them. Interagency cooperation in research presents considerable challenges for researchers but the growth of familiarity and trust can result in more successful future projects.

## 12.5 The aspirations project

In 2002 the research team was invited to conduct an evaluation of a new project being commenced by the education provider. For the most part, relations between the provider and the researchers were collegial. However, there was one instance of note during the commissioning phase of the project that caused some embarrassment to the researchers and this could be regarded as an instance of servant/master interaction, principally because information supplied by the provider was inaccurate and pointed to an assumption of superiority over the researchers.

This program was designed to support Indigenous students through high school and on to further studies or to gain employment. In discussions with the provider, we were informed that the project was an initiative of the provider based on models in other states. We were informed that it would be the researchers' role to explore the effectiveness of the innovation. However, the composition of the planning group that was overseeing the project's implementation should have alerted the researchers to seek clarification of the lines of authority: it comprised not just personnel from the provider but also representatives of industry and charitable foundations.

Initially, we were engaged to conduct research at three sites where the project was to be introduced. These were in high schools in regional towns, and a one-year pilot study was proposed. We engaged the services of a researcher to visit the towns, attend meetings of planning committees at each site and interview participants. He arranged to attend each site for their steering committee meetings, which were held four times a year. At one site, he was challenged as to his presence and it was made clear that he did not have approval from the committee to be present. There were no problems with his attendance at steering committees at the other two sites.

Our understanding that the project, at all sites, was being conducted by the education provider proved to be false: some sites were being managed by the charitable foundation that engaged industry sponsorship to fund much of the cost of operations. At these sites, the foundation was the appropriate authority that we should have contacted to seek consent to attend their meeting. The steering committee at the site which challenged the researcher's presence included high-powered people from industry, politics and law.

We were quite unaware of the different organisational structure of the project in this town. However, to continue the research at the site we had to apologise and seek retrospective approval for our involvement. While this was a failure on our part to ensure we were fully aware of the structure of the innovation, there was nothing to alert us to the primary role of the charitable foundation, and certainly not the claims being made by officers from the provider. We subsequently learned that the foundation developed the model of operation and the provider's sites were clones of the industry-sponsored sites, but without the sponsorship. The embarrassment for the researcher was considerable, all due to the hubris of the provider's officers to acknowledge that they were just one group of participants – and relatively minor ones – on the steering committee.

In hindsight, careful scrutiny of the origins of the project was essential if we were to embark on the study with a clear knowledge of the lines of authority. We were led up the garden path by false claims to ownership and initiation and it appeared that the provider's personnel wanted to claim the project as their construct. Subsequent involvement of the project at the various sites confirmed the foundation as the principal body initiating the projects.

Despite this initial hiccough, all contributors to the project were supportive of our role in the research study. A research grant was obtained to continue the study for five years to explore the mechanics and outcomes of the project. Throughout this period there was little effort on the part of stakeholders to influence the course of the study. This is likely due to the strong belief of all that the project was changing the lives of the participating students and our report was bound to demonstrate positive outcomes.

This was not the case with some projects, in particular a study into the role of Aboriginal and Islander Teacher Assistants in schools.

## 12.6 Teacher assistants' project

Ethical issues related to funded research most often focus on the medical and health fields (Dudgeon, Kelly & Walker, 2010; Laycock, Walker, Harrison & Brands, 2011). However, many organisations, both government and private, engage research organisations and individuals to conduct studies that respond to their research needs. Reasons include the decline – or absence – of internal research capacity within those organisations, the awareness of the importance of evidence in making planning decisions, or simply the financial benefits of outsourcing. In this study, researchers experienced pressure during all phases of the study, with the government department attempting to make the researchers "buckle under the pressure and produce the kind of politically supportive report the government wants" (LSE GV13, 2014, p. 225). However, they did not buckle, choosing instead to resist the pressure and produce a research report that adhered to principles of sound research and ethics.

This study was commissioned by an Australian educational provider to review its teacher assistant program following a negative review of the program by one of the state's leading Aboriginal health authorities. The director of the program was very concerned at this review and wanted evidence that would rebut it. At the time of the review, the program had been operating in schools for almost 40 years and had not been formally reviewed. The review came at a time when key state and Australian Government programs for Aboriginal and Torres Strait Islander students, particularly the Closing the Gap strategy, were being evaluated for their effectiveness in promoting school achievement, attendance and retention. In this project considerable pressure was placed on the research team to produce favourable outcomes from the study. The department negotiated the broad elements of the study with the research team but throughout the study attempted to direct the researchers in sample selection, identification of participants, data to include and the contents of the report. However, the research leader was not compliant (Allen, 2005) and insisted on a thoroughly ethical study.

The review process was extensive and comprised two major forms of data collection: an online survey using Survey Monkey (SurveyMonkey.com) which was sent out to schools which had employed at least one full-time teacher assistant, and school-based interviews with over 30 schools from across the state. The study principally examined the roles and responsibilities of Aboriginal teacher assistants, the match between the duties performed and the current job description, the effectiveness of the program at school and community level and how the program could be made more effective in schools. The major participants in the study were Aboriginal teacher assistants, school principals and teachers. The questions for the online survey and for the interviews were developed in consultation with representatives from the educational provider.

A reference group of key stakeholders was selected by the director to liaise with the research team during all stages of the study. The composition of the membership included representatives from the directorate's senior management, including the director overseeing the evaluation branch of the organisation who also had an interest in the project, a representative from the organisation's HR branch, an Area Director of Schools, Aboriginal Education Manager, Aboriginal teacher, and a representative for primary school principals. However, prior to the commencement of the reference committee's first meeting, the manager of the evaluation branch co-opted herself onto the reference group, and this was fortunate for the research team as her background in research and ethics was to provide a buffer from later interference by the directorate.

The reference group was regularly briefed by the research team and the provision of written reports as required. The reference group also provided feedback to the research team, including the monitoring of the identified requirements of the review. Despite these measures, the research team experienced a number of cases of "interference" from senior members of the educational provider that could possibly result in identification of participants and influence the outcomes of the study.

The first challenge was the selection of schools for the face-to-face interviews. For the study to be valid, participants needed the security of anonymity. Consequently, it was important that the education provider did not know the identity of the participants. However, the original list of schools supplied to the research team identified the schools that were to be selected from four parts of the state. In one area, only one school was nominated. Not only could the participants be identified, but also the school might have been listed in order to positively influence the outcomes of the study.

Fortunately, the reference group intervened. One member was equivalent in status to the head of the directorate and also was responsible for the conduct of evaluation in the organisation. His intervention resulted in a representation of schools which could demonstrate good or poor functioning of the Aboriginal teacher assistants program, and he advised that at least two schools in a regional area of the state were necessary.

A further, more direct effort at influence was the presentation of a list of recommended schools in each identified location from senior management for consideration. The research team were conscious that the use of recommended schools could sway the outcomes of the study. Concerned that they may be overruled by the director, the researchers approached the staff from the evaluation branch on the reference group to negotiate anonymity of schools. It was doubtful that the request for this anonymous list would have been achieved without "friends in court". But it was successful and the research team obtained an updated list of schools with Aboriginal teacher assistants. The research team then used this list to choose the schools in confidence. The research team advised senior management that the selection process was completed and that the location of each participating school would be kept strictly confidential.

The practice of providing lists of schools to researchers to refine the study or determine the participants recently occurred in a nationally funded project involving one of the authors on the use of information technology in the training of teacher assistants. In this study, the same educational provider produced a list of schools in which the research would take place. As with the teacher assistant project, the project leader refused the offer.

In the teacher assistant study, having secured a measure of anonymity for participants, the research team was informed by a senior officer that they could organise travel to the selected schools for the research team. The head of the project realised that such an arrangement would allow schools to be identified and once again identification of participants would be possible. The offer to organise travel was declined.

The extent to which the review would result in a comprehensive examination of the issues confronting Aboriginal teacher assistants in the schools was severely restricted when the research team were advised in an early reference group meeting that any discussion relating to human resources matters, such as working conditions and salary levels, could not be included in the research project. The research team felt that this instruction would not allow a full examination of the roles and responsibilities of staff and this became very clear throughout the interviews and in the online responses when many participants' principal issues were industrial matters, including salaries, responsibilities and workloads.

In a final example of "interference", when the final report was being written, the project team were approached by three senior members of the educational provider to include information in the report that did not result from the data collection process or any other process. By including the material in the report it would acquire the status of an independent finding and could have considerable impact on the future direction of the program in the state. The researchers were concerned at this request, which amounted to an ethical dilemma for them. Umphress, Bingham and Mitchell (2010, p. 770) report that individuals who strongly identify with their organisation "may choose to disregard personal moral standards and engage in acts that favour the organisation, possibly even at the expense of those outside it". This is a likely explanation for the behaviour of the staff in this instance.

Weiss (1970), cited in LSE GV13 Group, 2014, p. 225) noted that "evaluation has always had explicitly political overtones. It is designed to yield conclusions about the worth of programs and, in so doing, is intended to affect the allocation of resources", and this observation is relevant in this case. It is our view that the efforts of the directorate to influence the research from beginning to end was likely due to the high stakes for them: the researchers learnt that the directorate was in line for absorption into a larger internal entity, that the role of director was under threat of abolition, and that a good report could strengthen arguments for retention of both. The concern of administrators that the independent study they commissioned could highlight issues that they would prefer not to be revealed may have been the driving force behind their efforts to influence the study.

## 12.7 Conclusion

Researchers' careers are enhanced by the opportunity to conduct research, but this usually requires funds to buy out from teaching, to obtain the services of research assistants and to fund the projects they engage in. The strong competition for funds, particularly from government research funding bodies such as the Australian Research Council and from private foundations that sponsor research limits many researchers' opportunities. Universities also fund researchers within the institution but typically the amounts are relatively small. A more substantial source of research opportunity, for researchers who possess expertise in specific fields, is both state governments and industry. In particular, Australian state governments are willing to sponsor research to enable evidence-based decision-making, particularly in Indigenous education, due to the significant issues related to participation and achievement of Indigenous students.

In each project that has been discussed, there have been problems. However, most of the time the researchers have enjoyed a strong measure of autonomy in the conduct of their research, being required to consult and report progress regularly without the shadow of government pressure directing their study. The LSE GV13 Group noted this to be a fourth possibility in relation to government–researcher relationships: where government does not lean and researchers do not buckle – 'both parties have equivalent objectives and are committed to the goal of truth seeking" (Manzi & Smith-Bowers, cited in LSE GV13 Group, 2014, p. 226). The exception was the teacher assistants' project where the department attempted to lean but the researchers did not buckle – a case of resistance.

The authors of this paper have participated in several research projects either sponsored by an education provider, or in which the provider was a partner in an externally funded project. These projects have enabled the authors to conduct significant research that has the potential to improve the learning outcomes of Indigenous students. Despite this, there have been occasions when the smooth conduct of a research project has been disrupted at various stages of the studies by departmental demands and omissions (Greenwood & Levin, 2000). These include demanding information that infringes the confidential nature of data, preventing certain processes from occurring (such as interviews and support for teachers), and withholding information that would have been necessary for the smooth operation of the research.

Researchers will find that there are potential hazards in working with government departments in the conduct of research. The relationships developed between the researchers and the organisation will influence the quality of the research throughout, from commissioning to write-up (LSE GV13 Group, 2014). Partnerships between researchers and state departments can be sustained as long as the results of the research do not impinge negatively on the image or direction of the departments. It should be kept in mind that these departments have their own goals, motivations and limitations in the research endeavour and these may differ from those of the researcher. At best, these motivations can be incorporated seamlessly with the researchers' goals, and this has been their most common experience throughout their research careers.

Chapter 13

# When research, policy and practice disconnect

An educational leadership policy example

*Vicki Farwell*

## 13.1 Introduction

The increasing rate of educational reform over the last 30 years has made defining the aims and purposes of education, and therefore the best way to conceptualise educational leadership, management and administration of schools, more challenging (Cranston & Ehrich, 2006). As well, the context for education has become a large-scale global setting, placing complex and competitive performance pressures on governments, systems, schools and principals (Bredeson, 2013) within this context. Globalised measurements have created comparisons about educational effectiveness in a new, much broader scale than previously existed. This environment has led to a shift in the focus of educational policy as governments put in place strategies to improve student achievement based on these competitive comparisons in an international arena. Across countries politicians are under pressure to come up with answers to the universal aspiration to improve quality in education (Harris & Muijs, 2007) and many nations' governments are developing policy requiring schools to bring about significant, systematic, and sustained reform in order to improve student outcomes. The growth in international comparisons of educational results has seen this shift in policy-making reflect schooling as part of a market commodity, with the development of government policy based on the assumption that competition and information are the primary drivers of educational and economic improvement (Sahlberg, 2012) rather than research and evaluation.

The introduction of international comparative testing of students is symptomatic of this globally competitive trend and has become a major force in influencing the development of education policy across the globe. One of the most significant examples of this is The Programme for International Student Assessment (PISA) (The Organisation for Economic Co-operation and Development [OECD], 2013), which began international testing in 2000. The testing occurs through a triennial international survey which aims to evaluate the effectiveness of education systems worldwide and does so based on student achievement, established through testing the skills and knowledge of 15-year-old students (OECD, 2013, para. 1). This testing scheme is now used in over 70 different countries, where it creates a recognised impetus driving educational policy. Australia is one of the countries involved in PISA testing and the competitive nature of looking for strategies to improve student achievement is clearly reflected in the current development and articulation of education policy at both national and state government levels. Publishing the results of national literacy and numeracy testing, enabling the assessment of a school's 'effectiveness' based on their students' collective test results, is just one example of how policy has come to reflect this shifted perspective both nationally and at the state level.

Within this context, a focus on educational leadership has become a significant aspect of policy driven by education globalisation. This chapter aims to present a snapshot of how this has manifested in one Australian state's policy development as quick changes in policy language and discourse, rather than through considered and evaluative processes based on research. The review covers Queensland government education policy documents published between 2006 and 2013 that specifically describe expectations of school leaders. The information presented forms a small part of a broader literature review currently contributing to an ongoing unpublished case study identifying Queensland secondary principal leadership practices. Therefore, while the review presented in this chapter is not a fully completed case study, it does map the changes in educational leadership policy discourse and policy language as well as providing an avenue to consider the impact of political expediencies on the use (or non-use) of research in developing policy.

The review begins by providing background about how the globally competitive arena has brought about renewed interest in the concept of Instructional Leadership (IL) as a way to develop improved student achievement through the actions of school leaders. Next, a table is used to map the policy iterations of expectations of IL across the selected continuum of Queensland policies. The table shows the changes and alignments of various policy texts, which facilitates discussion about the reasons behind the shifts and transitions that characterise the language found in the policy discourse. Examples of the implementation associated with those policies is also considered, presenting evidence that the process used for implementation illustrates the lack of consistency between policy and practice, due to a disconnect between the intended policy, the research literature and educational leader's actions. The chapter ends by exploring and analysing the reasons behind this disconnect.

## 13.2 Background: the re-emergence of Instructional Leadership (IL)

Over the last 15 years in Australia, both federal and state governments have responded to growing international educational competitiveness by rapidly translating expectations for sustained improvement into educational policy (Caldwell & Lewis, 2005). The primacy of the principal's role in implementing mandated improvement agendas is acknowledged and chronicled in educational leadership research such as the 2010 *McKinsey and Company report*

(Barber, Whelan & Clark, 2010). In this report school principals, policymakers and system leaders were interviewed across eight countries, including Australia, aimed at identifying the emerging role of the principal within this global context. The outcome confirmed the expectation on all levels that the principal role was crucial in implementing systemic reform whose purpose was to facilitate international competitiveness in the education arena. However, across those levels it was also found that there was not a common basis or understanding backed up by research about what practices facilitated improvement. This lack of conceptual understanding for the development and implementation of educational leadership policy across the levels of organisation has been found to undermine the reform processes (Hargreaves, 2003). As well, when the impetus of the reform is not supported by research-based strategies it can create a gap between policy intent and practice.

Recently, policy aimed at improving student achievement in the international marketplace has embraced a global re-emergence in emphasising Instructional Leadership (IL) (Stewart, 2006). The origin of IL can be traced to the US in the 1970s, amidst public demand for school systems to raise standards and improve students' academic performance (Zigarelli, 1996). This demand for improvement created a search for a school model that would improve student achievement, eventually evolving into the effective schooling movement (Harris, Jamieson & Russ, 1996). Out of this focus on making schools more effective also emerged a search for the definitive characteristics of the effective leader, eventually giving rise to the concept of the Instructional Leader (Bossert, Dwyer, Rowan & Lee, 1982). Even though there was little research confirming a connection between IL and improvement, the concept became an integral part of the identified characteristics contributing to the 'school effect' (Harris et al., 1996, p. 8) in making a difference to student achievement. By the early 1990s IL became a focus in educational leadership research, and while there was still little empirical data linking IL and student improvement (Robinson, Lloyd & Rowe, 2008), it became a significant factor in educational policy in the US and the UK (Webb, 2005). By the 2000s, as broader, more encompassing trends in educational leadership emerged, IL was seen as only part of a leadership role (Hallinger, 2005).

Although the reasons for the more recent re-emergence of IL are debated in educational literature, it appears to be based once again on a belief that instructional leaders are able to impact student achievement (Anderson, Leithwood, Louis & Wahlstrom, 2010). This belief is seen by some, particularly policy developers, as having the capacity to make systems more globally competitive (Angel, Reitzug & West, 2008) in the current educational international arena. The resurgence in a focus on IL began to appear in government policy simultaneously in Australia and internationally (Horng & Loeb, 2010; Dinham, 2011) and is reflected in Australian educational reforms and policies beginning in the mid 2000s (Dinham, 2011; Drysdale & Gurr, 2012) at both a national and state level. This is despite the fact that ongoing research

(Horng & Loeb, 2010) confirms that the lack of understanding about the nature and construct of IL makes it difficult to judge the extent to which links between IL and student achievement exist. In terms of IL in educational policy, while the research demonstrating the link between IL and improved student achievement is debated (Robinson et al., 2008; Robinson, 2010; Townsend, Acker-Hocevar, Ballenger, Ballenger & William, 2013), the inference that instructional leaders can make a difference to student results has appealed to government policy makers (Cardno, 2010). At the Australian state level, in Queensland since 2006, these student achievement-based expectations of principal leadership have been described through a string of systemic policies and procedures beginning with the development of a leadership framework, the *Principal Capabilities and Leadership Framework* (DETA, 2007b; DETA, 2010).

## 13.3 A snapshot review of Queensland government policy focused on IL

Queensland government policies and reports taken from policy documents between 2006 and 2013 contributing to creating a focus on the leadership expectations for principals include:

- *Leadership Matters – leadership capabilities for Education Queensland principals* (Cranston & Ehrich, 2006);
- *Leadership Matters* (DETA, 2007b);
- *Principals' Capability and Leadership Framework* (DETA, 2007a);
- *A Shared Challenge Improving Literacy, Numeracy and Science Learning in Queensland Primary Schools* (The Masters Report) (Masters, 2009);
- *Principals' Capability and Leadership Framework* (DETA, 2010);
- *United in our pursuit of excellence – Agenda for improvement 2011–2015* (DETA, 2011a);
- *Principal Supervision and Capability Framework 2011–2012* (DETA, 2011b);
- *The School Planning, Reviewing and Reporting Framework 2012–2015* (DETE, 2012);
- *Education Queensland system review: Final report* (Fullan & Levin, 2012);
- *The Commission of Audit (CoA) Report* (Queensland Government, 2013a); and
- *Great Teachers = Great Results* (DETE, 2013).

These documents are reviewed in Table 13.1: *Instructional Leadership expectations: Queensland Government Reports and Policy Documents*[1]. The table lists each policy and then provides a description of the part of the document related to describing leadership expectations and, in particular, any description related to being or becoming Instructional Leaders. Other information in the table includes how the documents relate to each other and specific terms used when describing the concept of IL, especially within the context of the global emphasis on comparing student achievement.

To begin, the development of the technical paper, *Leadership Matters – leadership capabilities for Education Queensland principals* (Cranston & Ehrich, 2006) marked the start of a period in Queensland educational leadership policy focused on a specific framework. In the technical paper, the theory of educational leadership, as shown in the literature review, encompasses a very broad range of practices, including the concept of Instructional Leadership. As a precursor to policy development, this paper demonstrates the strength of using a considered approach based on research. Based on the capabilities notions of Duignan (2004) the suggested framework was to be built around five inter-related capabilities: Personal, Relational, Educational, Intellectual and Organisational (p. 1). The recommendations of the technical paper led to an overview policy, *Leadership Matters*.

In keeping with the recommendations of the technical paper, the original framework did not contain specific reference to IL but built on the research base to incorporate aspects attributed to instructional leaders. This framework was used unchanged for 2007, 2008 and 2009 as the capacity building tool for Queensland state educational leaders, particularly principals, in schools. The wording used in these initial documents is shown in Table 13.1 in rows 1 through 3 and provides an example of significant and thoughtful policy developed based on comprehensive research. In the remaining rows of Table 13.1, the subsequent strategic policies describing educational leadership up to 2013 are also traced, showing the leadership policy development pathway with an increasing use of language based on IL. Parallel to the development of the framework in 2007, the year also saw the introduction of national literacy & numeracy testing in Australia. This can be seen as a response to the globalised focus on improving student achievement (Lingard & Sellar, 2013; Lingard & Rizvi, 2010). For the first time, all the Australian states were ranked by overall student achievement results on a common set of standardised tests. Newspaper articles chronicling the Queensland results show that the state was rated sixth out of seven states and territories for the first three years students sat the tests (2007, 2008 and 2009) (Chillcott, 2009). It is within this context that the Queensland government commissioned *A Shared Challenge Improving Literacy, Numeracy and Science Learning in Queensland Primary Schools* (Masters, 2009), more commonly known as the Masters Report. The report was commissioned in order to 'analyse the reasons behind Queensland's poor results in the new national literacy and numeracy testing, particularly in state primary schools' (p. v).

This evaluative commissioned research demonstrated what Calzoni (Chapter 10) discusses as the advantages of using researchers to help establish policy, where, in some cases, researchers as evaluators are able to challenge the status quo. While the Masters Report (Masters, 2009) was specifically commissioned to investigate and make recommendations for numeracy, literacy and science education in Queensland primary schools, the report expanded on its terms of reference by also referring to the need for changes in school leadership. Although it was meant to be evaluative rather than developmental, it was in

Table 13.1 Instructional Leadership expectations: Queensland Government reports and policy documents.

| Row | Date | Document | Reference to Instructional Leadership | Document Reference: Relevant Leadership Characteristics | Alignment with Listed Documents |
|---|---|---|---|---|---|
| 1 | 2006 | *Leadership Matters – leadership capabilities for Education Queensland principals* | Instructional leadership found in the literature review of other frameworks and book chapters | Development of a diagrammatic representation of leadership with the components of:<br>• Educational Leadership<br>• Intellectual Leadership<br>• Organisational Leadership<br>• Personal Leadership<br>• Relational Leadership | The basis for developing: 2007 *Leadership Matters* and 2007 *Principal Capabilities and Leadership Framework* |
| 2 | 2007 | *Leadership Matters* | No mention of instructional leadership | Leadership developed through five categories, each with capabilities and elements. These are:<br>• Educational Leadership<br>• Intellectual Leadership<br>• Organisational Leadership<br>• Personal Leadership<br>• Relational Leadership | No match for instructional leadership but the basis for developing: 2010 *Principal Capabilities and Leadership Framework* – aligns in terms of categories of leadership. 2011 *Principal Supervision and Capabilities Framework* – aligns in categories but not the detail within categories. |
| 3 | 2007 | *Principals' Capabilities and Leadership Framework* | No mention of instructional leadership | Five sub-categories, each with capabilities and elements:<br>• Educational Leadership<br>• Intellectual Leadership<br>• Organisational Leadership<br>• Personal Leadership<br>• Relational Leadership | Aligns to *Leadership Matters* 2006 Technical Paper and *Leadership Matters* 2007 document. Is the basis for the 2010 version. |

*(continued)*

Table 13.1 (continued)

| Row | Date | Document | Reference to Instructional Leadership | Document Reference: Relevant Leadership Characteristics | Alignment with Listed Documents |
|---|---|---|---|---|---|
| 4 | **2009** | *A Shared Challenge – Improving Literacy, Numeracy and Science Learning in Queensland Primary Schools* (The Masters Report) | Instructional leadership as part of effective schools, where, as the driver of improvement in student achievement principals develop deep knowledge about IL | Essential component in high-performing systems. Uses the OECD focus for principals taking an 'active role in instructional leadership': <ul><li>monitoring and evaluating teacher performance, conducting and arranging;</li><li>mentoring and coaching;</li><li>planning teacher professional development; and</li><li>orchestrating teamwork and cooperative instruction.</li></ul> **This leads to Recommendation 5 from the report:** That the Queensland Government initiates an expert review of international best practice in school leadership development with a view to introducing a new structure and program of advanced professional learning for primary school leaders focused on effective strategies for driving improved school performances in literacy, numeracy and science. | Leads to an official response (see the next row). Appears to instigate changes to the *Principal Capabilities and Leadership Framework* (2010) and support leading to the development of *United in our Pursuit of excellence* (2011) |

| | | | | |
|---|---|---|---|---|
| 5 | 2009 | Queensland Government response to the Masters Report | No mention of instructional leadership | The Government affirms that educational leadership offered by principals and other school leaders is a critical factor in the performance of schools, the quality of teaching, and the educational experiences of students. | Relates specifically to Masters Report and indirectly to row 7, *United in our Pursuit of excellence* (2011a). |
| 6 | 2010 | *Principals' Capabilities and Leadership Framework* | Inserted statement: Instructional leaders create and lead a high performance, sustainable learning culture | Five sub-categories, each with capabilities and elements:<br>• Educational Leadership<br>• Intellectual Leadership<br>• Organisational Leadership<br>• Personal Leadership<br>• Relational Leadership | Is the same as the 2007 version except for the inserted statement |
| 7 | 2011 | *United in our pursuit of excellence – Agenda for improvement 2011–2015* | Strong leadership and Instructional leadership, with an unrelenting focus on improvement | All principals will be instructional leaders by focusing on:<br>• core learning priorities;<br>• quality curriculum;<br>• student achievement and improvement;<br>• pedagogical practice;<br>• teacher feedback;<br>• quality assessment. | Documents created to align with this include *Principal Supervision and Capabilities Framework 2011–2012* and the *School Planning, Reviewing and Reporting Framework 2012–2015* |
| 8 | 2011–2012 | *Principal Supervision and Capabilities Framework* | Instructional leaders create and lead a high performance, sustainable learning culture | Five sub-categories, each with capabilities and elements:<br>• Educational Leadership<br>• Intellectual Leadership<br>• Organisational Leadership<br>• Personal Leadership<br>• Relational Leadership | Initiated as a response to *United in our pursuit of excellence 2011–2015* and the *School Planning, Reviewing and Reporting Framework 2012–2015* |

*(continued)*

Table 13.1 (continued)

| Row | Date | Document | Reference to Instructional Leadership | Document Reference: Relevant Leadership Characteristics | Alignment with Listed Documents |
|---|---|---|---|---|---|
| 9 | 2011–2012 | *School Planning, Reviewing and Reporting Framework 2012–2015* | Instructional leadership, with an unrelenting focus on improvement | All principals will be instructional leaders by focusing on:<br>• core learning priorities;<br>• quality curriculum;<br>• student achievement and improvement;<br>• pedagogical practice;<br>• teacher feedback;<br>• quality assessment; | Initiated as a response to *United in our pursuit of excellence 2011–2015* and the *Principal Supervision and Capabilities Framework 2011–2012* |
| 10 | 2012 | *Education Queensland system review: Final report* | Provides two aspects of a research evaluation: Reviews the leadership focus by DETA and presents recommendations (Fullan & Levin, 2012). Incorporates the government response to recommendations. | • Review: The recommendations found that the instructional role of the principal is key and that currently the role is 'a vague notion that requires more definitional and developmental work' (p. 6);<br>• Government Response: Promises to create more consistent messages and to use instruction as the driver (p. 9). | Reviews the *Principal Supervision and Capabilities Framework 2001–2012*, *The School Planning, Reviewing and Reporting Framework 2012–2015* and *United in our pursuit of excellence – Agenda for improvement 2011–2015* |

| | | | | |
|---|---|---|---|---|
| 11 | 2013 | Commission of Audit (CoA) report | No direct mention of IL – reference to greater priority needing to be given to effective leadership focused on improving student performance as seen in other systems | • In Australia, the Productivity Commission's Schools Workforce research report identified innovation at the school level, supported by stronger school leadership.<br>• Conditions for success include appropriate leadership by principals, accountability for student outcomes, and support from central agencies on training, teacher standards and curriculum.<br>• One of the most significant impacts of school leadership is its influence on teachers' professional development and performance appraisal. | Whole of government review which initiates a DETE response (in Row 12 of this table) |
| 12 | 2013 | DETE Response to the CoA report: *Great Teachers = Great Results* | No mention of instructional leadership | Responds to the CoA in terms of leadership in four areas, none of which relate to instructional leadership:<br>• there are limitations on recognising and rewarding high performing staff;<br>• unlike leadership positions in many other industries, principals don't receive performance bonuses;<br>• there is no incentive for school leaders to focus on continuous improvement;<br>• there is little support for teachers and school leaders to undertake further study. | No linkages in discourse to any other documents other than to confirm expectations that principals still use the *Principal Capability and Leadership Framework* |

this report that IL first appears in the language used to describe the role of school leaders & also suggested a way to impact student achievement. The report stated that 'most high-performing systems recognise the importance of encouraging principals to take on instructional leadership roles' (p. 9) as is shown in row 4 of Table 13.1. This was based on the findings of a 2008 OECD study (Pont, Nusche & Moorman, 2008) of school leadership in 22 education systems, which found that 'instructional leadership is a key to improved learning outcomes' (p. 103).

While the Masters Report recommended changes in leadership based on relevant research, the recommended approach the report describes to achieve this was not acknowledged in the government response. The Queensland government response did not overtly recognise the inclusion of IL as a future focus for school leaders. A description of their response to the information on IL is shown in row 5 of Table 13.1. Unlike the development of the leadership framework after the 2006 technical paper, changes were made without further consultation with researchers. Instead, a shift in leadership discourse is introduced through a minimal change in language that is added to the existing principal leadership framework. This can be seen in the 2010 version of the *Principals' Capabilities and Leadership Framework*. In this new version of the framework, one change is made as an addition to what was already included. A single statement is inserted above the existing framework and the five areas for principal development (shown in row 6 of Table 13.1). No changes are made to the actual framework structure or descriptors of the leadership actions, nor is any explanation given for what the changes might mean for leadership practices. The sentence stated that 'Instructional leaders create and lead a high performance, sustainable learning culture' (DETA, 2010, p. 3). By simply adding one sentence, the approach did not incorporate the suggested structures in the Masters Report or those related to IL practices found in broader educational research. This would suggest that although the new sentence appears to be a response to the Masters Report it represents a disconnect between the research underpinning the suggestion for change and the development of consistency in the policy language.

Although the government response did not acknowledge the changes suggested by Masters, there are changes in language used in a number of the strategic policies that were developed directly after the report's release that do appear to link to the report. Phrases such as 'strong leadership' and 'instructional leadership', both used in the Masters Report, begin to appear in policy documents. For example, strong leadership is the focus of educational leadership in the *United in our pursuit of excellence – Agenda for improvement 2011–2015* document (DETA, 2011a, p. 1). However, how these changes link to still-existing policies about leadership is unclear. For example, the strong leadership mentioned in the *Agenda* document is not linked through any dialogue that aligns it to the five areas for principal leadership which still remain in the 2010 version of the leadership framework or the new inserted IL sentence. Instead, another new set of six new components as a focus for leaders appear. These are: core learning priorities, quality curriculum, student achievement and improvement, pedagogical practice, teacher feedback and quality assessment (DETA, 2011a, p. 2). The sources used to develop this new language are not cited, do not align to the leadership framework or the new inserted sentence, nor the Masters Report.

As further policies focused on leadership are developed from this time, mention of the concept of IL begins to appear in more documents. For example, the discourse about leadership in the *School Planning, Reviewing and Reporting Framework 2012–2015* (DETE, 2012), (found in row 9 of Table 13.1) describes four key strategies that were identified as crucial for effective schooling. The third of these key strategies is described as, 'Instructional Leadership, with an unrelenting focus on improvement' (p. 1). While this statement provided a clear message to Queensland principals that they had responsibility for being instructional leaders in a climate of competitive student achievement results, it does not mention or incorporate the new strong leadership description within the *Agenda* for improvement nor does it visibly link to the existing leadership framework.

The language in the policy discourse, even if inconsistent in terms of existing documents, created a message for principals that they needed to be developing their IL practices. How this was to be done was unclear. For example, if the *School Planning, Reviewing and Reporting Framework 2012–2015* (DETE, 2012) is aimed at working in tandem with the *Principals' Capabilities and Leadership Framework* (DETA, 2010), none of the documents included the same descriptor of IL or described how principals were to enact this new focus. The five areas of actions from the original leadership framework remained, but how these related to the new IL focus was not explained. Despite a significant body of educational leadership research being accessible, no connection with research was used to further develop the framework to clearly embrace and reflect the new IL perspective. It effectively meant that principals were to have new outcomes by continuing to implement the same practices that continued to form the leadership framework. This confirms the perspective concerning policy development that when the links between research, policy and implementation are unclear the result is 'neither linear, nor guaranteed' (Ahmed, 2005, p. 765).

In the Queensland context, this myriad of policies, with differing terms, created a broad and complex set of information that was unclear in terms of the actions to be taken by leaders. To make the situation even more complex, the process created to support the IL implementation by school leaders, was developed not through consistent use of research but through sometimes conflicting strategies used by members of the systemic leadership hierarchy.

## 13.4 Disconnect through the implementation of policy

The policy language ambiguity created around the concept and practices of IL that were expected to be implemented was reflected and increased through the range of approaches inculcated in state education regions after the release of the *School Planning, Reviewing and Reporting Framework* (DETE, 2012). The lack of clarity regarding IL practices in the succession of Queensland policies was then amplified by the processes developed regionally to support principals in the implementation process. It was decided that regional leaders would support principals to implement their IL focus. This was to be done through the development of regional and/or school-based implementation of pedagogical frameworks; that is, a framework for leaders to use as the tool that would support principals to build instructional capacity at their schools. However, the diversity of the initiatives and processes enacted across state regions created situations showing vastly different understandings about IL. For example, in one region principals were inducted into Marzano's *Art and Science of Teaching* (Marzano, 2007). This process focused on leaders observing teachers in classrooms and working to create a site-specific definition for learning. In contrast, another region offered opportunities to access a variety of different programs including one developed through the work of Fullan (2010) regarding the characteristics of effective principals in high-achieving schools, based on a study from across Canada and the US. Rather than a bottom-up instructional model building from students and teachers as in Marzano's (2007) process, this model used evidential data to frame a top-down process collaboratively led by principals. A range of other models were used across the state regions.

The confusing policy discourse on IL meant linking any of these pedagogic models to the policy leadership expectations was a confusing key issue for principals and for the development of a consistent way to instigate a state-wide approach to improving student achievement. With no common research-based understanding for the definition of IL being used or for building IL capacity to implement change, principals were left to decipher the situation themselves. This meant that across the state there was no clear interpretation for what IL meant or looked like. Evidence from the leadership literature (Hallinger, 2005) reveals that mixed messages for IL can be problematic in creating expectations for principals. Accessing and developing a common approach guided by significant research, as was done in the initial 2006 development of the leadership framework, could have supported a more cohesive outcome.

In a 2012-required evaluative review of the Queensland government's educational system focus, including educational leadership, the mixed messages created through this policy discourse and the implementation disconnection was recognised. The *Education Queensland system review: Final report* (Fullan & Levin, 2012), as shown in Table 13.1, indicated that there needed to be a reassessment of the processes and policies aimed at school leaders in order to build:

- common focus on goals and strategies;
- consistency of delivery across the seven regions; and
- instruction as the driver (p. 5).

As well, this evaluation recommended that there was a need to be globally competitive and to do so, there needed to be a 'common and consistent stance evident in relation to the reform strategy' (p. 5). The review also noted that the instructional role of the principal is key, and while this role was acknowledged, it is 'currently a vague notion that requires more definitional and developmental work' (p. 6). It is also noted that this has been a problematic aspect to instructional leadership shown in the research and implies that this should have been known. The government response, while stating that the recommendations are accepted and acknowledging the international research, does not put forward a convincing set of processes aimed at creating consistency. Instead, the existing range of models were to be added to with a 'suite of multi-layered strategies' (p. 10). Most of these strategies were never realised, as in 2012 a change in government in Queensland precipitated another shift in policy, policy language and discourse regarding leadership. This was to be implemented through policies that did not replace or clarify existing ones, but were created as additional to existing policy documents.

Added to this in 2013, as seen in Table 13.1, were both a *Commission of Audit* (CoA) (Queensland Government, 2013a) report, which included consideration of educational leadership, and a Queensland government (2013b) response to the CoA recommendations. The recommendations from the CoA mirrored those of the Fulton and Levin earlier evaluation. Once again the government response, rather than simplifying and responding to the most recent reseach to create a common language and process around IL, added more policies to augment the existing suite of policies. This meant that the ongoing issue relating to clarity and consistency became even more complex. As stated on the DETE website (July, 2013, para. 4), 'while these new policies do not replace the previous strategic focus of either the *Principals' Capabilities and Leadership Framework* (2010) or the *United in our Pursuit of excellence* (2011a) policy, they are meant to develop a stronger accountability context'. How this was to occur was not explicit.

## 13.5 Policy disconnect

Research into the processes used for developing government policy shows that a number of problematic situations can be responsible for a lack of convergence between policy and current research (Levin, 2010). The problematic use of research to shape policy, as shown in the review of Queensland educational leadership policy, can be analysed through the use of what Bowe, Ball and Gold (1992) refer to as the policy cycle. Figure 13.1 depicts their conceptual organisation of this cycle. The cycle describes the interaction between the development of policy and implementation strategies through the three contexts, including the context of influence on policy development, the context in which the policy language, text and discourse is developed and the context in which the policy is practised or implemented.

Within the cycle Bowe et al. suggest that when influences are urgent it creates the development of more and more policy to ensure the ongoing discourse. This is where the importance of research, as an influencing factor, and the lack of understanding for how research can support policy decision-making can

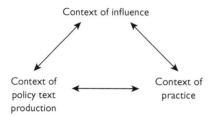

*Figure 13.1* The Bowe, Ball and Gold Policy Cycle (1992, p. 20).

impact the connection between the three areas of influence. This can lead to a disconnect between any of the three areas. For example, external factors, such as the growing international competitive situations, have been found to make increasingly substantial impacts on research and policy processes, especially in education (Levin, 2010). This can be seen in the current global trend where education is seen as a competitive commodity based on student testing results.

Another example is when the language of policy is compared to the hoped-for enacted practices and implementation strategies. Analysis shows (Adie, 2008) that development of policy-specific rhetoric, such as on the topic of educational leadership, can become a continuous discourse that responds to changing circumstances locally and globally. It also shows that continuing to develop the expected discourse as a response to these influential circumstances requires constant iteration and reiteration through a range of related policies. Without consolidation in policy, including identifying relevant research to support decisions, this constant and rapid change within the policy cycle is where the disconnect between research, policy and practice can occur.

In the case of the policy development reviewed, two issues clearly emerge:

1  the pressure for government policy to reflect the increasing importance, particularly in education, for being internationally competitive leading to inconsistent use of research to support change; and
2  problematic tensions created through inconsistencies in policy language contributing to development of inconsistent implementation strategies and practices.

### 13.5.1 The pressure to change

Increasingly, as found by Court and Young (2003), through the rush to develop policy addressing the globally competitive market, disconnection emerges between what is expected through policy and what has been found and established through research. Responding to the political pressure for change can create situations where policy is decided on the run and rather than a considered development and approach, new policy is added to old, creating an ever growing snowball of expanded policy that can create confusion. Without adequate understanding for building explicit policies, aligned to research and using consistent language, policy makers may not know how to identify suitable concepts and strategies for implementation in their context (Court & Young, 2003, p. 440). A body of international literature (Smith, 2005; Sahlberg; 2007) illustrates how different governments around the world have translated the global imperatives of competition and market-driven reform into their education policies. This has resulted in extensive resources being used to develop and implement policy that aims to reflect and enact strategies responding to this international environment. Use of resources in this way would indicate that governments expect their policies will act as change agents. However, as Adie (2008) found, 'producing policy documents does not necessarily result in changes to education practices in schools' (p. 252).

As seen in the Queensland context, adding to existing policies, without consolidation and the use of research to create a consistent message, led to a broad policy smorgasbord and eventually, a fractured implementation process. Elmore (1980) suggested that policy makers needed guidance in interpreting the literature and in determining the logic that ties policy and implementation strategies together. This lack of guidance can be seen in the new language and additional documents that were added to the suite of Queensland policies, such as the *Principal Supervision and Capability Development* (DETA, 2011b), where the existing leadership focus was added to and altered, in this case moving from a developmental focus to a performance one. This shift in focus, to not only create stronger statements about IL expectations but to also build in accountability measures, is one of the issues established by Bowe et al. (1992) as creating a policy cycle disconnect in the context of practice through exterior influences.

This can also lead to what Jenlink and Jenlink identify in their chapter as 'ethical drift' (Kleinman, 2006; Sternberg, 2012a). This outlines a concept where organisations are seen to 'drift' away from ethical practices in creating policy. Sternberg (2012a) saw ethical drift as the gradual ebbing of standards that occurs in organisational decision-making as the result of external pressures. This loss of standards can be seen as disconnection between the development of policy and the way in which the policies are enacted. One reason for this type of 'drifting' is when clear use of research does not support the design of consistent implementation processes and practices to back up policy decision-making. This can be seen in the selected Queensland policy context.

### 13.5.2 Policy discourse

These changes, without utilising consistent research-based decision-making processes, also highlight the problematic situations created through what is described in the policy cycle as the context of policy text. Reasons for this can relate to the capacity to understand the concepts by those responsible for translating policy into practice. In making this change to the *Principals' Leadership Capabilities Framework* (DETA, 2010), it would seem that this may be the case, as the shift in policy shown through the insertion of one sentence, does not represent a shift in a description of the actual practices. In the Queensland example, the combined set of reworded or additional policies provided a complex and confusing picture of the role of an instructional leader for school principals. While each policy and report identified the leadership as important in developing an educationally competitive system, they differed in describing these expectations in both terminology and format. The variance in the language and conceptual presentation of information prevented an automatic 'match' from one document to the next or a connection to a clear, common description of specific expectations. This variety of policy iterations created a situation where, while there were common expectations that Queensland principals would embrace and practice IL, exactly how principals were to implement the IL practices or build their 'instructional' capacity was not clear.

## 13.6 Conclusions

The comparison of the varying definitions of IL in the succession of Queensland policy documents, papers and regional initiatives supporting principal development, identifies that there was a lack of clarity in both the definition of IL and the processes used for implementation and the development of principal practice. Policy implementation as reflected across a sample of the state's regions demonstrates this same inconsistency. Based on the disparity in processes it is difficult to clearly see a significant, common core message or purpose that underpinned and drove the strategic direction for IL being developed across the Queensland system in the time period reviewed.

Across the seven-year period a disconnect in the policy cycle is visible between the pervasive research messages about IL and policy implementation. Ethical drift is also apparent in the profusion of strategic policy documents across this continuum. It is clear that the Queensland government educational policy development related to Instructional Leadership was impacted by the rise in the importance of the international and national high-stakes literacy and numeracy testing and that, although there were attempts to support making changes through commissioning the Masters Report (Masters, 2009) and the Fullan and Levin review (2012), the translation into policy and implementation were not developed through a consistent and considered response relying on research-based decisions. In reflecting on how this example relates to the Bowe, Ball and Gold Policy Cycle (1992), the use of research and researchers as an important influencing factor could have supported the development of a connected process.

## Note

1 It should be noted that at the time the documents were used for this study they were available from the Queensland Department of Education, Training and Employment (DETE) website.

Chapter 14

# The politics and complexity of research utilisation in the central education policy arena in Taiwan

*Hung-Chang Chen*

## 14.1 Introduction

This chapter provides a qualitative study which explores the impact of politics on the commissioning, conduct and utilisation of government-commissioned research in the formation of education policy in the Ministry of Education (MoE), Taiwan. It aims to illuminate how political dynamics in the policy-making arena could shape the way in which research is commissioned, conducted and used, which is an under-investigated area. This chapter seeks to make a contribution by providing examples of instances where politics was involved in government-sponsored research in an East Asian context that also reflects a key concern of this edited book.

The use of research in the policy-making process is a goal for many researchers (Carden, 2004) who hope that their work can be used and their ideas or suggestions can be adopted by policy-makers in some way. However, literature on the use of educational research in policy-making reveals a paucity of evidence of the extent to which policy reflects, is informed by, or is based on research evidence (Johnson, 1999; Levin, 2013; Lingard, 2013; Lubienski, Scott & DeBray, 2014; Weiss, 1979). This low utilisation of research is not just due to the inadequacies of the research itself (Levin, 2013), as notable attention has been paid to highlighting the key aspects of politics, which dominates the use of research in the education policy arena (Biesta, 2007; Gillies, 2014; Hess, 2008; Porter, 2010; Whitty, 2006). As Johnson (1999) points out, it is the political dynamics of the policy process that provides the context for research utilisation. Thus, it becomes more necessary for researchers to be aware of these political dynamics in policy-making when seeking to influence policy-making with their research findings or to analyse how research is used and for what.

Given the salience of political considerations, this chapter aims to examine how political dynamics in the policy-making arena shape and influence the commissioning, conduction and utilisation of research. In addressing this, this chapter focuses on the political side of commissioned research and the policy-making nexus, a dimension which is significant but often ignored by researchers. The chapter begins by briefly presenting the Taiwanese context of commissioning research in the MoE. It then reviews key aspects of political dynamics in the policy-making arena, and different meanings of research utilisation. Finally, it presents and discusses the findings of six commissioned research projects which drew upon in-depth, semi-structured interviews with researchers and Ministry policy-makers, and the analysis of relevant documents.

## 14.2 MoE research commissioning in Taiwan

Taiwan, like other East Asian countries, has historically and culturally placed great emphasis upon education, and makes great investments in its education system. In order to enhance educational standards under the pressure of international competition in educational achievement, such as the PISA, the Taiwanese MoE has been devoted to educational improvement for years. Research evidence has been recognised as an essential foundation of policy formation and an approach of evidence-informed policy-making has been increasingly prioritised by the government since the 1990s. The government's prioritisation of evidence-informed policy-making is indicated by statements found in official policy documents, such as the following: *'The education policy cannot be made simply by practical experiences or academic theories, but instead it should be based upon research evidence'* (The Education Research Committee, 2011, pp. 46–47).

In particular, during the period of 2006–2011, the MoE, including its affiliations, commissioned a total of 533 research projects to academics, research institutions or non-profit foundations, with the total funding amounting to about 7.3 million pounds (Research Development and Evaluation Commission, 2014). This considerable number of commissioned research projects forms a clear contrast to the austerity budgets in government. However, there have been a considerable amount of research projects being commissioned to seek feasible reform approaches or to identify problems in education. There has been surprisingly little research into the examination of research utilisation in MoE policy-making, an arena which is understood to be heavily politicised. Consequently, little has been known about how these commissioned research results were used by civil servants, or what dilemmas occurred in researchers' conduct of research within a highly politicised policy context.

## 14.3 The salience of political considerations in research utilisation

Literature on the policy-research nexus has indicated that research and politics are intertwined, and the relationship between research, politics and policy-making is always complex (Wong, 2008). It is recognised that the policy-making process is much more complex, dynamic and political than it is static and rational (Taylor et al., 1997; Weaver-Hightower, 2008). The well-known work of Ball (1998) perhaps best summarises such a politically dynamic view of policy-making:

National policy-making is inevitably a process of bricolage: a matter of borrowing and copying bits and pieces of ideas from elsewhere, drawing upon and amending locally tried and tested approaches, cannibalising theories, research, trends and fashions and not infrequently flailing around for anything at all that looks as though it might work.

(p. 126)

Ball's work vividly depicts the complex and dynamic context of research use. Research information should play an indispensable role in these policy-making activities, especially when information is input into the policy-making process to resolve highly complex social problems (Johnson, 1999). It is argued that there is an inescapable political dimension to educational research use (Cohen, Manion & Morrison, 2011). In this sense, politics is seen by many researchers to be the main determinant to shape the utilisation of research in the policy-making process and determine the policy direction accordingly (Biesta, 2007; Johnson, 1999; Monaghan, 2010; Porter, 2010). In his influential work on agenda setting, Kingdon (2003, p. 228) elucidates the different concerns of the 'policy community' and the 'political people'. Johnson (1999) points out the political features of the policy process, namely its agenda-driven nature, the incentive structure that guides the behaviour of policy actors, the value and perspective-driven nature of the interpretative act, and the interactive nature of the policy-making process. All of these factors and conditions provide a context for capturing the politics of research utilisation. Similarly, as Wong (2008, p. 220) iterates, echoed by Porter (2010), electoral interests, distribution of power, partisan-oriented agendas, the tension between the electoral-policy cycle and the timeliness of research undertakings, intra-organisational politics and bureaucratic inertia must each be taken into consideration in understanding the use and the influence of research in the policy process. These features provide meaningful insights into the context of research undertakings and research utilisation in the policy-making arena for this study.

## 14.4 Meanings of research use

What it means to 'use' research is a complicated and contested phenomenon, and is still open to debate. Central to these debates is the issue of how research use can be conceptualised. The following section reviews the different ways of conceptualising this issue.

### 14.4.1 Research-use typologies

Much research has attempted to classify different models of research utilisation. Some of the most influential work in this area is that offered by Weiss (1979), a leading scholar of the research-policy nexus during 1970s and 1980s

(Hess, 2008). The following brief review has mainly drawn upon Weiss' (1979) typology of research use, coupled with two new models proposed by Stevens (2007) and Monaghan (2010). *The enlightenment model* and *the interactive model* are seen to be the most visible and influential paradigms in the field of education policy (Nutley, Walter & Davies, 2007; Weiss, 1979). Central to these two models is that what influences policy perhaps is not the findings of a single study or set of related studies, but rather the new way of thinking about an issue or a range of ideas and opinions in a policy area. It is seldom the case that a social science research study has the direct impact on policy-making promised by *the knowledge-driven model* (Weiss, 1979) in which research knowledge has a leading role in identifying its potential value and utilisation to policy. However, it is usually assumed that social science research projects are purposefully commissioned by governments as in the case of *the problem-solving model* (Lingard, 2013; Ouimet et al., 2009; Weiss, 1979) which assumes that researchers help policy-makers find a solution to a consensually agreed upon problem. Although this direct research influence on policy remains the prevailing expectation of research use (Carden, 2004), chances of this actually taking place are rare (Elliott & Popay, 2000).

More specifically, policy-makers would primarily use research to support their political survival as in the case of *the political model* (Hammersley, 2002; McDonnell, 2008). In this model, research is often used if it is considered to be politically expedient (Cohen, Manion & Morrison, 2011), as in what Brown (2015, pp. 7, 25) terms 'ornamental evidence use'. Similarly, in *the tactical model* research is used as a tactic for delaying action or deflecting criticisms; hence, the utility of the research exists irrespective of its findings, but in the research itself diverting attention or supporting other goals (Weiss, 1979). Thus, policy-makers' use of research is sometimes governed, to a large extent, by political pragmatism rather than rational consideration.

The above Weiss (1979) models have proved highly influential in the research utilisation literature and have also been extensively applied to studies of the use of research in a variety of contexts (Elliott & Popay, 2000; Nutley, Walter & Davies, 2007). Meanwhile, others, who are dissatisfied with the high level of abstraction of these existing models of research utilisation have turned to exploring the subtle interactions and relationships between research information and policy-making. Drawing upon classic evolutionary social theory of 'survival of the fittest', Stevens' (2007, p. 26) *evolutionary model* seeks to explain how evidence can be used selectively to further the interests of powerful social groups. Based on Stevens (2007), Monaghan's (2010) work of *the processual model* aptly synthesises the evolutionary model and the enlightenment model, providing valuable insights into the use of research. It both emphasises the operation of strategic evidence selection and acknowledges the indirect research impact on policy processes. These new models further enrich the understanding of research use in policy-making.

### 14.4.2 Research-use stages

A different set of frameworks view research use as a cumulative and ongoing process, incorporating a more dynamic perspective. The best known work on this is perhaps Knott and Wildavsky's (1980) *'research use scale'* which manifests a cumulative process progressing through a number of stages: reception, cognition, reference, effort, adoption, implementation and impact (p. 546). Central to such a 'stage' approach is that research use is not fixed in a static model but has the potential to flow through many levels or stages of uses in a given context. Knott and Wildavsky's (1980) work has been extensively adopted in policy research (for example, Cherney et al., 2012; Landry, Amara & Lamari, 2001; Ouimet et al., 2009). However, the stages approach has its limitations. It fails to capture the prevailing instances of tactical and strategic uses of evidence and the political influence on research use, which, as noted earlier, forms an indispensable dimension to research use. This is perhaps related to its second downside, which is that it assumes research use 'proceeds in a linear and logical way' (Nutley, Walter & Davies, 2007, p. 50), and that the later stage can only be progressed from once the former one has been achieved.

Thus far, this chapter has reviewed different ways of conceptualising the utilisation of research. Static typologies provide a method of understanding various ways of research use in time, for example integrating political considerations into the research utilisation. The advantages of the stages approach rely on the conceptualisation of the flow process through various stages of research use in different periods of time. Both the typology and stage models of research use have respective advantages and form part of the conceptual framework of this study.

## 14.5 Qualitative multiple-case study design

This qualitative-oriented study attempts to better understand the dynamics within government-commissioned research projects in the MoE in Taiwan, using the cases as examples to explore the real-life, complex dynamic and unfolding interactions (Cohen, Manion & Morrison, 2011) between commissioned research and policy-making. In order to increase the understanding of the cases and situations studied, a qualitative multiple-case approach was adopted (Patton, 2002, p. 14). The government-commissioned research projects by the MoE were used as the unit of analysis in this multiple-case study. The six commissioned research projects conducted during 2006–2008 were chosen through purposive sampling (Silverman, 2013, p. 148) from a total of 533 Ministry-commissioned research projects.

Data were mainly collected through in-depth, semi-structured interviews and the analysis of relevant documents from 2013. A total of 11 face-to-face interviews for the six cases were carried out and these included five researchers from different higher education institutions and six MoE policy-makers who were involved in the six case study research projects. Due to the different positions of respondents, two sets of interview questions were used for each of the groups. For researchers, the focus of the interview questions were on their interactions with relevant MoE policy-makers, and difficulties or dilemmas they faced in conducting research; for policy-makers, the focus was more on how they were involved in the research projects and used the research results. All the interviews were audio-recorded and then transcribed and analysed based on the research questions. Data analysis was conducted with thematic analysis, developing codes and themes in the data through Boyatzis' (1998, pp. 31–37) 'hybrid approach' which included 'theory-driven', 'prior-research-driven' and 'data-driven'. To ensure anonymity, all the titles of the research projects and identifiable information in terms of people and research content have been deleted or re-named with a pseudonym to maintain research confidentiality.

## 14.6 Political constraints and researchers' pressure

The commissioned research for the MoE is conducted to respond to a specific problem, need or pressure that the MoE confronts. The research purposes, questions or frameworks are usually tailored to the specifications set by the MoE staff. Then, public bidding for the research project is invited and bidders normally prepare their research proposals in accord with the pre-framed research purposes and questions. After the bidding invitation, a review committee will decide which research proposal best fits with the needs of the MoE. The best-fitting bidder, usually a research group from a university, is then selected to undertake the commissioned research and their research results are presumably expected to be taken on board by policy-makers. Nevertheless, this study finds that the process of research commissioning, conduct and use is not so straightforward and that a number of political dynamics can disturb, distract, and obstruct the research process.

First of all, it was evident that research projects were likely to be offered to 'the preferred' researchers although there were diverse ways of commissioning research projects. The data indicated that these preferred persons were normally either those who had had good interactions or relationships with the MoE senior officials or those who were deemed to be able to cooperate with and satisfy the MoE, as one civil servant reported:

> For the most part, we would commission research projects to the academics with whom we are familiar. By so doing, it would reduce the shock of the research, and also benefit our collaboration.
>
> (Policy-maker, A2-19)

Once the MoE officials had selected the preferred person, the review committee would be a simple formality. Thus, what was selected in the policy arena would be, in the context of Taiwan, not only research evidence, but also the researcher as well. This issue of selection of the researcher seems to be less identified in the literature on research utilisation.

This study also finds that a number of political demands could constrain the conduct of research and put researchers under pressure. These political dynamics can be categorised into 'the external politics' and 'internal political constraints'. First, the evidence showed that the political pressure from external groups penetrated through to civil servants and was directly imposed on researchers. One example in this study was that an official, who was confronted with heavy pressure from legislators and lobbying groups, passed this pressure on to the researchers and ultimately requested that they corroborate the MoE's stance by fabricating the needed evidence. As one researcher reported, '*This is obviously against research ethics and the thing we don't want to do*'. Another case, under similar political pressure, was that researchers were asked unexpectedly by officials to change research direction and add additional tasks into a research project within a very tight timetable. These changing demands, as noted by the respondent, '*kept the researchers tired and constantly on the run*'.

Second, internal political constraints also put pressure on researchers and gave them dilemmas. The data revealed that MoE policy-makers in some cases had taken certain predetermined positions around a policy and sought to shape, guide and direct the research towards their own stance through either face-to-face communication or '*review mechanisms*'. The review mechanisms, which included the administration review conducted by the MoE officials as well as interim and terminal review committees chaired by specialists who were designated by the MoE, were reported as a powerful and useful tool to rectify the conduct of research. The way that they operated was clearly captured by a policy-maker, as she noted:

> Although most researchers would follow your (policy-makers') framework, you would sometimes find that some researchers have deviated from the predetermined direction. What you can do is not to monitor all the time but to utilise either the administration review or specialist review to pull them back, to focus them on what you think is the right trajectory. You can use the interim or terminal review to do this.
>
> (Policy-maker, A6–48)

The consequences were that these researchers had to revise their interim or terminal research reports until they could satisfy the official. This does not only produce a more laborious job, increase workload and a sense of frustration for researchers, but also jeopardises research ethics either through the external political pressure or internal bureaucratic interventions. It is this dual-effect on both researchers' work practice and ethical concerns that are critical to consider.

## 14.7 The dynamics and complexity of research utilisation

A significant theme penetrating through the six cases reveals the dynamics and complexity of research utilisation. In particular, this dynamic assemblage manifests the flow or shift of research-use models and political dynamics embedded in the research-use process. The dynamic flow of research use for each research case is summarised in Table 14.1, and will be briefly presented in the following sub-sections.

### 14.7.1 Case 1: the shift of research-use models

According to the MoE policy-maker interviewed, this research project was initially commissioned to find out different solutions to compete with other MoE Departments on a predetermined but contentious teacher education policy. That is to say, the commissioned research had expected to function as a political model of research use, as it was set up to give officials an edge in political debates within the MoE. However, the research conclusions finally dissatisfied the officials and failed to help them use the research results to achieve their goal. As the official reported, the research conclusion

Table 14.1 The flow of research-use models.

|  | Intended model of research use | Resultant model of research use | The main reason for the model shift/continuity |
|---|---|---|---|
| Case 1 | Political → | Processual | Research conclusion; dissatisfied officials; research use was postponed |
| Case 2 | Tactical → | Tactical | Electoral cycle: the turnover of elected politicians (Legislators); the intervention from the Office of the President |
| Case 3 | Enlightenment → | Processual | Party alternation; the turnover of elected MoE officials; agenda shift; realistic constraints |
| Case 4 | Tactical → | Tactical | Electoral cycle: the turnover of elected politicians (Legislators) |
| Case 5 | Problem-solving → | Enlightenment | Difficulties in identifying the extent of research use |
| Case 6 | Problem-solving → | Processual | Discordant perspectives on solutions of problem-solving between two communities |

was too conceptual to provide concrete alternatives and to persuade the Minister to change the determined policy. Although the initial political model of research use failed, the policy-maker noted that he still developed new initiatives by selecting and assembling some concepts from the commissioned research conclusions.

The research utilisation in this case was postponed and was undertaken in a nonlinear and selective way, which fits much more closely with the processual model. It should be noted that this case clearly showed the difference between the initially anticipated research-use model and the resultant one, namely a shift of research-use model from the political to the processual.

### 14.7.2 Case 2: a consistent tactical model

Faced with the advocacy of a particular higher education initiative from elected officials of the Office of President and some elected Legislators, the MoE then decided to commission a research project to respond to this external pressure. Both the interviewed researcher and MoE civil servant noted that this contested initiative was not on the MoE's policy agenda and not preferred by the MoE at all. Thus, the commissioned research was used as a tactic for delaying action. Ultimately two key issues enabled the MoE to delay action. A shift in the position of the advocating legislators weakened the issue and the necessity of the commissioned research. Additionally, the opposition regained power and successfully persuaded the Office of the President to suspend the initiative as well as the commissioned research. This case can be categorised into the tactical model of research use as it illustrates an instance when policy-makers achieve their goals of using research for delaying action.

### 14.7.3 Case 3: different expectations and perspectives on research use

The data from case 3, which involved the issue of providing schooling to remote and mountainous areas, showed that the researchers' expectations for the research use differed from those of the policy-makers. The researchers seemed to embrace a problem-solving model while civil servants simply held the view that the research might provide them with different and alternative ways of thinking about the problem. Both respondents pointed to the low degree of research use. The researcher asserted that this was owing to a change in the political party and the subsequent turnover of the higher-echelon elected officials during the research process, which had resulted in a lack of officials' involvement in this particular research project. In sum, the newly elected officials seemed to have different policy agendas. In contrast, the policy-maker reported that it was external realistic factors and statutory and budgetary limitations within the MoE that ultimately constrained the impact of the research on policy. Nonetheless, this study finds that MoE officials still selected some useful concepts and information from the research report to further develop other policies. So, the way in which this commissioned research was used is much closer to the processual model.

### 14.7.4 Case 4: a consistent tactical model

Case 4 revealed how the MoE tactically used a research project to respond to external political forces. As a new special education policy was enacted by the MoE, it triggered great resistance from certain stakeholders – most of them were parent groups. The timing of this issue was crucial; it was before the legislative election in 2008, a pivotal period for politicians hoping for re-election. Many legislators thus aligned closely with these parents and put pressure on the MoE to halt the policy. One of the rationales for these legislators' action was to accumulate political goodwill for the next election cycle through helping their constituents. Confronted with these external political demands, the MoE officials responded by commissioning a research project. As the newspaper documented:

> The official of the Ministry of Education says that with regard to the issue of [. . .] of special education, the Ministry is doing research on it now. It is scheduled to publish the research report at the end of April. The Ministry will further discuss and consult with relevant agencies and actors after the publication of the commissioned research report.
>
> (Chuang, 2008)

It was clear in this case that the commissioned research was used as a proof of policy makers' responsiveness to camouflage their own pre-determined stance and delay action. When the research report was published two months after the legislative election, the political demands gradually faded. The MoE thus successfully got through this highly politicised demand. Data from the policy-maker revealed that the final research conclusions accorded with policy-makers' predetermined positions. Thus, in case number 4 research use was a tactic in bureaucratic politics irrespective of its conclusions.

### 14.7.5 Case 5: the ambiguity of research use

In order to deal with education inequality, the MoE launched a large-scale commissioned research project with several sub-projects. It seemed that both officials and researchers reached a consensus on the purpose of the research which was very *problem-solving oriented* at the beginning. However, the interviewed respondents found it difficult to identify the extent to which the research was used. Data from researchers indicated the following reasons: firstly, the large-scale research provided numerous suggestions which were divided into immediate, mid-term and long-term suggestions. Many of these suggestions were related to ongoing policies or initiatives. To concisely distinguish research contribution was difficult. Second, there were too many policies and initiatives and too much research information in process, which meant the officials could not clearly tell whether their own decision-making was influenced by research suggestions or other inputs. Therefore, the research was believed to be used merely to help officials clarify problems and understand the problematic contexts, rather than adopting concrete action plans to solve problems.

### 14.7.6 Case 6: leading researchers

Faced with increasing cases of student suicide, the MoE urgently hoped to propose active policy strategies for schools to protect students' well-being. A research project with the intended *problem-solving purpose* of aiming to investigate the status of student stress and also present concrete suggestions for policy strategies was commissioned. What use was finally made of the research shifted due to the different perspectives on the research direction between researchers and civil servants. The research leader, who was an experienced director-general of a local education authority, successfully convinced the MoE officials to change the research direction from proposing policy strategies to curriculum design. Due to this shift the commissioned research was unable to fulfil the MoE's initial expectation for providing policy strategies. In the end, the MoE could only publish this curriculum-oriented research as a guidance model for schools' reference and did not directly take research evidence on board. This process, reflecting the dynamic selection and the dispersive nature of research influence, is a manifestation of *the processual model* of research use.

## 14.8 Discussion

Much literature has attempted to identify the factors shaping the use of research (Johnson, 1999; Levin, 2013; Nutley, Walter & Davies, 2007; Tseng, 2012), but less attention has been given to the way in which the 'commission' and 'conduct' of research is shaped by the inescapable political dimension of the research–policy nexus. Drawing upon empirical findings, the study finds the 'preferred researchers' who had a close relationship with or who could better satisfy the MoE staff seemed likely to receive the commissioned research. This finding echoes Brown's (2012a) work of the policy-preferences mode, where preferred people are considered as one of the preconditions of knowledge adoption. Furthermore, this study also fills the gap by identifying the salient influences of the external and internal political pressures on researchers' undertakings. Data showed that researchers might be requested to fabricate evidence, to undertake additional research tasks or to change research direction, so as to respond to external demands and officials' preferred ideology or predetermined positions. In their research process, researchers might not only be faced with ethical dilemmas, but might also get caught up in a laborious workload and tight timetable.

Findings in the study also reflect recent research on the political influence on research utilisation. For instance, the party alternation and the electoral cycle of politicians and officials (see Porter, 2010; Wong, 2008) would often alter the priorities of policy agendas and then shift the attention given to the commissioned research. Furthermore, data also confirms that civil service officials who had a predetermined position might 'squash' research findings which were deemed deviant from given policy (Brown, 2012b, p. 67). More specifically, power relations within the interaction between policy-makers and researchers could also influence the research and its future use. The researcher's background, while indicated in this study is seldom documented in the literature, but also contributes to the asymmetrical power relations.

Findings from this study also uncover some unique contributions with specific implications for conceptualising research use. The research data revealed the fluid and multifaceted nature of research use, presenting a flow or shift of the anticipatory intention(s) of research use to the resultant one. As can be seen in Table 14.1, there could be a change between the anticipatory research-use model at the beginning of research commissioning and the later model at the time when the investigation is conducted. Exceptions to this are case 2 and case 4, which consistently maintained their tactical use of research. The *tactical* and *problem-solving models* were most often the intended model in this study. This finding is supported by most of the previous studies (for example, Weiss, 1979) showing that research tends to be used for achieving organisational or individuals' instrumental goals, either rational problem-solving or as a bureaucratic tactic. The other four cases turn to either the processual or the enlightenment model. However, no case in this study showed the problem-solving model as a resultant model. As most studies have indicated, chances of direct research utilisation are rare (Elliott & Popay, 2000; Johnson, 1999), and research knowledge 'creeps' in with the diffuse process of research use (Weiss, 1982, p. 635).

## 14.9 Conclusion

This chapter has provided insights into the political influences on the commissioning, and conduct of research. Seeking to bring attention to an important but neglected aspect of this topic, this chapter has explored the ways in which political pressure disturbs researchers' undertaking of research, and the consequences of these disturbances. It then suggests that further attention should be given to how researchers can cope with these inescapable political pressures and dilemmas. There is little discussion of this issue in the literature in the research-policy nexus, and further studies are needed.

The empirical data in this chapter also presents the ways in which the commissioned research projects were 'used'. A significant contribution of this study is the emergence of a fluid research-use model from the research fieldwork. The fluid model not only views research use as a much more fluid process than a static state, but also enables us to identify political considerations in the research process, along with ethical dilemmas and pressures that researchers often confront when undertaking commissioned research projects. This research, and the research-use model that emerged from the project, therefore add to the body of knowledge related to the use of commissioned research projects in the education policy arena in Taiwan.

# Chapter 15

# The pressures within

Dilemmas in the conduct of evaluation from within government

*Karen Trimmer*

## 15.1 Background

This concluding chapter reflects on the lived experience of the author as a government employee responsible for the conduct of performance reviews and evaluations of State government initiatives in Australia over a period of 17 years. Two specific cases are discussed that illustrate points raised throughout the book and strategies explored for addressing issues and challenges encountered. Over the 17-year period I was employed in four State government agencies, including education and training departments and an audit office. In these roles I was involved in leading, managing and conducting evaluations and performance reviews, the reports of which were used by the departments to advise on the effectiveness of policy, its implementation and development, and in the case of audit, tabled in State parliament.

## 15.2 The politics of research and evaluation

The literature clearly acknowledges that evaluation is an inherently political process (Markiewicz, 2005; Palumbo, 1987; Patton, 2008; Simons, 2000; Slattery, 2010) and in recent years, the work of evaluation has become even more politicised as have its uses and non-uses (Cohen, Manion & Morrison, 2011). Weiss's (1970) seminal work regarding the politicisation of evaluation has been acknowledged and cited by many authors since its publication. She regards politics and evaluation as being linked in three main ways.

First, the programs and policies which evaluation examines are the products of political decisions. This means that discussion, debate and operational management by many officers has already occurred prior to the implementation of any policy and program so politics are already part of the landscape before decisions about conducting an evaluation are made. Second, the product of the evaluation ultimately feeds into a further decision-making process so the evaluation report itself becomes a political entity. Third, evaluation as a process is political because it involves assessing and judging. Fundamentally, Weiss (1987, 1993) contends, evaluation takes place in a political context and is subject to political pressures.

Patton's (2008) more recent work in the field of utilisation-focused evaluation purports that politics are never absent from evaluation work, although the degree of politicalisation may vary. Patton expanded on Weiss's (1987) work to argue that politics are involved in all aspects of evaluation, including the data collection stage, and he offers six sources of political inherency:

1. The involvement of people in evaluation means that their own values, perceptions and politics are involved.
2. Because evaluation requires the classification and categorisation of data, this means that decisions are made regarding the way the data is filtered.
3. The fact that empirical data underpins evaluation makes it a political process because data always requires interpretation.
4. Because actions and decisions follow from evaluations, and such decisions affect the allocation of resources and distribution of power, politics are involved.
5. The fact that programs and organisations are involved in evaluations makes them political. Organisations allocate power, status and resources and evaluation affects that.
6. The involvement of information in evaluations makes them political because information leads to action and the accumulation of power.

Notably, Patton's (2008) second and third points above regarding data manipulation relate to the work of the researcher and evaluator, thus inferring that the researcher and evaluator themselves unwittingly bring politics into the arena of evaluation. This is where the issue of ethical drift raised by Jenlink and Jenlink (Chapter 4) may arise. Patton's other points relate to the stakeholders and participants. Stakeholders involved in allocation of resources and distribution of power for higher education researchers include their employing institutions, government policy-makers and funders of research (Brown, Chapter 2; Normand, Chapter 3; Viseu, Chapter 5; Doyle & McDonald, Chapter 8; Bendix Petersen, Chapter 9).

Markiewicz (2008) views the links between politics and evaluation as being all-encompassing. She argues that political influence begins from the moment that decisions to evaluate are made, when discussions about the purpose and role of the evaluation occur. Further political decisions are then made with respect to budget, timelines, scope, detail, findings, recommendations and dissemination of results. In addition to these considerations are discussions about what is methodologically necessary to ensure that an evaluation is credible, what is pragmatically appropriate, and what is politically desirable. While Pawson (2006) acknowledges the politics that impact on evaluation work, he suggests that their contribution to the policy and program development process is overstated because evaluation takes place after program design and implementation cycles. All evaluation takes place in a social context and political overtones are generally present in all branches of evaluation research. The politics involved may be at a small-group, wider-organisation, national or international level (Barlow, 2005). The policy agora and its influence on evidence based decision-making were discussed by Brown in Chapter 2.

The agency that has responsibility for the policy or program is generally the agency that commissions the evaluation (Weiss, 1993), so it has ownership of the program as well as the product of the evaluation. At the conclusion of the evaluation, the findings are reported to those who commissioned the evaluation, i.e. the decision-makers and managers. The extent to which attention is given to an evaluation is often dependent upon the political attractiveness of the findings to decision-makers (Cohen, Manion & Morrison, 2011) and it is likely to be taken more seriously when its findings confirm the already-held beliefs of the decision-makers (Weiss, 1993). Decision-makers can also distort or only partially use the findings of evaluations to their own ends (Barton, 2002) and can select to publicise only those findings that support desired policy directions (Guenther, Williams & Arnott, 2010). If the findings are negative or politically sensitive, the report may be buried and the findings ignored in any future decision-making (Guenther, Williams & Arnott, 2010). Alternatively, findings may be released with the decision-makers' own facts and interpretations (Schram & Soss, 2001). A number of these issues were experienced and discussed by Gower and Partington (Chapter 12) and Chen (Chapter 14). Sometimes, it is not even the outcome which is considered to be important, but simply the mere process of conducting an evaluation or research into a policy or program which can be used by decision-makers to legitimise actions (Glass, 1987; Gorard, 2010) or pre-empt research or evaluation of other sensitive issues (Doornbos, 2012). In a recent study in the United States, it was found that education district leaders did not utilise research in relation to policy decision-making, but often utilised research to legitimise and substantiate a policy decision that had already been made, even where there was not a good match of context (Coburn, 2015). Gower and Partington (Chapter 12) provided examples of how this pressure arises in the context of commissioned research conducted by academic researchers, and they and Chen (Chapter 14) considered the changes in purpose and policy position of departments commissioning research throughout the research or evaluation process. Farwell (Chapter 13) provided an example of where policy development has occurred in isolation of related research to become disconnected to evidence that may have informed the process.

Even while evaluations are underway, political pressures can affect them. If evaluations or research are lengthy, other changes may be occurring so that the political climate at the completion of an evaluation may not be the same as it was at its commencement. For example, the programs and policies being evaluated may also be subject to influences such as budget cuts, administrative changes, varying government support, public appraisal, media coverage, and the implementation of additional or competing programs (Pawson, 2006; Weiss, 1993; Chen, Chapter 14). As examples of the changing landscape that can affect evaluation work, Pawson's (2006) personal experience involved:

- a program being declared dead by one government department in the same month that funding for its evaluation was announced by a different government department;
- a large-scale restructure of programs and services being announced at the same time that evaluators were still in the field collecting data;
- a research team reporting to four different managers as a consequence of the commissioning organisation undergoing restructuring during an evaluation.

In Chapter 14, Chan provided a taxonomy to analyse how these uses and outcomes of evaluations may be categorised and how this focus can change during the course of the research or evaluation. Guenther, Williams and Arnott's (2010) experience while working with Charles Darwin University demonstrated how an evaluation can have no impact in a political environment. In 2005, Guenther and his team were engaged by the Northern Territory Government to conduct an evaluation of the territory government's family violence strategies. Just after the completion of the report, a number of staffing changes took effect, as did a restructure of the entire section responsible for the management and implementation of the policy supporting the strategies. The management responsibility for the policy was then transferred to a different government department. Subsequent to this, all staff previously involved with managing the policy and strategies left the department and the entire initiative lapsed.

Any political tension that arises during an evaluation is due to differing value systems between the evaluator and the policy-maker (Weiss, 1993). Evaluators and researchers view their work as being objective, unbiased and non-political whereas policy-makers see their work as clearly anchored in a political arena and the products of evaluations are seen as political tools. Many researchers experience pressure, both subtle and unsubtle, in the conduct of evaluation activity even to the extent of producing findings that substantiate existing policy or support a policy favoured by the funding or commissioning body (Gorard, 2010; Winch, 2002). Pressures may be felt at any stage of an evaluation. During the design phase, pressures may be exerted by sponsors and stakeholders. During the data collection and data analysis phases, pressure is most likely to come from stakeholders and at the end of the evaluation when findings and recommendations emerge, pressure may come from sponsors and stakeholders (Chelimsky, 2007; Markiewicz, 2008). While those pressures may be felt at any stage of the conduct of an evaluation, they are often particularly highlighted during the stage of formulating findings and recommendations (Markiewicz, 2008). Managing those pressures and aiming to maintain a neutral, independent and objective orientation to the evaluation work can be challenging for the evaluator (Markiewicz, 2005; Slattery, 2010).

Trade-offs between evaluators and stakeholders are often involved in evaluations and the scope of evaluations is often constrained as a result of limitations relating to mandate, resources, time and methodologies (Slattery, 2010). Evaluators and researchers need to recognise that the purposes, roles and uses of evaluation are subject to change, but still remain legitimate, and that they themselves may need to change in response to government change (Slattery, 2010). However, in doing so they need to remain conscious of the influences acting upon them and how this may impact the rigor and ethics of their work (Jenlink & Jenlink, Chapter 4; Calzoni, Chapter 10).

## 15.3 Case studies of political influence and associated strategies for research and evaluation

The literature cites various examples which demonstrate the intersection of politics and research and evaluation (Brandon, Smith, Trenholm & Devaney, 2010; Duckett, Sixsmith & Kagan, 2008; Guenther, Williams & Arnott, 2010). In particular, Chelimsky (2007, 2008), who managed the Program Evaluation and Methodology Division (PEMD) within the US Government Accountability Office during the 1980s and 1990s, offered a range of examples where political influence made its presence felt at various stages of evaluations she was asked to undertake.

- Issues arising during the design phase – the PEMD was commissioned to undertake an evaluation with the evaluation question "To what degree has the secretary of education distorted the evaluation findings on bilingual education?" The highly politicised evaluation question was responded to by the PEMD through adopting a fair and unbiased methodology, including unbiased selection of participants.
- Issues arising during evaluations in progress – with some evaluations in the area of defence regarding weapon-system testing, the PEMD was often deprived of negative test measurement data by the US Department of Defense. The Department released favourable test results but kept the unfavourable results invisible. The PEMD responded to this situation by using a flexible methodology, refraining from answering questions using distorted test data, and publishing honest arguments about why evaluation questions could not be answered objectively.
- Issues arising during the final stages of evaluations – when the PEMD examined the extent to whether American businesses were sustaining an increased burden of paperwork, the findings showed no change. The sponsor of the evaluation requested the evaluators to maintain the data without adjustments for changed procedures so that he could argue business mistreatment as a consequence of government procedural change. The PEMD responded by refusing to change its findings, citing a lack of credibility that would ensue from doing so.

Chelimsky (2007, 2008) contends that being flexible with a choice of methods but also having methodological persuasiveness is the key to maintaining credibility with respect to findings that may not be palatable to sponsors and stakeholders. The following two case studies relate to evaluations of education initiatives undertaken within a State government department in Australia.

### 15.3.1 Case study 1

In this case a trial was announced by the Minister to explore school-level issues relating to an educational option for students that was of current interest for potential future policy development. Whilst the key aim was to contribute evidence and advice to the relevant department, the announcement of the trial included invitations to five schools based on their positive response to an offer of specific, and generous, funding to conduct a trial. No project parameters were set for the year levels, courses or format of classes at this stage. The request to conduct an evaluation of the trial came following the announcement, which then did not allow any selection process or flexibility in the proposed methodological approach.

The implementation of the trial and its evaluation, therefore, commenced at a stage where planning of an appropriate and rigorous methodology was restricted by circumstances already in place. Each school determined their own individual proposal regarding how they would conduct the trial and implemented the initiative in different ways. Different year groups, subject areas, and pedagogical approaches were used in each school. A case-study approach and an empowerment evaluation process (Fetterman & Eiler, 2001; Fetterman & Bowman, 2002) was therefore adopted to address the different monitoring and evaluation requirements of each school. In addition, a set of "agreed measures" was developed that outlined the monitoring requirements for each school for each year of the trial. The agreed measures allowed interim feedback to be provided to each school in each year of the trial, hence enabling schools to use the collected and analysed data to iteratively adjust their trial program consistent with the empowerment evaluation process.

Whilst this evaluation approach provided some positive outcomes for the participating schools, a consequence of the design was that there were a range of issues that impacted on the rigor of the evaluation. These included:

- a wide variation in the approaches taken by the participating schools;
- schools were not provided with guidelines regarding the use of financial resources provided to fund the trial, and therefore were allocated the funding in vastly different ways;
- staff changes within schools impacted on the continuity of the trial programs;
- teachers' access to professional development varied widely according to school circumstances and staff changes within the schools.

Whilst the empowerment process ensured outcomes were attained within each participating school, there was no possibility of generalising findings and limited capacity to provide sound evidence in relation to the conditions that supported learning in relation to the educational initiative or a policy direction that may be applicable across schools.

The researchers within the government department in case study 1 had severe limitations placed on the research methodology imposed by the political circumstance prior to the development of clearly defined research questions or a consistent approach or direction for the education initiative being investigated. This created a dilemma in trying to develop a methodology that was rigorous and could meet stated outcomes for the project. Whilst the research team adopted an approach, within the limitations, that provided a way forward in assessing the effectiveness of the initiative there were problems that could not be fully overcome and a subsequent impact on the veracity of the conclusions that could be drawn at the conclusion of the research.

Researchers and evaluators aim to approach their roles in conducting evaluations with independence and objectivity. In adopting a high level of independence, researchers and evaluators aim to produce neutral and unbiased results, and this ensures the credibility of their findings (Chelimsky, 2008; Markiewicz, 2008). Their independence arises from a freedom to pursue rigorous evaluation without submitting to political pressures that might compromise the quality of the work. Their objectivity relates to an impartiality with regard to methodology, conduct and interpretation of findings (Markiewicz, 2008). These aims were not able to be met in this case study and caused significant dissonance within the team, and between the team and the executives commissioning the research project.

While evaluators have strong methodological backgrounds that equip them to pursue unbiased research, they also need to be aware that their work is carried out in politicised contexts and that the outcomes of their evaluations have a high level of application to the positions of individual stakeholders (Chelimsky, 2008; Markiewicz, 2005). By understanding and acknowledging the political context of their work, evaluators need to select approaches and methods that will maximise the benefits of their evaluations (Slattery, 2010) and attempt to preserve their independence and objectivity (Markiewicz, 2008). The adoption of the case-study methodology and empowerment evaluation approach were the option that this team took to achieve this in this instance.

The literature offers few strategies to evaluators working strictly inside agencies and government departments to address the politics that infiltrate evaluations they undertake. A few authors (Chelimsky, 2008; Simons, 1995), though, have suggested various strategies that can be employed by researchers and evaluators undertaking contract work for such agencies and departments.

Chelimsky's (2008) strategies for evaluators working within a political context are suggested as a means of preserving the credibility of their evaluations. She suggests the following:

1. Expand the design phase.

   Including an analysis of program histories and values, past and present political controversies, and an account of probable stakeholder positions with respect to the evaluation can highlight any elements of the evaluation design that may be considered politically or methodologically weak. It also enables the evaluator to focus upon the elements of the evaluation design so that they can defend its credibility both politically and technically.

2. When relevant, include public groups.

   The credibility of an evaluation is enhanced when the perspectives of public groups are included, especially when they possess important knowledge that helps to inform the evaluation questions. There may be occasions when there is stakeholder conflict within a program, however this is the very time when the opinions of a diversity of public groups needed to be included, thereby averting the risk that some views may overwhelm others.

3. Lean heavily on negotiation.

   The ability to negotiate enables the evaluator to overcome things such as vagueness about evaluation issues, unclear work feasibility, and uncertainty about the dissemination of findings and use of the final report. Sometimes in the face of political pressure, the willingness to negotiate represents an unwillingness to be intimidated.

4. Never stop pursuing credibility.

   An evaluation needs to be technically transparent, defensible, and objective and needs to be perceived by others as such. These can be achieved through: the selection of appropriate methods; an honesty of reporting the confidence in the data and analysis; the clarity of how findings flow from the data and do not exceed them; and neutrality in the language and presentation of the report.

5. Develop a dissemination strategy.

   Ensure that the evaluation report is focused and free of jargon and able to be understood by policy makers as well as members of the public. Prepare an individual dissemination strategy for every evaluation that may include: articles in journals; simple statements of findings to relevant interest groups; and briefings to reporters and other organisations. When the findings are especially politically displeasing, the dissemination strategy helps to ensure that the findings are heard.

These strategies are more effective when the evaluator who is contracted to undertake the work is outside the organisation commissioning the work, and the work is conducted, ostensibly, to inform the public. If the evaluation is to provide information for policy use, there may be no need for a dissemination strategy. Greater difficulties arise when the evaluator works inside the organisation, especially when it is a government agency. Because of the nature of some evaluation contracts, evaluators may be powerless to disseminate or publish findings of their work without agency permission (Chelimsky, 2008). Evaluators of government programs or policies must also be cognisant that some reports may not even be acted on due to the political landscape into which the report is forwarded (Schram & Soss, 2001). This was the scenario that impacted on the evaluators who conducted the rigorous, longitudinal study described in case study 2.

## 15.3.2 Case study 2

This evaluation, in contrast to the previous case, was a longitudinal study that utilised a scientifically rigorous methodology to critically investigate the impact of an educational initiative on a broad range of school and student outcomes. This methodology incorporated large samples across multiple cohorts using control groups that were matched across a range of factors identified as influencing student outcomes, so that effects of these variables could be minimised. Multiple quantitative and qualitative measures were used at an individual, rather than aggregated, level to allow for corroboration of data and outcomes analysed across sub-groups of students to determine if there were differentiated effects for some groups.

This educational initiative was of key strategic import for the current government in regard to shaping future educational strategy and promotion of standards. Significant funds had been invested over a number of years into infrastructure to support the initiative on the basis of a worldwide educational trend that had not been rigorously researched. The resulting report and subsequent ministerial briefings challenged the current strategic direction and provided information that could be interpreted as in opposition to preferred ministerial strategy. Initially, the methodology was questioned with a suggestion that the findings were not rigorous or reliable. However, as this was not the case and could not be sustained, the report was subsequently shelved for over 12 months rather than being published. As a consequence the sound evidence was unable to be considered for the development of policy related to the initiative. Given the complexity of issues surrounding the initiative and related initiatives, the report was eventually released 18 months later with caveats regarding its interpretation on related initiatives that it was not commissioned to evaluate or inform. It was then able to be utilised to inform strategic policy in education in regard to the specific initiative investigated.

Two strategies offered by Simons (1995) address evaluations conducted for government and non-government agencies, especially with regard to the publication of findings. First of all, she suggests that when politics become involved in evaluations conducted for government agencies the evaluator could simply accept the agency's requests entirely and do the work, and not be at all concerned about whether the findings will be published. This is a position that is accepted by many, however it does not ensure any professional check on the quality of the work or ensure that mechanisms are in place to allow access to or publication of the findings. In this case, whilst the evaluation team accepted the requirement not to publish, the professional check on quality was countered via delivery of an unpublished paper at a national conference that discussed the methodology but omitted all results. The paper was highly commended by peers and won an evaluation award which confirmed the veracity and rigour of the work.

Simons' (1995) second strategy may be considered extreme by some and relates to the publication or release of findings. She suggests that evaluators take on evaluation work and sign contracts where necessary. Then, regardless of any contractual restrictions on the release of findings, employ various mechanisms to ensure that this occurs. She suggests using tactics such as leaking findings, seeking to have questions raised in parliament, and sending anonymous letters and articles to the press. Such tactics involve a high degree of risk for those working within government in regard to job security, and Gower and Partington (Chapter 12) indicate that this is not without risk for a university tenderer, as it can result in not being considered for future work. Since Simons' (1995) original writing, there is now much greater scope to publish online and create online or social media discussion on various matters.

Mohan and Sullivan (2006) contend that evaluators need to recognise the various political pressures present in the milieu of their work, identify the key sponsors and stakeholders, and have an understanding of the interactions among those key players who often have competing and conflicting interests in the outcomes of evaluations. They argue that evaluators need to have a measure of both impartiality and responsiveness. It is the impartiality of evaluators' work that gives their reports prestige and credibility, and their responsiveness to stakeholders' perspectives and positions that help to ensure that evaluation reports have some usage.

Mohan and Sullivan (2006) suggest various strategies for addressing the politics present in evaluations as means of maximising impartiality and responsiveness. These strategies include:

- consulting extensively with policy-makers to identify their evaluation questions and other information needs;
- considering the political context, such as agency sensitivity to issues that form the focus of the evaluation;
- identifying and understanding the relationships among key stakeholders;
- managing the project's scope to ensure the feasibility of work completion within the designated time frame;
- responding to sponsors' and stakeholders' needs for information;
- carefully assessing the pros and cons of obtaining certain information, if required, through exercising statutory authority of appropriate evaluation offices; and
- using professional standards to guide the evaluation work.

Brandon et al.'s (2010) congressionally mandated evaluation of Title V abstinence education programs being delivered in US schools won an American Evaluation Association Best Evaluation Award in 2009 due to its balance of impartiality and responsiveness to stakeholders. Both the program and the evaluation took place in a politically and ideologically contentious climate, but the evaluation contained a number of features that contributed to its consideration of being a model of exemplary practice. A higher profile and significant circumstance, but similar situation to case study 2 above.

With respect to independence and impartiality, the methodology of Brandon et al.'s (2010) evaluation and case study 2 were technically sound and the evaluators included a large sample. In both cases during the term of the evaluation, the evaluators themselves recognised and considered several potential threats to the integrity of the study and they took immediate steps to mitigate them. When the work of the evaluation was labelled as being biased or flawed, the evaluators addressed such criticisms immediately. As a means of being responsive to stakeholders, the evaluators established a technical work group which operated as a reference group and consisted of people who were trusted by the community and represented a range of perspectives and expertise. The evaluators engaged in constant contact with the reference group and ensured that all members of the group clearly understood and appreciated the evaluation design and the program outcomes that were being measured. The technical work group was also provided with ongoing evaluation briefings as well as preliminary results. At the conclusion of the evaluation, the team of evaluators worked with a government deputy secretary or senior executive officer whose communications and public relations skills were used to help facilitate the release of the report.

The issues of evaluator impartiality and responsiveness are also addressed by Vestman and Conner (2006) in their model of three positions in which politics and evaluation are connected, and the strategies they offer to address each position. Their model relates to whether it is possible and/or desirable to separate politics from evaluation.

Vestman and Conner's (2006) first position is that it is desirable and possible to separate politics and evaluation with the aim of producing objective and neutral evaluation findings. In pursuing this objective, they suggest that evaluators:

- determine who has commissioned the evaluation and the motivation and reasons for the undertaking of an evaluation;
- uncover all aspects of the policy or program and involve participants who are officially as well as unofficially involved in it;
- develop peer review procedures;
- utilise expert panels and/or outside consultants in the entire evaluation process;
- wherever possible, use established and credible testing and assessment instruments;

- include a "limitations" section in the report that discusses any political influences and critical decisions made during the evaluation that may impact on the findings.

The second position as viewed by Vestman and Conner (2006) relates to it being desirable and possible to separate politics and evaluation with respect to the provision of information but not with respect to the provision of judgements. In this position, the authors suggest that evaluators seek to understand the political context in which the policy or program is situated and the information needs of those commissioning the evaluation. Vestman and Conner's (2006) third position is that it is neither desirable nor possible to separate politics and evaluation, in which case the evaluator is unable to adopt a neutral perspective because judgements are involved. In this instance, the evaluator accepts the involvement of politics. This was clearly the position accepted by Gaitskell (Chapter 11) in relation to evaluation of boards.

## 15.4 Conclusion

Researchers and evaluators seek to deliver neutral and unbiased results about the work they undertake through adopting technically sound methodologies and work practices. The reality is, though, that evaluation operates in highly politicised and interests-driven environments and is inevitably influenced and affected by them.

Evaluators should be encouraged not to ignore the politics or pretend to be immune to politics involved with their work, but to face the reality that politics are present (Mohan & Sullivan, 2006) and be armed with strategies to deal with the intersection of those politics and their undertaking of evaluation.

This and the preceding chapters have discussed a number of ways in which the researcher and evaluator can encounter the incursion of politics on their work. It has also offered a range of perspectives, issues and strategies for the researcher and evaluator to consider and to implement to guard against any potential political inroads and to address any political trespass that may occur during the conduct of a piece of research or evaluation. Ultimately, it is up to the researcher and evaluator to be mindful of the potential of politics to become involved in their work, recognise when politics is becoming involved, and to take steps, as necessary and appropriate, to constructively address any political encounter.

# References

Abma, T. & Schwandt, T. (2005). The practice and politics of sponsored evaluations. In B. Somekh and C. Lewin (Eds.), *Research methods in the social sciences*, 105–112. London: Sage.

Abramo, G., Cicero, T., & D'Angelo, C. A. (2011). The dangers of performance-based research funding in non-competitive higher education systems. *Scientometrics*, 87 (3), 641–654.

Adelle, C., Jordan, A., & Turnpenny, J. (2012). Proceeding in parallel or drifting apart? A systematic review of policy appraisal research and practices. *Environment and Planning C*, 30 (3), 401.

Adie, L. (2008). The hegemonic positioning of 'Smart State' policy. *Journal of Education Policy*, 23 (3), May 2008, 251–264.

Ahmed, M. (2005). Bridging research and policy. *Journal of International Development*, 17, 765–773.

Allen, C. (2005). On the social relations of contract research production. *Housing Studies*, 20 (6), 989–1007.

Alton-Lee, A. (2007). The iterative best evidence synthesis programme, New Zealand. In *Evidence in education: linking research and policy*. Paris, Centre for Educational Research and Innovation: OECD.

Alton-Lee, A. (2012). The use of evidence to improve education and serve the public good. Paper prepared for the New Zealand Ministry of Education and the annual meeting of the American Educational Research Association, Vancouver, Canada, April 2012.

Alvino, L. A. (2003). Who's watching the watchdogs? Responding to the erosion of research ethics by enforcing promises. *Columbia Law Review*, 103, 893–924.

Amos, S. K, Keiner, E., Proske, M. & Radtke, F. (2002). Globalisation: autonomy of education under siege? Shifting Boundaries between politics, economy and education. *European Educational Research Journal*, 1 (2), 193–213.

Andersen, H. C. (1837). *The Emperor's new clothes*. Available at: http://hca.gilead.org.il/emperor.html

Anderson, S., Leithwood, K., Louis, K. & Wahlstrom, K. (2010). *Investigating the links to improved student learning*. Final Report on the Learning from Leadership Project to The Wallace Foundation, Center for Applied Research and Educational Improvement, The University of Minnesota and Ontario Institute for Studies in Education, University of Toronto.

Ang, I. (2006). From cultural studies to cultural research: engaged scholarship in the twenty-first century. *Cultural Studies Review*, 12 (2), 183–197.

Angel, R., Reitzug, U. & West, D. (2008). Conceptualising instructional leadership: the voices of principals. *Education and Urban Society*, 40 (6), 694–714.

Angelo, T. A. & Cross, K. P. (1993). *Classroom assessment techniques*. San Francisco: Jossey-Bass.

Anholt, S. (2009). *Places: identity, image and reputation*. London: Palgrave.

Annas, G. J. (1992). The changing landscape of human experimentation: Nuremberg, Helsinki, and beyond. *Health Matrix*, 2 (2), 119–140.

Annas, G. J. & Grodin, M. A. (1992). *The Nazi doctors and the Nuremberg Code: human rights in human experimentation*. New York: Oxford University Press.

Argyris, C. & Schön, D. (1974). *Theory in practice: increasing professional effectiveness*. San Francisco: Jossey-Bass.

Armstrong, K. & Kendall, E. (2010). Translating knowledge into practice and policy: the role of knowledge networks in primary health care. *Health Information Management Journal*, 39 (2), 9.

Aronczyk, M. (2013). *Branding the nation: mediating space, value and identity in global culture*. New York: Oxford University Press.

Åström, F. (2014). The context of paratext: a bibliometric study of the citation contexts of Gérard Genette's texts. In N. Desrichers & D. Apollon (Eds.), *Examining paratextual theory and its applications in digital culture*, 1–23. Hershey, PA: IGI Global.

Atkinson, E. (2000). In defence of ideas, or why 'what works' is not enough. *British Journal of Sociology of Education*, 21 (3), 317–330.

Australasian Evaluation Society. (2014, December 18). AES code of ethics and professional practice. Retrieved from Australasian Evaluation Society: http://www.aes.asn.au/join-the-aes/membership-ethical-guidelines/7-aes-codes-of-behaviour-ethics.html

Australia Department of Finance. (2015). National collaboration framework. Downloaded from http://www.finance.gov.au/resource-management/cooperation/ncf/ on 13 October 2015.

Australian Government. (2010). *National standards for mental health services*. Commonwealth of Australia.

Australian Research Council. (2014). Glossary of terms for research impact. Retrieved from http://www.arc.gov.au/general/impact.htm on 17 July 2014.

Babbie, E. (2014). *The basics of social research*. Belmont, CA: Wadsworth.

Baehr, M. (2005). Distinctions between assessment and evaluation. *Program Assessment Handbook*, 7.

Baez, B. (2002). Confidentiality in qualitative research: reflections on secrets, power and agency. *Qualitative Research*, 2 (1), 35–58.

Ball, S. (2008). *The education debate*. Bristol: The Policy Press.

Ball, S. (2012). *Global Education Inc. new policy networks and the neo-liberal imaginary*. Abingdon: Routledge.

Ball, S. J. (1998). Big policies/small world: an introduction to international perspectives in education policy. *Comparative Education*, 34 (2), 119–130.

Ball, S. J. (2001). 'You've been NERFed!' Dumbing down the academy: National Educational Research Forum: 'a national strategy consultation paper': a brief and bilious response. *Journal of Education Policy*, 16 (3), 265–268.

Ball, S. J. (2010). New voices, new knowledges and the new politics of education research: the gathering of a perfect storm? *European Educational Research Journal*, 9 (2), 124–137.

Bansel, P. (2015). A narrative approach to policy analysis. In Gulson, K., Clarke, M. & Petersen, E. B. (Eds.), *Education policy and contemporary theory*. New York: Routledge.

Barber, M., Whelan, F. & Clark, M. (2010). Capturing the leadership premium. *Mckinsey & Company report*, 1–33. Retrieved from: http:// mckinseyonsociety.com/capturing-the-leadership-premium/

Barcan, R. (2014). *Academic life and labour in the new university: hope and other choices*. Farnham: Ashgate.

Barlow, A. (2005). Evaluation: what is it really for? *Evaluation Journal of Australasia*, 5 (1), 11–17.

Barnhouse Walters, P., Lareau, A. & Ranis, S. H. (2009). *Educational research on trial: policy reform and the call for scientific rigor*. New York: Routledge.

Barroso, J. (2005). Les nouveaux modes de régulation des politiques éducatives en Europe: de la régulation du système à un système de régulations. In Dutercq, Y. (Ed.), *Les régulations des politiques d'éducation*. Rennes: Presses Universitaires de Rennes, 151–171.

Barton, A. (2002). Evaluation research as passive and apolitical? Some reflections from the field. *Social Research Methodology*, 5 (4), 371–378.

Bastow, S., Dunleavy, P., & Tinkler, J. (2014). *The impact of the social sciences: how academics and their research make a difference*. London: Sage.

Bazeley, P. (2003). Defining 'early career' in research. *Higher Education*, 45 (3), 257–279.

Bazerman, M. H. & Gino, F. (2012). Behavioral ethics: toward a deeper understanding of moral judgment and dishonesty. *Annual Review of Law and Social Science*, (8), 85–104.

Bence, V. & Oppenheim, C. (2005). The evolution of the UK's research assessment exercise: publications, performance and perceptions. *Journal of Educational Administration and History*, 37 (2), 137–155.

Bennis, W. G. & O'Toole, J. (2005). How business schools lost their way. *Harvard Business Review*, 83 (5), 96–104.

Berg, M. (1997). *Rationalizing medical work: decision support techniques and medical practices*. Cambridge, MA: MIT Press.

Besley, A. C. (2008). *Assessing the quality of educational science in higher education*. Rotterdam: Sense Publications.

Beyrer, C. & Kass, N. E. (2002). Human rights, politics, and reviews of research ethics. *Lancet*, 360, 246–251.

Biesta, G. (2007). Why 'what works' won't work: evidence-based practice and the democratic deficit in educational research, *Educational Theory*, 57 (1), 1–22.

Biesta, G. (2009). Good education in an age of measurement: on the need to reconnect with the question of purpose in education. *Educational Assessment, Evaluation and Accountability*, 21 (1), 33–46.

Bitan-Friedlander, N., Dreyfus, A. & Milgrom, Z. (2004). Types of 'teachers in training': the reactions of primary school science teachers when confronted with the task of implementing an innovation. *Teaching and Teacher Education*, 20, 607–619.

Bledsoe, C. H., Sherin, B., Galinsky, A. G. et al. (2007). Regulating creativity: research and survival in the IRB iron cage. *Northwestern Law Rev.*, 101 (2), 593–642.

Boaz, A., Fitzpatrick, S. & Shaw, B. (2008). *Assessing the impact of research on policy: a review of the literature for a project on bridging research and policy through outcome evaluation*. Policy Studies Institute. London: Kings College.

Boaz, A., Grayson, L., Levitt, R. & Solesbury, W. (2008). Does evidence-based policy work? Learning from the UK experience. *Evidence & Policy: A Journal of Research, Debate and Practice*, 4 (2), 233–253.

Bobis, J., Shore, S., Bennett, D., Bennett, S., Chan, P., Harrison, N. & Seddon, T. (2013). Education research in Australia: where is it conducted? *The Australian Educational Researcher*, 40 (4), 453–471.

Bok, S. (1989). *Secrets*. New York: Vintage Books.

Bølstad, J. (2014). I hurtigforskningens tid. *Aftenposten*. Retrieved from http://www.aftenposten.no/viten/I-hurtigforskningens-tid-7424856.html

Borgatti, S. P., Everett, M. & Freeman, L. C. (2002). *Ucinet for Windows: software for social network analysis*. Harvard, MA: Analytic Technologies.

Borko, H., Davinroy, K. H., Bliem, C. L. & Cumbo, K. B. (2000). Exploring and supporting teacher change: two third-grade teachers' experiences in a mathematics and literacy staff development project. *The Elementary School Journal*, 100 (4), 273–306.

Bossert, S., Dwyer, D., Rowan, B. & Lee, G. (1982). The instructional management role of the principal. *Educational Administration Quarterly*, 18 (3), 34–64.

Boulton, G. & Lucas, C. (2011). What are universities for? *Chinese Science Bulletin*, 56 (23), 2506–2517.

Bourdieu, P. (2001). *Science de la science et réflexivité*. Paris: Raisons d'agir.

Bowe, R., Ball, S. & Gold, A. (1992). *Reforming education and changing schools: case studies in policy sociology*. London: Routledge.

Boyatzis, R. E. (1998). *Transforming qualitative information: thematic analysis and code development*. London: Sage.

Brandon, P., Smith, N., Trenholm, C. & Devaney, B. (2010). Evaluation exemplar: the critical importance of stakeholder relations in a national, experimental abstinence education evaluation. *American Journal of Evaluation*, 31 (4), 517–531.

Bredeson, P. (2013). Distributed instructional leadership in urban high schools: transforming the work of principals and department chairs through professional development. *Journal of School Leadership*, 23, 362–390.

Brewer, J. D. (2011). The impact of impact. *Research Evaluation*, 20 (3), 255–256. doi: 10.3152/095820211x12941371876869.

Bridges, D. (2003). *Fiction written under oath: essays in philosophy and educational research*. The Netherlands: Kluwer Academic Publishers.

Broadbent, G. (2014). Legal Education Research Network (LERN) workshop: What's the point if no-one knows about your research? Embedding effective dissemination into research design, 5 Nov 2014, London.

Broady, D., Börjesson, M., Dalberg, T., Krigh, J. & Lidegran, I. (2011). *Inventering av svensk utbildningsvetenskaplig forskning. Redovisning av ett uppdrag för vetenskapsrådets utbildningsvetenskapliga kommitté*. (An inventory of educational science in Sweden.) UVK rapport 2011-03-16.

Brown, C. (2009). *Effective research communication and its role in the development of evidence-based policy making: A case study of the training and development agency for schools*. Unpublished MRes Dissertation, University of London, Institute of Education.

Brown, C. (2011). *What factors affect the adoption of research within educational policy making? How might a better understanding of these factors improve research adoption and aid the development of policy?* Unpublished DPhil Dissertation, University of Sussex.

Brown, C. (2012a). The 'policy-preferences model': a new perspective on how researchers can facilitate the take-up of evidence by educational policy makers. *Evidence & Policy: A Journal of Research, Debate and Practice*, 8 (4), 455–472.

Brown, C. (2012b). The policy agora: how the epistemological and ideological preferences of policy-makers affect the development of government policy. *Human Welfare*, 1, 57–70.

Brown, C. (2013). *Making evidence matter: new perspectives on evidence-informed policy making in education*. London: IOE Press.

Brown, C. (2014). *Evidence-informed policy and practice in education: a sociological underpinning*. London: Bloomsbury.

Brown, C. (2015). *Evidence-informed policy and practice in education: a sociological grounding*. London: Bloomsbury Publishing.

Brown, J. S., Collins, A. & Duguid, P. (1989). Situated cognition and the culture of learning. *Educational Researcher*, 18 (1), 32–42.

Brown, R. H. & Schubert, J. D. (2000). *Knowledge and power in higher education: a reader*. New York: Teachers College Press.

Brown, R. H. & Malone, E. L. (2004). Reason, politics, and the politics of truth: how science is both autonomous and dependent. *Sociological Theory*, 22 (1).

Brown, W. (2003). Neo-liberalism and the end of liberal democracy. *Theory and Event*, 7, 1–43.

Brownson, R. C. & Jones, E. (2009). Bridging the gap: translating research into policy and practice. *Preventive Medicine*, 49 (4), 313–315.

Bruford, W. H. (1975). *The German tradition of self-cultivation: Bildung from Humboldt to Thomas Mann*. Cambridge: Cambridge University Press.

Butler, D. (2008). Translational research: crossing the valley of death. *Nature*, 453 (11 June). Retrieved from http://www.nature.com/news/2008/080611/full/453840a.html on 30 September 2014.

Butler, N. & Spoelstra, S. (2015). *How the REF's regime of excellence is changing research for the worse* (6 February). Retrieved from https://theconversation.com/how-the-refs-regime-of-excellence-is-changing-research-for-the-worse-37187 on 16 February 2015.

Buxton, M. (2011). The payback of 'payback': challenges in assessing research impact. *Research Evaluation*, 20 (3), 259–260.

Buxton, M. & Hanney, S. (1994). *Assessing payback from Department of Health research and development: preliminary report*. HERG research report.

Buykx, P., Humphreys, J., Wakerman, J., Perkins, D., Lyle, D., McGrail, M. & Kinsman, L. (2012). 'Making evidence count': a framework to monitor the impact of health services research. *Australian Journal of Rural Health*, 20 (2), 51–58. doi: 10.1111/j.1440-1584.2012.01256.x

Cabinet Office. (2001). *Better policy-making*. London: Cabinet Office.

Cabinet Office. (1999). *Modernising government*. London: The Stationery Office.

Cabinet Office. (2001). *Professional policy-making for the twenty-first century*. London: Cabinet Office.

Cai, Y. & Kivistö, J. (2010). *Towards a fee-based education Finland: Where to go?* Paper presented at the Organisation for Economic Co-operation and Development Institutional Management Higher Education.

Calandar, F. (2004). *Mellan Akademi och Profession: nitton svenska lärarutbildares berättelser om lärarutbildning igår och idag*. Lärom-rapport 4. Uppsala Universitet: Department of Education.

Caldwell, B. J. & Lewis, J. (2005). Evidence-based leadership. *The Educational Forum*, 69 (2), 182.

Calver, M. & Beattie, A. (2015). *Our obsession with metrics is corrupting science*. The Conversation. https://theconversation.com/our-obsession-with-metrics-is-corrupting-science-39378

Cambrosio, A., Keating, P. & Bourret, P. (2007). Objectivité régulatoire et systèmes de preuves en médecine: le cas de la cancérologie. In V. Tournay (Ed.), *La gouvernance des innovations biomédicales*. Paris: Presses Universitaires de France, 155–175.

Campbell, D. T. & Stanley, J. (1963). *Experimental and quasi-experimental designs for research*. Chicago: Rand McNally.

Campbell, D. T. (1969). Reforms as experiments. *American Psychologist*, 24, 409–429.

Cantwell, B. & Kauppinen, I. (Eds.) (2014). *Academic capitalism in the age of globalization*. Baltimore, MD: John Hopkins University Press.

Carden, F. (2004). Issues in assessing the policy influence of research. *International Social Science Journal*, 56 (179), 135–151.

Cardno, C. (2010). Focusing educational leadership on creating learning conditions that sustain productive relationships: the case of a New Zealand primary school. *Leading and Managing*, 16 (1), 40–57.

Carney, S. (2009). Negotiating policy in an age of globalization: exploring educational 'policyscapes' in Denmark, Nepal, and China. *Comparative Education Review*, 53 (1), 63–88.

Carpenter, C. (2012). 'You talk of terrible things so matter-of-factly in this language of science': constructing human rights in the academy. *Perspectives on Politics*, 10 (2), 363–383.

CBR Country Brand Report. (2010). *Mission for Finland: final report of the country brand delegation*.

Chan, A.-W., Song, F., Vickers, A., Jefferson, T., Dickersin, K., Gøtzsche, P. C. & van der Worp, H. B. (2014). Increasing value and reducing waste: addressing inaccessible research. *The Lancet*, 383 (9913), 257–266.

Chandler, C. (2014). What is the meaning of impact in relation to research and why does it matter? A view from inside academia. In P. Denicolo (Ed.), *Achieving impact in research*. London: Sage.

Charle, C., Schriewer, J. & Wagner, P. (2004). Preface. In Charle, C., Schriewer, J. & Wagner, P. (Eds.), *Transnational intellectual networks: forms of academic knowledge and the search for cultural identities*, 9–14. Frankfurt/New York: Campus Verlag.

Chelimsky, E. (2007). Factors influencing the choice of methods in federal evaluation practice. *New Directions for Evaluation*, 113, 13–33.

Chelimsky, E. (2008). A clash of cultures: improving the 'fit' between evaluative independence and the political requirements of a democratic society. *American Journal of Evaluation*, 29 (4), 400–415.

Cherney, A., Povey, J., Head, B., Boreham, P. & Ferguson, M. (2012). What influences the utilisation of educational research by policy-makers and practitioners? The perspectives of academic educational researchers. *International Journal of Educational Research*, http://dx.doi.org/10.1016/j.ijer.2012.08.001.

Chillcott, T. (2009). Queensland schools again among the worst NAPLAN performers. *The Courier-Mail*, 11 September 2009. Retrieved from http://www.couriermail.com.au/news/queensland-schools-again-among-worst-naplan-performers/story-e6freon6-1225771851143.

Chomsky, N. & Foucault, M. (1974). Human nature: justice versus power. In Elders, F. (Ed.), *Reflexive water: the basic concerns of mankind*. London: Souvenir Press.

Chuang, H.-C. (2008). Special education classes: legislators seek for solutions (1 April). *NOWnews*. Available [online] at: http://legacy.nownews.com/2008/04/01/11478-2253824.htm#ixzz2qMq7kylQ.

Chubb, J. (2014). How does the impact agenda fit with attitudes and ethics that motivate research? In Denicolo, P. (Ed.), *Achieving impact in research*. London: Sage.

Chung, J. (2015). International comparison and educational policy learning: looking north to Finland. *Compare*, 45 (3), 475–479.

Cleaver, F. & Franks, T. (2008). Distilling or diluting? Negotiating the water research-policy interface. *Water Alternatives*, 1 (1), 157–176.

Coburn, C. (2015). *Pathways from research to policy*. Keynote lecture, British Educational Research Association Conference, Queens University, Belfast, UK, 17 September 2015.

Cohen, L., Manion, L. & Keith, M. (2007). *Research methods in education*. New York: Routledge.

Cohen, L., Manion, L. & Morrison, K. (2011). *Research Methods in Education* (7th edn). Oxon: Routledge.

Cole, A. L. (2000). Academic freedom and the publish or perish paradox in schools of education. *Teacher Education Quarterly*, 27 (2), 33–48.

Commaille, J. (2006). Sociologie de l'action publique. In L. Boussaguet, S. Jacquot, & P. Ravinet, *Dictionnaire des politiques publiques*. Paris: Science Po, 415–423.

Commonwealth of Australia & Department of Industry Innovation Climate Change Science Research and Tertiary Education. (2013). Assessing the wider benefits arising from university-based research: discussion paper (Vol. June). Canberra.

Conlon, D., Gill, N., Tyler, I. & Oeppen, C. (2014). Impact as odyssey. *ACME: An International E-Journal for Critical Geographies*, 13 (1), 33–38.

Court, J. & Young, J. (2003). Bridging research and policy: insights from 50 case studies. *ODI Working Paper 213*. London: ODI.

Cranston, N. & Erich, L. with reflections by Lindsay, J. (2006). *Leadership matters – leadership capabilities for Education Queensland principals, technical paper*. Education Queensland. Retrieved from http://education.qld.gov.au/staff/development/docs/leadershipmatterstechpaper.doc

Cronin, B. (2010). *The hand of science: academic writing and its rewards*. Lanham, MD: Scarecrow Press.

Crozier, M., & Friedberg, E. (1977). *L'acteur et le systéme*. Paris: Èditions du Seuil.

Curtis, B. (2008). The performance-based research fund: research assessment and funding in New Zealand. *Globalisation, societies and education*, 6 (2), 179–194.

Czarnitzki, D., Grimpe, C. & Toole, A. (2011). *Delay and secrecy: does industry sponsorship jeopardise disclosure of academic research?* Department of Managerial Economics, Strategy and Innovation, Katholieke Universiteit Leuven.

Dahllöf, U. (1989). Doctoral studies and public policies affecting the labour market for PhDs in Norway and Sweden. *Scandinavian Journal of Educational Research*, 33 (3), 165–184.

Dale, R. (2005). Globalisation, knowledge economy and comparative education. *Comparative Education*, 41 (2), 117–149.

Dale, R., & Robertson, S. (Eds.). (2009). *Globalisation and Europeanisation in education*. Didcot: Symposium Books.

Davies H. T. O., Nutley, S. M. & Smith, P. C. (2007). *What works? Evidence-based policy and practice in public services*, Bristol: The Policy Press.

Davies, B. (2000). *A body of writing 1990–1999*. Walnut Creek: AltaMira Press.

Davies, B. & Petersen, E. (2005) Intellectual workers (un)doing neoliberal discourse. *International Journal of Critical Psychology*, 13, 32–54.

Davies, B., & Bansel, P. (2005). The time of their lives? Academic workers in neoliberal time(s). *Health Sociology Review*, 14 (1), 47–58.

Davies, B. & Bansel, P. (2010). Governmentality and academic work: shaping the hearts and minds of academic workers. *Journal of curriculum theorizing*, 26 (3).

Davies, H., Nutley, S. & Walter, I. (2005). *Assessing the impact of social science research: conceptual, methodological and practical issues*. Paper presented at the ESRC Symposium on Assessing Non-Academic Impact of Research, London.

Davies, P. (2006). *Scoping the challenge: a systems approach*. National Forum on Knowledge Transfer and Exchange Toronto Canada, 23–24 October 2006. Available at: www.chsrf.ca/migrated/pdf/event_reports/philip_davies.ppt.pdf, accessed 14 August 2015.

Declaration of Constitution of the Council of Education Research Centres. (2010). http://webs.ie.uminho.pt/ccce/declara%C3%A7%C3%A3o%20constituicao.htm

Deem, R. & Brehony, K. J. (2005). Management as ideology: the case of 'new managerialism' in higher education. *Oxford Review of Education*, 31 (2), 217–235.

Denzin, N. K. (2009). The elephant in the living room: or extending the conversation about the politics of evidence. *Qualitative Research*, 9 (2), 139–160.

Department of Education Training and The Arts (DETA). (2007a). *Principals' leadership and capabilities framework*. Department of Education and Training. Published by the Queensland Government, 61 Mary Street, Brisbane Qld 4000.

Department of Education, Training and The Arts (DETA). (2007b). *Leadership matters: leadership capabilities for Education Queensland principals*. Queensland Government. Retrieved from http://education.qld.gov.au/staff/development/docs/leadershipmatterspdf.pdf

Department of Education Training and The Arts (DETA). (2010). *Principals' leadership and capabilities framework*. Department of Education and Training. Published by the Queensland Government, 61 Mary Street, Brisbane Qld 4000.

Department of Education Training and The Arts (DETA). (2011a). *United in our pursuit of excellence: agenda for improvement 2011–2015 document*. Department of Education and Training. Published by the Queensland Government, 61 Mary Street, Brisbane Qld 4000.

Department of Education Training and The Arts (DETA). (2011b). *Principal supervision and capability development*. Department of Education and Training. Published by the Queensland Government, 61 Mary Street, Brisbane Qld 4000.

Department of Education Training and Employment (DETE). (2012). *School planning, reviewing and reporting framework 2012–2015*. Department of Education and Training. Published by the Queensland Government, 61 Mary Street, Brisbane Qld 4000. Retrieved from http://education.qld.gov.au/strategic/accountability/pdf/sprr-framework.pdf

Department of Education, Training and Employment. (DETE). (2013). *Great teachers = GREAT results: a direct action plan for Queensland schools*. Queensland Government.

Department of Education, Training and Youth Affairs. (2000). *National English literacy and numeracy strategy*. Canberra: Department of Education, Training and Youth Affairs.

Department of Innovation Industry Science and Research. (2011). *Focusing Australia's publicly funded research review: maximising the innovation dividend review key findings and future direction*.

Department of the Prime Minister and Cabinet. (2014). *Reform of the federation white paper: Issues paper 1* (September). Canberra: Commonwealth of Australia.

Dervin, F. (2013). *La meilleure éducation au monde? Contre-enquête sur la Finlande*. Paris: L'Harmattan.

Dervin, F. (2015). Towards post-intercultural teacher education: analysing 'extreme' intercultural dialogue to reconstruct interculturality. *European Journal of Teacher Education*, 38 (1), 71–86.

Dill, D. D. (2014). Public policy design and university reform: insights into academic change. In *Reforming Higher Education*, 21–37. Netherlands: Springer.

Dinham, S. (2011). Breakthroughs in school leadership development in Australia. *School Leadership & Management*, 31 (2), 139.

Doornbos, M. (2012). Research, policy and politics: connections, collusions and collisions. *Administrative Culture*, 13 (1), 39–48.

Dostaler, I. & Tomberlin, T. J. (2013). The great divide between business schools research and business practice. *Canadian Journal of Higher Education*, 43 (1), 115–128.

Drysdale, L. & Gurr, D. (2012). Tensions and dilemmas in leading Australia's schools. *School Leadership & Management*, 32 (5), 403–420.

Duckett, P., Sixsmith, J. & Kagan, C. (2008). Researching pupil well-being in UK secondary schools: community psychology and the politics of research. *Childhood*, 15 (1), 89–106.

Dudgeon, P., Kelly, K. & Walker, R. (2010). Closing the gap in and through Indigenous health: guidelines, processes, and practices. *Australian Aboriginal Studies*, 2, 81–91.

Duignan, P. (2004). Forming capable leaders: from competence to capabilities. *New Zealand Journal of Educational Leadership*, 19 (2), 5–13.

duToit, B. M. (1980). Ethics, informed consent, and fieldwork. *Journal of Anthropological Research*, 36 (3), 274–286.

Eco, U. (1989). *The open work*. Cambridge: Harvard University Press.

Edgar, F. & Geare, A. (2013). Factors influencing university research performance. *Studies in Higher Education*, 38 (5), 774–792.

Egginger, J.-G. (2013). Aux sources de l'Éden éducatif nordique. Images véhiculées en France de l'instruction primaire finlandaise au cours de la deuxième moitié du XIXe siècle (1851–1911). *Recherches en Education*, 16, 13–19.

Elliott, H. & Popay, J. (2000). How are policy makers using evidence? Models of research utilisation and local NHS policy making. *Journal of Epidemiology and Community Health*, 54 (6), 461–468.

Ellis, C., Adams, T. E. & Bochner, A. P. (2010). Autoethnography: an Overview [40 paragraphs]. *Forum Qualitative Sozialforschung/Forum: Qualitative Social Research*, 12 (1), http://nbn-resolving.de/urn:nbn:de:0114-fqs1101108.

Elmore, R. (1980). Backward mapping: implementation research and policy decisions. *Political Science Quarterly*, 94 (4), 601–616.

Emihovich, C. (1999). Compromised positions: the ethics and politics of designing research in the postmodern age. *Educational Policy*, 13 (1), 37–46.

Estabrooks, C. A., Floyd, J. A., Scott-Findlay, S., O'Leary, K. A. & Gushta, M. (2003). Individual determinants of research utilization: a systematic review. *Journal of Advanced Nursing*, 43 (5), 506–520.

European Commission. (2007). *Towards more knowledge-based policy and practice in education and training* (Commission staff working document). Brussels: Directorate-General for Education and Culture.

European Commission. (2008). *Scientific evidence for policy-making*. Luxembourg: Publications Office of the European Union.

European Commission. (2010). *Communicating research for evidence-based policymaking: a practical guide for researchers in socio-economic sciences and humanities*. Luxembourg: Publications Office of the European Union.

Eurostat. (2013). *Eurostat*. http://epp.eurostat.ec.europa.eu/portal/page/portal/eurostat/home/

Eurydice Network. (2012). *Entrepreneurship education in schools in europe*. Available at http://eacea.ec.europa.eu/education/eurydice/documents/thematic_reports/135EN.pdf, accessed 26 May 2012.

FCT. (2015). *About FCT*. http://www.fct.pt/index.phtml.en

Fetterman, D. & Bowman, C. (2002). Experiential education and empowerment evaluation: Mars rover educational program case example. *The Journal of Experiential Education*, 25 (2), 286–295.

Fetterman, D. & Eiler, M. (2001). *Empowerment evaluation and organizational learning: a path toward mainstreaming evaluation*. St Louis, MO: American Evaluation Association.

Fetterman, D. M. (2013). Empowerment evaluation: learn to think like an evaluator. In Alkin, M. C. *Evaluation roots: a wider perspective of theorists' views and influences*, 304–322. Thousand Oaks, CA: Sage.

Finnish Ministry of Education and Culture. (2010). *Finnish education export strategy: Summary of the strategic lines and measures*. Helsinki: Ministry of Education and Culture. http://www.minedu.fi/export/sites/default/OPM/Julkaisut/2010/liitteet/okm12.pdf?lang=en

Fitzgerald, T. (2012). Tracing the fault lines. *International Perspectives on Higher Education Research*, 7, 1–22.

Fontana, A. & Frey, J. H. (2005). The interview: from neutral stance to political involvement. In Denzin, N. K. & Lincoln, Y. S. (Eds.) *The Sage handbook of qualitative research*. Thousand Oaks, CA: Sage.

Foucault, M. (1978). *The history of sexuality, vol 1: an introduction*. Harmondsworth: Penguin.

Foucault, M. (1980). *Power/knowledge: selected interviews and other writings, 1972–1977*. New York: Pantheon.

Foucault, M. (1988). Practicing criticism. In Kritzman, L. (Ed.), *Politics, philosophy, culture: interviews and other writings, 1977–1984*, 152–158. New York: Routledge.

Foucault, M. (2004). *Society must be defended*. London: Penguin.

Fransson, K. & Lundgren, U. P. (2003). Utbildningsvetenskap – ett begrepp och dess sammanhang (Educational Science – a concept and its context). *Rapport*, 2003: 1. Stockholm: Vetenskapsrådet. http://www.cm.se/webbshop_vr/pdfer/VR2003_1.pdf

Freeman, M. (2004). Data are everywhere: narrative criticism in the literature of experience. In Daiute, C. & Lightfoot, C. (Eds.), *Narrative analysis: studying the development of individuals in society*, 63–81. Thousand Oaks, CA: Sage.

Fujii, L. A. (2012). Research ethics 101: dilemmas and responsibilities. *PS: Political Science and Politics*, 45 (4), 717–723.

Fullan, M. & Levin, B. (2012). *Education Queensland system review: final report*. Education Queensland.

Fullan, M. (2010). The big ideas behind whole system reform. *Education Canada*, 50 (3), 24–27.

Furlong, J. & Lawn, M. (2011). *The disciplines of education: their role in the future of education research*. London & New York: Routledge.

Garrett-Jones, S. (2000). International trends in evaluating university research outcomes: what lessons for Australia? *Research Evaluation*, 9 (2), 115–124.

Gaultier, J. de (1902). *Bovarysme*. Paris: Mercure de France.

German Institute for International Educational Research (DIPF). (2007). *Knowledge for action: research strategies for an evidence-based education policy*. Frankfurt: Deutsche Institut für Internationale Pädagogische Forschung.

Gibbons, M. (1999). Science's new social contract with society. *Nature*, 404, C81–C84.

Gibbons, M., Limoges, C., Nowotny, H., Schwartzman, S., Scott, P. & Trow, M. (1994). *The new production of knowledge: the dynamics of science and research in contemporary societies*. London: Sage.

Giddens, A. (1990). *The consequences of modernity*. Stanford, CA: Stanford University Press.

Gieryn, T. F. (1983). Boundary-work and the demarcation of science from non-science: strains and interests in professional ideologies of scientists. *American Sociological Review*, 48 (6), 781–795.

Gillies, D. (2014). Knowledge activism: bridging the research/policy divide. *Critical Studies in Education*, 1–17.

Gino, F. & Bazerman, M. H. (2009). When misconduct goes unnoticed: the acceptability of gradual erosion in others' unethical behavior. *Journal of Experimental Social Psychology*, 45, 708–719.

Gino, F., Ayal, S. & Ariely, D. (2009). Contagion and differentiation in unethical behavior: the effect of one bad apple on the barrel. *Psychological Science*, 20, 393–398.

Girvan, C. & Savage, T. (2012). Ethical considerations for educational researchers in a virtual world. *Interactive Learning Environments*, 20 (3), 239–251.

Glass, G. (1987). What works: politics and research. *Educational Researcher*, 16 (5), 5–10.

Goldstein, H. (2004). International comparisons of student attainment: some issues arising from the PISA study. *Assessment in Education: Principles, Policy and Practice*, 11, 319–330.

González-López, G. (2011). Mindful ethics: comments on informant-centered practices in sociological research. *Qual. Sociol.*, 34, 447–461.

Goodson, I. (2006). The rise of the life narrative. *Teacher Education Quarterly*, 7–21.

Gorard, S. (2010). Political control: a way forward for educational research? *British Journal of Educational Studies*, 50 (3), 378–389.

Gordon, C. (2000). Introduction. In J. D. Faubion (Ed.), *Michel Foucault: power*, xi–xli. New York: The New Press.

Gough, D., Tripney, J., Kenny, C. & Buk-Berge, E. (2011). *Evidence informed policy in education in europe: EIPEE final project report*. London: EPPI-Centre, Social Science Research Unit, Institute of Education, University of London.

Greenwood, D. J. & Levin, M. (2000). Reconstructing the relationships between universities and society through action research. In Denzin, N. K. & Lincoln, Y. S. (Eds.). *Handbook of qualitative research* (2nd edn), 85–106. Thousand Oaks, CA: Sage.

Grek, S. (2009). Governing by numbers: the pisa 'effect' in Europe. *Journal of Education Policy*, 24 (1), 23–37.

Group of Eight. (2011). Measuring the impact of research: the context for metric development. In Rymer, L. (Ed.), *Go8 Backgrounder*. Turner: ACT.

Guenther, J., Williams, E. & Arnott, A. (2010). *The politics of evaluation: evidence-based policy or policy-based evidence?* Paper presented to the NARU Public Seminar Series, Darwin, 30 November 2010.

Guillemin, M. & Gillam, L. (2004). Ethics, responsibility, and 'ethically important moments' in research. *Qualitative Inquiry*, 10 (2), 261–280.

Gunasekara, C. (2006). Reframing the role of universities in the development of regional innovation systems. *The Journal of Technology Transfer*, 31 (1), 101–113.

Gunsalus, C. K. (2004). The nanny state meets the inner lawyer: overregulating while underprotecting human participants in research. *Ethics Behav.*, 14 (4), 369–382.

Gunter 3rd, H. (2012). Hard labour? Academic work and the changing landscape of higher education. *Academic Work and the Changing Landscape of Higher Education*, 7. Bingley: Emerald Group Publishing.

Gustavsson, S. (1971). *Debatten om forskningen och samhället: en studie i några teoretiska inlägg*. [The debates about research and society: a study of some theoretical articles]. Uppsala: Almqvist & Wicksell.

Guthrie, J. & Neumann, R. (2007). Economic and non-financial performance indicators in universities. *Public Management Review*, 9 (2), 231–252.

Habermas, J. (1990). *Moral consciousness and communicative action*. Cambridge, MA: MIT Press.

Habermas, J. & Cooke, M. (Ed.) (1999). *On the pragmatics of communication*. Cambridge, MA: MIT Press.

Hallinger, P. (2005). Instructional leadership and the school principal: a passing fancy that refuses to fade away. *Leadership and Policy in Schools*, 4 (3), 1–20.

Hammersley, M. (2002). *Educational research, policymaking and practice*. Thousand Oaks, CA: Sage.

Hammersley, M. (2013). *The myth of research-based policy and practice*. Thousand Oaks, CA: Sage.

Hargreaves, A. (2003). *Teaching in the knowledge society: education in the age of insecurity*. New York: Teachers College.

Hargreaves, A. & Fullan, M. (2000). Mentoring in the new millennium. *Theory into Practice*, 39 (1), 50–56.

Hargreaves, A. & Harris, A. (2011). *Performance beyond expectations*. Nottingham: National College for School Leadership.

Hargreaves, D. H. (1996). *Teaching as a research-based profession: possibilities and prospects*. London: Teacher Training Agency.

Hargreaves, David H. (2003). *From improvement to transformation*. Keynote speech presented at the International Congress for School Effectiveness and Improvement, 'Schooling the knowledge society' Sydney, Australia, 5 January 2003.

Harré, R. & Van Langenhove, L. (Eds.). (1998). *Positioning theory: moral contexts of international action*. London: Wiley-Blackwell.

Harris, A. & Muijs, D. (2007). *Improving schools through teacher leadership*, 174. New York: McGraw-Hill Education.

Harris, A., Jamieson, I. & Russ, J. (1996). *School effectiveness and school improvement: a practical guide*. London: Pitman Publishing.

Henry, M., Lingard, B., Rizvi, F. & Taylor, S. (2001). *The OECD, globalization, and education policy*. Oxford: Pergamon-Elsevier.

Hess, F. M. (2008). *When research matters: how scholarship influences educational policy*. Cambridge: Harvard Education Press.

Hicks, D. (2012). Performance-based university research funding systems. *Research Policy*, 41 (2), 251–261.

Higher Education Funding Council of England. (2014a). *Annual report and accounts 2013–14*.

Higher Education Funding Council of England. (2014b). *Higher education in England 2014: key facts*.

Hilderbrand, M., Simon, J. & Hyder, A. (2000). The role of research in child health policy and programs in Pakistan. *Lessons in Research to action and policy: case studies from seven countries*, 77–85.

Hillage, J., Pearson, R., Anderson, A. & Tamkin, P. (1998). *Excellence in research on schools*. The Institute for Employment Studies, London: DfEE.

Hitt, M. A. & Greer, C. R. (2011). The value of research and its evaluation in business schools: killing the goose that laid the golden egg? *Journal of Management Inquiry*, doi: 1056492611428721.

Hofstetter, R. & Schneuwly, B. (2002). Institutionalisation of educational sciences and the dynamics of their development. *European Educational Research Journal*, 1 (1), 3–26.

Holliday, A. (2010). *Intercultural communication and ideology*. London: Sage.

Homer-Vanniasinkam, S. & Tsui, J. (2012). The continuing challenges of translational research: clinician-scientists' perspective. *Cardiology Research and Practice*.

Hooks, B. (1994). *Teaching to transgress: education as the practice of freedom*. New York: Routledge.

Horng, E. & Loeb, S. (2010). New thinking about instructional leadership. *Kappan*, 92 (3), 66–69.

Howe, K. & Moses, M. (1999). Ethics in educational research. *Review of Research in Education*, 24, 21–60.

Huberman, M. & Miles, M. B. (Eds.) (2002). *The qualitative researcher's companion*. London: Sage.

Hughes, M. & Bennett, D. (2013). Survival skills: the impact of change and the ERA on Australian researchers. *Higher Education Research & Development*, 32 (3), 340–354.

Hunt, S. (2009). *Stand up for research*. Undated statement circulated in October–December. Available online at www. ucu. org. uk/index. cfm.

Hunter, I. (1994). *Rethinking the school: subjectivity, bureaucracy, criticism*. St Leonards, NSW: Allen & Unwin.

Israel, M. (2014). *Research ethics and integrity for social scientists: beyond regulatory compliance* (2nd edn). Thousand Oaks, CA: Sage.

Jacob, M. (2014). Europe needs a single system for competitive research. *Research Europe*, 17 (4), 214.

Jasanoff, S. (2011). The practices of objectivity in regulatory science. In Camic, C., Gross, N. & Lamont, M. (Eds.), *Social knowledge in the making*, 307–337. Chicago: University of Chicago Press .

Jenkins-Smith, H. & Sabatier, P. (1993). The study of public policy processes. In Sabatier, P. & Jenkins-Smith, H., *Policy change and learning: an advocacy coalition approach*, 1–9. Boulder: Westview Press.

Johnson, B. L. (1999). The politics of research-information use in the education policy arena. *Educational Policy*, 13 (1), 23–36.

Jump, P. (2014). *The (predicted) results for the 2014 REF are in*, 27 November. Retrieved 6 February 2015.

Kaarbo, J. & Gruenfeld, D. (1998) The social psychology of inter- and intragroup conflict in governmental politics. *Mershon International Studies Review*, 42 (2), 226–233.

Kalleberg, R. (2007). Robert K. Merton: a modern sociological classic. *Journal of Classical Sociology* (JCS), 7 (2), 131–136.

Kant, I. (1803). *On education* ('Über pädagogik'). Translated by Annette Churton, with an Introduction by C. A. Foley Rhys Davids, MA. Boston, MA: DC Heath and Co., Publishers, 1906.

Keller, E. & Lee, S. (2003). Ethical issues surrounding human participants research using the internet. *Ethics and Behavior*, 13 (3), 211–219.

Kelly, A. (2014). The impact of impact on the REF, 18 December. Retrieved 16 February 2015 from https://theconversation.com/the-impact-of-impact-on-the-ref-35636

Kelly, R. (1987). The politics of meaning and policy inquiry. In Palumbo, D. (Ed.), *The Politics of Program Evaluation*, 270–296. Newbury Park, CA: Sage.

Kelly, U. & McNicoll, I. (2011). *Through a glass, darkly: measuring the social value of universities*. Bristol: National Coordinating Centre for Public Engagement.

Kiesinger, C. E. (2002). My father's shoes: the therapeutic value of narrative reframing. In A. P. Bochner & C. Ellis (Eds.), *Ethnographically speaking: autoethnography, literature, and aesthetics*, 95–114. Walnut Creek, CA: AltaMira.

Kimber, M. (2003). The tenured 'core' and the tenuous 'periphery': the casualisation of academic work in Australian universities. *Journal of Higher Education Policy and Management*, 25 (1), 41–50.

Kingdon, J. W. (2003). *Agendas, alternatives, and public policies* (2nd edn). Longman: Pearson.

Kleinman, C. S. (2006). Ethical drift: when good people do bad things. *JONA's Healthcare Law, Ethics, and Regulation*, 8 (3), 72–76.

Knott, J. & Wildavsky, A. (1980). If dissemination is the solution, what is the problem? *Knowledge: creation, diffusion, utilization,* 1 (4), 537–78.

Koro-Ljungberg, M. (2008). A social constructionist framing of the research interview. In Holstein, J. A. & Gubrium, J. F. (Eds.), *Handbook of Constructionist Research.* New York: The Guildford Press.

Kristjanson, P., Place, F., Franzel, S. & Thornton, P. (2002). Assessing research impact on poverty: the importance of farmers' perspectives. *Agricultural Systems,* 72 (1), 73–92.

Kumashiro, K. K. (2014). Troubling the politics of engagement, ethics, and educational research: reframing our work. *Disapora, Indigenous, and Minority Education,* 8, 44–54.

Kuruvilla, S., Mays, N. & Walt, G. (2007). Describing the impact of health services and policy research. *Journal of Health Services Research and Policy,* 12 (suppl 1), 23–31.

Kuruvilla, S., Mays, N., Pleasant, A. & Walt, G. (2006). Describing the impact of health research: a research impact framework. *BMC Health Services Research,* 6 (134), 1–18. doi: 10.1186/1472-6963-6-134.

Kwok, J. T. (2013). *Impact of ERA research assessment on university behaviour and their staff.* Melbourne: NTEU National Policy and Research Unit. Retrieved 27 May, 2013.

Lakey, J., Rodgers, G. & Scoble, R. (2013). *What are the different characteristics of research impact? Developing transferable skills: enhancing your research and employment potential,* 33.

Lamont, M. (2009). *How professors think: inside the curious world of academic judgment.* Cambridge, MA: Harvard University Press.

Landry, R., Amara, N. & Lamari, M. (2001). Climbing the ladder of research utilization evidence from social science research. *Science Communication,* 22 (4), 396–422.

Lascoumes, P. & Le Gales, P. (2007a). Introduction: understanding public policy through its instruments: from the nature of instruments to the sociology of public policy instrumentation. *Governance,* 20 (1), 1–21.

Lascoumes, P. & Le Galès, P. (2007b). *Sociologie de l'action publique.* Paris: Armand Colin.

Lather, P. (2012). *Getting lost: feminist efforts toward a double (d) science.* New York: Suny Press.

Lawn, M. & Normand, R. (2014). *Shaping of European education. Interdisciplinary approaches.* London: Routledge.

Lawn, M. & Grek, S. (2012). *Europeanizing Education: governing a new policy space.* Oxford: Symposium Books.

Laycock, A., Walker, D., Harrison, N. & Brands, J. (2011). *Researching indigenous health: a practical guide for researchers.* Melbourne, Victoria: The Lowitja Institute.

Lehti, M. (2011). *Performing identity, looking for subjectivity: marginality, self-esteem and ontological security.* Paper presented at the 'Comparative Baltic Sea Building' seminar, Uppsala Centre for Russian and Eurasian Studies, Uppsala University, 14–15 March 2011.

Leisey, M., Holton, V. & Davey, T. L. (2012). Community engagement grants: assessing the impact of university funding and engagements. *Journal of Community Engagement and Scholarship,* 5 (2).

Levin, B. (2010). Leadership for evidence-informed education. *School leadership & management,* 30 (4), 303.

Levin, B. (2013). To know is not enough: research knowledge and its use. *Review of Education,* 1 (1), 2–31.

Lindberg, L. (2006). Disciplinen och den dubbla kompetensen. Noteringar i anslutning till ett kvalifikationskrav. (The discipline and the double competence. Notes in relation to a qualification demand). *Studies in Educational Policy and Educational Philosophy.* E-tidskrift 2006:2/2007.

Lindblad, S. (1984). The practice of school-centred innovation: a Swedish case. *Journal of Curriculum Studies*, 16 (2), 165–172.

Lindblad, S. & Foss Lindblad, R. (2013). Educational research: the state of Sweden and the Australian 2.2 world. *The Australian Educational Researcher*, 40 (4), 527–534.

Lincoln, S. H. & Homes, E. K. (2007). *A need to know: an ethical decisions-making model for research administrators*. Paper presented at the annual October Society of Research Administrators International meeting, Nashville, TN.

Lincoln, Y. S. & Guba, E. G. (2000). Paradigmatic controversies contradictions and emerging confluences. In Denzin, N. K. & Lincoln, Y. S. (Eds.), *Handbook of qualitative research* (2nd Ed, 163–188). Thousand Oaks, CA: Sage.

Lingard, B. (2013). The impact of research on education policy in an era of evidence-based policy. *Critical Studies in Education*, 54 (2), 113–131.

Lingard, R. & Rizvi, F. (2010). *Globalizing Education Policy*. Abingdon: Routledge.

Lingard, R. & Sellar, S. (2013). Globalization, edu-business and network governance: the policy sociology of Stephen J. Ball and rethinking education policy analysis. *London Review of Education*, 11 (3), 265–280.

LSE GV13 Group. (2014). Evaluation under contract: government pressure and the production of policy research. *Public Administration*, 92 (1), 224–239.

Lubienski, C., Scott, J. & DeBray, E. (2014). The politics of research production, promotion, and utilization in educational policy. *Educational Policy*, 28 (2), 131–144.

Lucas, L. (2006). *The research game in academic life*. Berkshire: Open University Press.

Lukes, S. (2005). *Power: a radical view* (2nd edn). Basingstoke: Palgrave Macmillan.

MacLean, L. M. (2006). The power of human subjects and the politics of informed consent. *Qualitative Methods*, 4 (2), 13–15.

MacLure, M. (2005). 'Clarity bordering on stupidity': where's the quality in systematic review? *Journal of Education Policy*, 20 (4), 393–416.

Mannay, D. (2014). Storytelling beyond the academy: exploring roles, responsibilities and regulations in the open access dissemination of research outputs and visual data. *Journal of Corporate Citizenship*, 2014 (54), 109–116.

Marginson, S. (2014). *Game-playing of the REF makes it an incomplete census*. The Conversation.

Markiewicz, A. (2005). 'A balancing act': resolving multiple stakeholder interests in program evaluation. *Evaluation Journal of Australasia*, 4 (1 & 2), 13–21.

Markiewicz, A. (2008). The political context of evaluation: what does this mean for independence and objectivity? *Evaluation Journal of Australasia*, 8 (2), 35–41.

Marks, H. M. (2000). *The progress of experiment: science and therapeutic reform in the United States, 1900–1990*. Cambridge: Cambridge University Press.

Maroy, C. (2008). Vers une régulation post-bureaucratique des systèmes d'enseignement en Europe? *Sociologie et sociétés*, 40 (1), 31–55.

Martin, B. R. (2011). The research excellence framework and the 'impact agenda': are we creating a Frankenstein monster? *Research Evaluation*, 20 (3), 247–254. doi: 10.3152/095820211x13118583635693.

Marzano, R. (2007). *The art and science of teaching: a comprehensive framework for effective instruction*. Australia: Hawker Brownlow.

Masters, G. (2009). *A shared challenge improving literacy, numeracy and science learning in Queensland primary schools*. Victoria, Australia: Australian Council for Educational Research (ACER).

McAdams, D. P., Josselson, R. E. & Lieblich, A. E. (2006). *Identity and story: creating self in narrative*. Washington, DC: American Psychological Association.

McDonnell, L. M. (2008). Foreword. In F. M. Hess (Ed.), *When research matters: how scholarship influences educational policy*, vii–ix. Cambridge, MA: Harvard Education Press.

McLaughlin, M. W. (2005). Listening and learning from the field: tales of policy implementation and situated practice. In Lieberman, A. (Ed.), *The roots of educational change*, 58–72. Dordrecht, The Netherlands: Springer.

Meagher, L., Lyall, C. & Nutley, S. (2008). Flows of knowledge, expertise and influence: a method for assessing policy and practice impacts from social science research. *Research Evaluation*, 17 (3), 163–173. doi: 10.3152/095820208x331720.

Menon, A., Jaworski, B. J. & Kohli, A. K. (1997). Product quality: impact of interdepartmental interactions. *Journal of the Academy of Marketing Science*, 25 (3), 187–200.

Mertens, D. M. (2009). *Transformative research and evaluation*. New York: Guilford Press.

Mertens, D. M. (2013). Social tranformation and evalaution. In Alkin, M. C. (Ed.), *Evaluation roots: a wider perspective of theorists' views and influences*, 229–240. Thousand Oaks, CA: Sage.

Merton, R. K. (1942). A note on science and democracy. *Journal of Legal and Political Sociology* (1/2), 115–126.

Merton R. K. (1968). Science and the social order. *Social theory and social structure*. New York: Free Press.

Messick, D. M. & Bazerman, M. H. (1996). Ethics for the 21st century: a decision making approach. *Sloan Management Review*, 37, 9–22.

Messick, D. M. & Tenbrunsel, A. E. (Eds.) (1996). *Codes of conduct: behavioral research into business ethics*. New York: Russell Sage.

Middleton, S. (2005). Disciplining the subject: The impact of PBRF on education academics. *New Zealand Journal of Educational Studies*, 40 (1/2), 131.

Ministerial Council on Education Employment Training and Youth Affairs. (2000). *Report of MCEETYA taskforce on indigenous education*. Canberra: MCEETYA.

Mitscherlich, A. & Mielke, F. (1949). *Doctors of infamy: the story of the Nazi medical crimes*. New York: Schuman.

Moed, H. F. (2008). UK research assessment exercises: informed judgments on research quality or quantity? *Scientometrics*, 74 (1), 153–161.

Mohan, R. & Sullivan, K. (2006). Managing the politics of evaluation to achieve impact. *New Directions for Evaluation*, 112, 7–23.

Molas-Gallart, J., Salter, A., Patel, P., Scott, A. & Duran, X. (2002). *Measuring third stream activities*. Final report to the Russell Group of Universities. Brighton: SPRU, University of Sussex.

Molina, J. L., Muñoz, J. M. & Domenech, M. (2002). Redes de publicaciones científicas: un análisis de la estructura de coautorías. *REDES-Revista hispana para el análisis de redes sociales*, 1 (3), 3–15.

Monaghan, M. (2010). The complexity of evidence: reflections on research utilisation in a heavily politicised policy area. *Social Policy and Society*, 9 (01), 1–12.

Moody, J. (2004). The structure of social science collaboration network: disciplinary cohesion from 1963 to 1999. *American Sociological Review*, 9, 213–238.

Moore, C. (2009). Psychological perspectives on corruption. In D. De Cremer (Ed.), *Psychological perspectives on ethical behavior and decision making*, 35–71. Charlotte, NC: Information Age Publishing.

Moore, C. & Gino. F. (2013). Ethically adrift: how others pull our moral compass from true North, and how we can fix it. *Research in Organizational Behavior*, 33, 53–77.

Moore, C., Detert, J. R., Treviño, L. K., Baker, V. L. & Mayer, D. M. (2012). Why employees do bad things: moral disengagement and unethical organizational behavior. *Personnel Psychology*, 65, 1–48.

Moreno, J. D. (1997). Reassessing the influence of the Nuremberg Code on American medical ethics. *Journal of Contemporary Health Law & Policy*, 13 (2), 347–360.

Morris, M. (1999). Research on evaluation ethics: what have we learned and why is it important? *New Directions for Evaluation*, 82 (Summer), 15–24.

Morris, M. (2006). From criticism to research: the 'textual' in the academy. *Cultural Studies Review*, 12 (2), 17–32.

Morton, S. (2015). Progressing research impact assessment: a 'contributions' approach. *Research Evaluation*, rvv016.

Mosteller, F. & Boruch, R. (eds.), (2002). *Evidence matters: randomised trials in education research*. Washington, DC: Brookings Institution Press.

Mountfield, R. (1999). *'Politicisation' and the civil service*. Available at: www.civilservant.org.uk/politicisation.pdf, accessed 5 September 2012.

Mulkay, M. J. (1976). Norms and ideology in science. *Social Science Information*, 15 (4/5), 637–656.

Mundine, W. (2014). This insane spending must stop (June 10). *The Australian*. Retrieved from http://www.theaustralian.com.au/national-affairs/opinion/this-insane-spending-must-stop/story-e6frgd0x-1226948643258, accessed 7 August 2015.

Munro, C. L. & Savel, R. H. (2014). Stepping forward in practice through research. *American Journal of Critical Care*, 23 (1), 4–6.

National Audit Office. (2001). *Modern policy-making: ensuring policies deliver value for money*, London: The Stationery Office.

National Audit Office. (2003). *Getting the evidence: using research in policy making*. London: The Stationery Office.

National Consumer and Carer Forum. (2004). *Consumer and carer participation policy: a framework for the mental health sector*. National Consumer and Carer Forum Australia.

National Health and Medical Research Council (NHMRC). (2007). *National statement on the ethical conduct of health research involving humans*. Canberra: Commonwealth of Australia.

National Health and Medical Research Council. (2014). Measuring the impact of research: not just a simple list of publications (1 April). Retrieved 10 October 2014, from http://www.nhmrc.gov.au/media/newsletters/ceo/2014/measuring-impact-research-not-just-simple-list-publications

Niemi, H., Toom, A. & Kallioniemi, A. (Eds.). (2012). *Miracle of education: the principles and practices of teaching and learning in Finnish schools*. Rotterdam: Sense Publishers.

Normand, R. (2009). Expert measurement in the government of lifelong learning. In Mangenot, E. & Rowell, J. (Coords.), *What Europe constructs: new sociological perspectives in european studies*. Manchester: Manchester University Press.

Nóvoa, A. (2015). Looking for freedom in contemporary universities: what is educational research for? *European Educational Research Journal*, 14 (1), 3–10.

Nowotny, H., Scott, P. & Gibbons, M. (2001). *Rethinking science: knowledge and the public in an age of uncertainty*. Cambridge: Polity Press.

Nowotny, H., Scott, P. & Gibbons, M. (2003). 'Mode 2' revisited: the new production of knowledge. *Minerva*, 41, 179–194.

Nutley, S. M., Walter, I. & Davies, H. T. O. (Eds.) (2007). *Using evidence: how research can inform public services*. Bristol: Policy Press.

O'Brien, T., Payne, S., Nolan, M. & Ingleton, C. (2010). Unpacking the politics of evaluation: a dramaturgical analysis. *Evaluation*, 16 (4), 431–444.

O'Flynn, J. (2008). Elusive appeal or aspirational ideal? The rhetoric and reality of the 'collaborative turn' in public policy. In *Collaborative governance: a new era of public policy in Australia?*, 181–195. Canberra: ANU EPress.

Oakley, A. (2000). *Experiments in knowing: gender and method in the social sciences*. Cambridge: Polity Press.
Oakley, A. (2003). Research evidence, knowledge management and educational practice: early lessons from a systematic approach. *London Review of Education*, 1 (1), 21–33.
Oancea, A. (2005). Criticisms of educational research: key topics and levels of analysis. *British educational research journal*, 31 (2), 157–183.
OECD. (2003). *Knowledge management: New challenges for educational research*. Paris: Publications de l'OCDE.
OECD. (2007). *Evidence in education. linking research and policy*. Paris: Publications de l'OCDE.
OECD. (2013). *What makes schools successful? Resources, policies and practices – Volume IV*, 70. PISA, OECD Publishing.
OERI. (1985) *What works: Research about teaching and learning*. Department of education. Washington, DC: Office of Educational Research and Improvement.
Office for Learning and Teaching. (2014). *2015 innovation and development grants: programme information and application instructions* (Version 1.0 ed.), 49. Australian Government.
O'Leary, Z. (2004). *The essential guide to doing research*. London: Sage.
Østerud, Ø. (2015). Det vitenskapelige vurderingssystemet er i alvorlig krise. *Aftenposten*: http://www.aftenposten.no/viten/uviten/Uviten-Et-varslet-sammenbrudd-8026619.html
Otley, D. (1999). Performance management: a framework for management control systems research. *Management accounting research*, 10 (4), 363–382.
Ouimet, M., Landry, R., Ziam, S. & Bédard, P.-O. (2009). The absorption of research knowledge by public civil servants. *Evidence & Policy: A Journal of Research, Debate and Practice*, 5 (4), 331–350.
Oxman, A., Lavis, J., Lewin, S. & Fretheim, A. (2009). SUPPORT tools for evidence-informed health policymaking (STP) 1: what is evidence-informed policymaking? Available at: http://www.health-policy-systems.com/content/7/S1/S1, accessed on 14 November 2010.
Ozga, J. (2000). Resources for policy research. In J. Ozga, *Policy Research in Educational Settings*, 68–113. Buckingham: Open University Press.
Ozga, J., Dahler-Larsen, P., Segerholm, C. & Simola, H. (2011). *Fabricating quality in education: data and governance in Europe*. London: Routledge.
Ozga, J., Seddon, T. & Popkewitz, T. (2006). Education research and policy: steering the knowledge-based economy. In J. Ozga, T. Seddon, & T. Popkewitz (Eds.), *World yearbook of education 2006: education research and policy: steering the knowledge-based economy*, 1–14. London: Routledge.
Pain, R., Kesby, M. & Askins, K. (2011). Geographies of impact: power, participation and potential. *Area*, 43 (2), 183–188.
Palumbo, D. (1987). Politics and evaluation. In D. Palumbo (Ed.), *The politics of program evaluation*. Newbury Park, CA: Sage.
Parsons, W. (2002). From muddling through to muddling up: evidence-based policy making and the modernising of British government. *Public Policy and Administration*, 17 (3), 43–60.
Patton, M. Q. (2002). *Qualitative research and evaluation methods* (3rd edn). London: Sage.
Patton, M. Q. (2008). *Utilization-focused evaluation* (4th edn). Thousand Oaks, CA: Sage.
Patton, M. Q. (2012). *Essentials of utilisation focused evaluation*. Thousand Oaks, CA: Sage.
Pawson, R. (2006). *Evidence-based policy: a realist perspective*. London: Sage.
Payne-Gifford, S. (2013). What is the meaning of the impact agenda: is it a repackaged or a new entity? Views from inside the research councils. *Developing Transferable Skills: Enhancing Your Research and Employment Potential*, 10.

Penfield, T., Baker, M., Scoble, R. & Wykes, M. (2013). Assessment, evaluations, and definitions of research impact: a review. *Research Evaluation*, 23 (1), 21–32. doi: 10.1093/reseval/rvt021.

Perry, L. & McWilliam, E. (2007). Accountability, responsibility and school leadership. *Journal of Educational Enquiry*, 7 (1), 32–43.

Peters, D. H., Adam, T., Alonge, O., Agyepong, I. A. & Tran, N. (2014). Implementation research: what it is and how to do it. *British Journal of Sports Medicine*, 48 (8), 731–736.

Petersen, E. B. (2014). Re-signifying subjectivity? A narrative exploration of 'non-traditional' doctoral students' lived experience of subject formation through two Australian cases. *Studies in Higher Education*, 39 (5), 823–834.

Petersen, E. B. (2011). Staying or going? Australian early career researchers' narratives of academic work, exit options and coping strategies. *Australian Universities Review*, 53 (2), 34–42.

Phillips, R. (2006). Consumer participation in mental health research (March). *Social Policy Journal of New Zealand* (27), 177–182.

Phillips, R. (2010). The impact agenda and geographies of curiosity. *Transactions of the Institute of British Geographers*, 35 (4), 447–452.

Pickerill, J. (2014). The timeliness of impact: impacting who, when, and for whose gain? *ACME: An International E-Journal for Critical Geographies*, 13 (1), 24–26.

Piper, H. & Simons, H. (2005). Ethical responsibility in social research. In Somekh, B. & Lewin, C. (Eds.), *Research methods in the social sciences*, 56–63. London: Sage.

Pittenger, D. J. (2003). Internet research: opportunity to revisit classic ethical problems in behavioral research. *Ethics and Behavior*, 12 (1), 45–60.

Polkinghorne, D. E. (1988). *Narrative knowing and the human sciences*. Albany, NY: State University of New York Press.

Polonsky, M. J. & Waller, D. S. (2010). *Designing and managing a research project* (2nd edn). Thousand Oaks, CA: Sage.

Pont, B., Nusche, D. & Moorman, H. (2008). *Improving school leadership: volume 1: policy and practice*. Paris: Organisation for Economic Cooperation and Development.

Pope, J. & Jolly, P. (2008). *Working in partnership: practical advice for running effective partnerships*. Melbourne, Victoria: Department of Planning and Community Development.

Pope, J., Bond, A., Morrison-Saunders, A. & Retief, F. (2013). Advancing the theory and practice of impact assessment: setting the research agenda. *Environmental Impact Assessment Review*, 41, 1–9. doi: 10.1016/j.eiar.2013.01.008.

Porter, C. (2010). *What shapes the influence evidence has on policy? The role of politics in research utilisation*. Oxford: Young Lives: Department of International Development, University of Oxford.

Queensland Government. (2013a). *The commission of audit report, volume 3*. Retrieved from: http://www.commissionofaudit.qld.gov.au/reports/coa-final-report-volume-3.pdf

Queensland Government. (2013b). *A plan for better services for Queenslanders: Queensland government response to the independent commission of audit final report*. Retrieved from: https://www.treasury.qld.gov.au/publications-resources/better-services-for-queenslanders/better-services-for-queenslanders.pdf

Randall, E. V., Cooper, B. S. & Hite, S. J. (1999). Understanding the politics and ethics of research in education. *Educational Policy*, 13 (1), 7–22.

Read, J. (2009). A Genealogy of homo-economicus: neoliberalism and the production of subjectivity. *Foucault Studies*, 6, 25–36.

Reinikainen, P. (2012). Amazing PISA results in Finnish comprehensive schools. In H. Niemi, A. Toom, & A. Kallioniemi (Eds.), *Miracle of education: The principles and practices of teaching and learning in Finnish schools*, 3–180. Rotterdam: Sense Publishers.

Research Assessment Exercise. (2002, 21 May 2002). *What is the RAE 2001?* Retrieved 14 July 2014 from http://www.rae.ac.uk/2001/AboutUs/

Research Development and Evaluation Commission. (2014). *The annual report of the development and the achievement of commissioned research at agencies subordinate to the executive yuan* [Online]. Available at: http://archive.rdec.gov.tw/lp.asp?CtNode=11981&CtUnit=1671&BaseDSD=7&mp=100, accessed 25 October 2015.

Research Excellence Framework. (2011). *Decisions on assessing research impact.*

Research Excellence Framework. (2013). *Research excellence framework 2014.* Retrieved 15 November 2013 from http://www.ref.ac.uk/

Reynaud, J.-D. (2003). Régulation de contrôle, régulation autónome, régulation conjoint. In G. Terssac, *La théorie de la régulation sociale de Jean-Daniel Reynaud*, 103–113. Paris: Éditions La Découverte.

Rickinson, M., Sebba, J. & Edwards, A. (2011). *Improving research through user engagement.* London: Routledge.

Riessman, C. K. (2008). *Narrative methods for the human sciences.* London: Sage.

Roberts, S. F., Fischhoff, M. A., Sakowski, S. A. & Feldman, E. L. (2012). Perspective: transforming science into medicine: how clinician–scientists can build bridges across research's 'valley of death'. *Academic Medicine*, 87 (3), 266–270.

Roberts, S. G. (2003). *Review of research assessment.* London: RA Review.

Robinson, V. (2010). From instructional leadership to leadership capabilities: empirical findings and methodological challenges. *Leadership and Policy in Schools*, 9 (1), 1–26.

Robinson, V. M. J., Lloyd, C. & Rowe, K. J. (2008). The impact of leadership on student outcomes: an analysis of the differential effects of leadership types. *Education Administration Quarterly*, 44, 635–674.

Rogers, A., Bear, C., Hunt, M., Mills, S. & Sandover, R. (2014). Intervention: the impact agenda and human geography in UK higher education. *ACME: An International E-Journal for Critical Geographies*, 13 (1).

Romano, D. (2006). Conducting research in the Middle East's conflict zones. *Political Science and Politics*, 39 (3), 439–441.

Rosengren, K. & Öhngren, B. (Eds.). (1977). *An evaluation of Swedish research to education.* Stockholm: HSFR.

Rossoni, L., & Graeml, A. (2009). A influência da imersão institucional e regional na coperação entre pesquisadores no Brasil. *REDES – Revista hispana para el análisis de redes sociales*, 16 (9), 228–249.

Rowe, D. & Brass, K. (2008). The uses of academic knowledge: the university in the media. *Media, Culture & Society*, 30 (5), 677–698.

Ryan, S., Burgess, J., Connell, J. & Groen, E. (2013). Casual academic staff in an Australian university: marginalised and excluded. *Tertiary Education and Management*, 19 (2), 161–175.

Sahlberg, P. (2007). Education policies for raising student learning: the Finnish approach. *Journal of Education Policy*, 22 (2), 147–171.

Sahlberg, P. (2011). *Finnish lessons: what can the world learn from educational change in Finland?* New York: Teachers College Press.

Sahlberg, P. (2012). A model lesson: Finland shows us what equal opportunity looks like. *American Educator*, 36 (1), 20.

Sahlberg, P. (2012). Stanford Center for Opportunity Policy in Education, verbal communication, March 2012.

Sahlberg, P. (2015). *Finnish lessons 2.0*. New York: Teachers College Press.

Sahlgren, G. H. (2015). *Real finnish lessons. The true story of an education superpower*. London: Center for Policy Studies. http://www.cps.org.uk/files/reports/original/150410115444-RealFinnishLessonsFULLDRAFTCOVER.pdf

Sampson, C. (2014). *What counts as an academic publication?* The Conversation.

Sanderson, I. (2002). Making sense of 'what works': evidence-based policy making. *Public Policy and Administration*, 17 (3), 61–75.

Satyanarayana, K. (2013). Journal publishing: the changing landscape. *The Indian Journal of Medical Research*, 138 (1), 4–7.

Schatz, M., Popovic, A. & Dervin, F. (2015). From PISA to national branding: exploring Finnish education. *Discourse: Studies in the Cultural Politics of Education*.

Schram, S. & Soss, J. (2001). Success stories: welfare reform, policy discourse, and the politics of research. *Annals of the American Academy of Political and Social Science*, 577, 49–65.

Schriewer, J. & Keiner, E. (1992). Communication patterns and intellectual traditions in educational sciences: France and Germany. *Comparative Education Review*, 25–51.

Schuller, T., Jochems, W., Moos, J. & Van Zanten, A. (2006). Evidence and policy research. *European Educational Research Journal*, 5 (1), 57–70.

Schuman, J. (2010). Beyond Nuremberg: a critique of informed consent in third world humans subject research. *Journal of Law and Health*, 25 (1), 123–153.

Scott, S., Knapp, M., Henderson, J. & Maughan, B. (2001). Financial cost of social exclusion: follow up study of antisocial children into adulthood. *British Medical Journal*, 323, 1–5.

Scott, D., Posner, C., Martin, C. & Guzman, E. (2015). *Interventions in education systems: reform and development*. London: Bloomsbury.

Scott, J. (2000). *Social network analysis: a handbook*. London: Sage.

Scriven, M. (1996). Types of evaluation and types of evaluator. *American Journal of Evaluation*, 17, 151–161.

Seals, G. (2013). An ethics paradigm for the service organization. *American International Journal of Social Science*, 2 (3), 1–9.

Senate Select Committee on Mental Health. (2006). *A national approach to mental health: from crisis to community: final report*. Parliament of Australia.

Shalvi, S., Dana, J., Handgraaf, M. J. J. & De Dreu, C. K. W. (2011). Justified ethicality: observing desired counterfactuals modifies ethical perceptions and behavior. *Organizational Behavior and Human Decision Processes*, 115, 181–190.

Shamoo, A. E. & Resnick, D. E. (2009). *Responsible conduct of research*. Oxford: Oxford University Press.

Shaw, I. (2003). Ethics in qualitative research and evaluation. *Journal of Social Work*, 3 (1), 9–29.

Shore, C. (2010). Beyond the multiversity: neoliberalism and the rise of the schizophrenic university. *Social Anthropology*, 18, 15–29.

Shore, C. & Wright, S. (1999). Audit culture and anthropology: neo liberalism in British higher education. *The Journal of the Royal Anthropological Institute*, 5, 557–575.

Sidhu, R. K. (2006). *Universities and globalization: to market, to market*. New York: Routledge.

Silverman, D. (2013). *Doing qualitative research: a practical handbook*. London: Sage.

Simons, H. (1995). The politics and ethics of educational research in England: contemporary issues. *British Educational Research Journal*, (4), 435–449.

Simons, H. (2000). Damned if you do, damned if you don't: ethical and political dilemmas in evaluation. In Simons, H. & Usher, R. (Eds.), *Situated ethics in educational research*, 39–55. London: Routledge.
Simons, H. (2006). Ethics in evaluation. In Shaw, I. F., Greene, J. C. & Mark, M. M. (Eds.), *The Sage handbook of evaluation*, 243–265. London: Sage.
Sitra. (2015). *Finnish education is based on meeting yesterday's standards* http://www.sitra.fi/en/news/new-education/finnish-education-based-meeting-yesterdays-standards.
Slattery, D. (2010). The political inherency of evaluation: the impact of politics on the outcome of 10 years of evaluative scrutiny of Australia's mandatory detention policy. *Evaluation Journal of Australasia*, 10 (1), 17–27.
Slaughter, S. (2014). Foreword. In Cantwell, B. & Kauppinen, I. (Eds.). *Academic capitalism in the age of globalization*, i–iii. Baltimore, MD: John Hopkins University Press.
Smith, E. (2005). Raising standards in American schools: the case of No Child Left Behind. *Journal of Education Policy*, 20 (4), 507–524.
Smith, R. (2006). Research misconduct: the poisoning of the well. *J R Soc Med*, 99 (5), 232–237.
Smith, S. (2007). *Applying theory to policy and practice: issues for critical reflection*. Abingdon: Routledge.
Smith, S., Ward, V. & House, A. (2011). 'Impact' in the proposals for the UK's research excellence framework: shifting the boundaries of academic autonomy. *Research Policy*, 40 (10), 1369–1379.
Spaapen, J. & van Drooge, L. (2011). Introducing 'productive interactions' in social impact assessment. *Research Evaluation*, 20 (3), 211–218.
Spring, J. (2005). *Political agendas for education: from the religious right to the Green Party*. Mahwah, NJ/London: L. Erlbaum.
Spring, J. (2015). *Globalization of education: an introduction*. New York: Routledge.
Squires, J. E., Hutchinson, A. M., Boström, A.-M., O'Rourke, H. M., Cobban, S. J. & Estabrooks, C. A. (2011). To what extent do nurses use research in clinical practice? A systematic review. *Implement Sci*, 6 (1), 21.
Staeheli, L. A. & Mitchell, D. (2005). The complex politics of relevance in geography. *Annals of the Association of American Geographers*, 95 (2), 357–372.
Staley, L. (2008). *Evidence-based policy and public sector innovation*. Melbourne: Institute of Public Affairs.
Stark, L. (2012). *Behind closed doors: IRBs and the making of ethical research*. Chicago, IL: The University of Chicago Press.
Steffens, P. R., Weeks, C. S., Davidsson, P. & Isaak, L. (2014). Shouting from the ivory tower: a marketing approach to improve communication of academic research to entrepreneurs. *Entrepreneurship Theory and Practice*, 38 (2), 399–426.
Steneck, N. H. (1994). Research universities and scientific misconduct: history, policies, and the future. *The Journal of Higher Education*, 65 (3), 310–330.
Sternberg, R. J. (2012a). Ethical drift. *Liberal Education*, 98 (3), 58–60.
Sternberg, R. J. (2012b). A model of ethical reasoning. *Review of General Psychology*, 16 (4), 319–326.
Sternberg, R. J. (2012c). Teaching for ethical reasoning. *International Journal of Educational Psychology*, 1 (1), 35–50.
Stevens, A. (2007). Survival of the ideas that fit: an evolutionary analogy for the use of evidence in policy. *Social Policy and Society*, 6 (1), 25.

Stewart, J. (2006). Transformational leadership: an evolving concept. *Canadian Journal of Educational Administration and Policy*, 54, (June), 1–29.

Stipp, S. L. (2010). Strategic or blue sky research? *Elements* (June 2010).

Strengthening Non-profits (2015). A capacity builder's resource library. Available at www.strengtheningnonprofits.org, accessed 13 July 2015.

Sullivan, G. M. (2011). Education research and human subjects protection: crossing the IRB quagmire. *Journal of Graduate Medical Education*, 3 (1), 1–4.

Sultana, F. (2007). Reflexivity, positionality and participatory ethics: negotiating fieldwork dilemmas in international research. *ACME: An International E-Journal for Critical Geographies*, 6 (3), 374–385.

SurveyMonkey.com

Sylva, K., Taggart, B., Melhuish, E., Sammons, P. & Siraj-Blatchford, I. (2007). Changing models of research to inform educational policy. *Research papers in Education*, 22 (2), 155–168.

Taggart, B., Siraj-Blatchford, I., Sylva, K., Melhuish, E. & Sammons, P. (2008). Influencing policy and practice through research on early childhood education. *International Journal of Early Childhood Education*, 14 (2), 7–21.

Taylor, J. (2001). The impact of performance indicators on the work of university academics: evidence from Australian universities, *Higher Education Quarterly*, 55 (1), 42–61.

Taylor, J. & Taylor, R. (2003). Performance indicators in academia: an x-efficiency approach? *Australian Journal of Public Administration*, 62, 71–82.

Taylor, S., Rizvi, F., Lingard, B. & Henry, M. (1997). *Educational policy and the politics of change*, (Vol. 54). London: Routledge.

Team Finland. (2014). Future learning Finland and Finnish education export 2014. http://team.finland.tfi/etusivu

Team Finland, (2015). *Strategy update 2015*. Helsinki: Prime Minister's Office Publications. http://vnk.fi/documents/10616/1098657/J0714_Team+Finland+Strategy+2015.pdf/19ff0f61-1f74-4003-8b7b-8b029ba00d8e

Team Finland. (n. d.) *Finland country image communications workbook*. Helsinki: Ministry of Foreign Affairs of Finland. http://213.214.149.79/public/download.aspx?ID=127539&GUID={FEAB1518-AF20-43FC-AE69-4CDD8004D93B}

Tenbrunsel, A. E. & Messick, D. M. (2004). Ethical fading: the role of self-deception in unethical behavior. *Social Justice Review*, 17 (2), 223–236.

The Education Research Committee. (2011). *The education report of the Republic of China, Taiwan*. Taipei: Ministry of Education.

Thornton, M. (2008). The retreat from the critical: social science research in the corporatised university. *Australian Universities Review*, 50 (1), 5–10.

Timmer, C. P. (2004). Adding value through policy-oriented research: reflections of a scholar-practitioner. *What's economics worth*, 129–152.

Timmermans, S. & Berg, M. (2003). *The gold standard: the challenge of evidence-based medicine and standardization in health care*. Philadelphia, PA: Temple University Press.

Timmermans, S. & Kolker, E. S. (2004). Evidence-based medicine and the reconfiguration of medical knowledge. *Journal of Health and Social Behavior*, (45), extra issue: health and health care in the United States: origins and dynamics, 177–193.

Tooley, J. & Darby, D. (1998). *Educational research: a critique*. London: Ofsted.

Torrance, H. (2010). When is an 'evaluation' not an evaluation? When it's sponsored by the QCA? A response to Lindsay and Lewis. *British Educational Research Journal*, 29 (2), 169–173.

Townsend, T., Acker-Hocevar, M., Ballenger, A., Ballenger, J. & William, A. (2013). Voices from the field: what have we learned about instructional leadership? *Leadership and Policy in Schools*, 12 (1), 12–40.

Trowler, P. (2003). *Education policy*. London: Routledge.

Tseng, V. (2012). The uses of research in policy and practice. *Social Policy Report*, 26 (2), 1–16.

Umphress, E. E., Bingham, J. B. & Mitchell, M. S. (2010). Unethical behavior in the name of the company: the moderating effect of organizational identification and positive reciprocity beliefs on unethical pro-organizational behavior. *Journal of Applied Psychology*, 95 (4), 769–780.

van den Besselaar, P., Hemlin, S. & van der Weijden, I. (2012). Collaboration and competition in research. *Higher Education Policy*, 25 (3), 263–266. doi: 10.1057/hep.2012.16.

Vestman, O. & Conner, R. (2006). The relationship between evaluation and politics. In Shaw, I., Mark, M. & Green, C. (Eds.), *The Sage handbook of evaluation*, 225–242. London: Sage.

VicHealth. (2011). The partnership analysis tool. Retrieved from http://www.vichealth.vic.gov.au/search/the-partnerships-analysis-tool

Villani, M. & Normand, R. (2015). *The new ways of entrepreneurship among academics*. Paper delivered at European Conference for Educational Research, Corvinus University, Budapest, Hungary, 9 September 2015.

Vincent-Lancrin, S. (2006). What is changing in academic research? Trends and futures scenarios. *European Journal of Education*, 41 (2), 169–202.

Viseu, S. (2015). Redes de investigadores que transportam representações e dilemas sobre o trabalho científico. *REDES-Revista hispana para el Análisis de redes sociales*, (26) (1), 203–219.

Waitere, H. J., Wright, J., Tremaine, M., Brown, S. & Pause, C. J. (2011). Choosing whether to resist or reinforce the new managerialism: the impact of performance-based research funding on academic identity. *Higher Education Research and Development*, 30 (2), 205–217.

Walsh, K., Kitson, A., Cross, W., Thoms, D., Thornton, A., Moss, C., Campbell, S. & Graham, I. (2012). A conversation about practice development and knowledge translation as mechanisms to align the academic and clinical contexts for the advancement of nursing practice. *Collegian*, 19 (2), 67–75.

Walter, I., Nutley, S. & Davies, H. (2003). *Research impact: a cross sector review*. Literature review. St. Andrews: University of St. Andrews.

Watermeyer, R. (2014). Issues in the articulation of 'impact': the responses of UK academics to 'impact' as a new measure of research assessment. *Studies in Higher Education*, 39 (2), 359–377.

Watson, H. (2003). *Final report of the national evaluation of the National English Literacy and Numeracy Strategy (NIELNS)*. Canberra: Department of Education, Science and Training.

Weaver-Hightower, M. B. (2008). An ecology metaphor for educational policy analysis: a call to complexity. *Educational Researcher*, 37 (3), 153–167.

Webb, R. (2005). Leading teaching and learning in the primary school, from educative leadership to pedagogical leadership. *Educational Management Administration & Leadership*, 33 (1), 69–91.

Weber, J. M., Kopelman, S. & Messick, D. M. (2004). A conceptual review of decision making in social dilemmas: applying a logic of appropriateness. *Personality and Social Psychology Review*, 8, 281–307.

Weingart, P. (2008). Socially robust knowledge and expertise. In Carrier, M., Howard, D., & Kourany, J. (Eds.), *The challenge of the social and the pressure of practice: science and values revisited*, 131–145. Pittsburgh, PA: University of Pittsburgh Press.
Weiss, C. (1970). The politicization of evaluation research. *Journal of Social Sciences*, 26 (4), 57–68.
Weiss, C. (1980). Knowledge creep and decision accretion. *Knowledge: Creation, Diffusion, Utilisation*, 1 (3), 381–404.
Weiss, C. (1982). Research in the context of diffuse decision making. *The Journal of Higher Education*, 53 (6), 619–639.
Weiss, C. (1987). Where politics and evaluation research meet. In Palumbo, D. (Ed.), *The politics of program evaluation*, 47–70. Newbury Park, CA: Sage.
Weiss, C. (1993). Where politics and evaluation research meet. *American Journal of Evaluation*, 14 (1), 93–106.
Weiss, C. H. (1979). The many meanings of research utilization. *Public Administration Review*, 39 (5), 426–431.
Wells, P. (2007). New Labour and evidence based policy making, 1997–2007. *People, Place & Policy*, 1 (1), 22–29.
Whitley, R. (2000). *The intellectual and social organization of the sciences* (2nd edn). Oxford: Oxford University Press.
Whitney, S. N., Alcser, K., Schneider, C. E., McCullough, L. B., McGuire, A. L. & Volk, R. J. (2008). Principal investigator views of the IRB system. *Int. J. Med. Sci.*, 5 (2), 68–72.
Whitty, G. (2006). Education(al) research and education policy making: is conflict inevitable? *British Educational Research Journal*, 32 (2), 159–176.
Winch, C. (2002). Accountability and relevance in educational research. In McNamee, M. & Bridges, D. (Eds.), *The ethics of educational research*, 151–170. Oxford: Blackwell.
Winckler, G. & Fieder, M. (2012). The contribution of research universities in solving 'grand challenges'. *Global Sustainability and the Responsibilities*, 179.
Winefield, A. H., Gillespie, N., Stough, C., Dua, J. & Hapuararchchi, J. (2002). *Occupational stress in Australian universities*. National Tertiary Education Union, downloaded 010815 http://www.researchgate.net/profile/Con_Stough/publication/45705774_Occupational_stress_in_Australian_universities_A_national_survey_2002/links/02bfe512411176115f000000.pdf
Wolf, B., Lindenthal, T., Szerencsits, M., Holbrook, J. B. & Heß, J. (2013). Evaluating research beyond scientific impact: how to include criteria for productive interactions and impact on practice and society. *GAIA-Ecological Perspectives for Science and Society*, 22 (2), 104–114.
Woliver, L. R. (2002). Ethical dilemmas in personal interviewing. *Political Science and Politics*, 35 (1), 677–678.
Wong, K. K. (2008). Considering the politics in the research policymaking nexus. *When research matters: how scholarship influences education policy*, 219–237. Cambridge: Harvard Education Press.
Zafirakis, E. (2010). Curing the revolving door phenomenon with mentally impared offenders: applying a theraputic jurisprudence lens. *Journal of Judicial Administration*, (20), 81–84.
Zigarelli, M. (1996). An empirical test of conclusions from effective schools research. *The Journal of Educational Research*, 90 (2), 103–110.
Ziman, J. (1994). *Prometheus bound: science in a dynamic steady state*. Cambridge: Cambridge University Press.
Ziman, J. (2002). *Real science: what it is and what it means*. Cambridge: Cambridge University Press.

# Index

academic relevance 70
agreed measures 185
agreement to participate 142
applied research 72, 95
assessing research impact 97-8
assessing research value 98
assessment 56, 77, 90, 94, 95, 96, 97, 98, 99, 100, 101, 102, 105, 123, 151, 161, 190
autoethnography 8, 79, 91
autonomy 62-4, 67-8, 73, 75, 99, 148

board power 126, 135
boards social cohesion 127

co-authorship 57
collaborative research 97-8, 101
company performance 127
consumer involvement 121
contested relevance 70, 73
contrasting board roles 127
cooperation 40, 63, 70, 72, 75, 86, 142-3
corporate boards 126-7, 135
country branding 82, 85, 90
court diversion 120
CUDOS 68

decision-making 48, 54
discourse 11-18, 24-5, 33, 69, 88, 151, 159, 160-64
dissemination strategy 187
docile relationship 137

early career researchers 104, 114
education export 77, 79, 80, 83, 88, 89

empowerment 121, 124, 185
empowerment evaluation 123, 185, 186
epistemology 14-15, 26, 33
ethical choices 123, 124
ethical dilemmas 41, 44, 45, 46, 47, 52, 119, 120, 122, 124, 125, 178, 179
ethical drift 8, 41, 46-9, 51-3, 165-6, 181
ethical issues 5, 44, 119, 125
ethical practice 5, 41, 47-8
ethical trade-offs 125
ethics clearance 142
European commission 35, 37-8, 40
evaluating boards 128
evaluation 3-9, 25, 26-8, 31-3, 39, 40, 54, 55, 57-9, 61-4, 68, 72, 76, 90, 98, 99, 119-25, 126, 128-30, 132-33, 135, 143, 145, 146, 162-3, 168, 180-91
evaluation theoretical approaches 123
evaluative 25, 119, 154, 162
evidence 10-12, 14-32, 35-40, 64, 98-9, 101-02, 136, 145, 151, 162, 167-8, 170-1, 173, 177, 182, 185-6, 188
evidence misuse 11, 21-4
evidence-based policy 3, 8, 25, 27-30, 32-5, 39
expertise 25, 36, 39, 40, 74, 82, 86, 127, 148
external research funding 110, 114

Finland 77-78, 80-91
Foucaultian 15, 24
funding 3-9, 32, 34, 39, 41, 45, 47-51, 54-9, 61, 63-4, 66-67, 69, 73, 76, 84, 94-6, 98, 101-03, 109-11, 113-14, 123, 136-9, 148, 168, 183, 185

globalisation 35
grant game 110-11

Habermassian 21-2
hidden agendas 138
higher education 4-8, 65-71, 73-6, 79-80, 83, 86, 89, 90, 94-5, 98, 101, 103, 171, 175, 181

ideology 14-16, 21, 76, 177
imaginaries 80, 81
impact 94-8, 100, 103, 170
impact agenda 94-6, 100
innovation 36, 39, 56-7, 91, 96, 102, 129
institutional review board (IRB) 41
instructional leadership 9, 151-4, 160, 163, 166
interagency cooperations 142-3
interculturality 92
interlocking directorates 128

knowledge 4-5, 8, 12-17, 19, 20, 23, 25, 26, 28, 31, 32, 35, 37-41, 43, 44, 52, 55, 57, 60, 67-8, 70, 74-6, 78, 79, 83, 94, 98-103, 123, 129, 139-40, 144, 150, 170, 177, 178-9, 187

marketisation 8, 17, 105
mental health 120-2
metrology 39
mode 1 and mode 2 knowledge 75
monetisation 94
moral covenant 53
multiple-case study design 171

negative effects of ethical drift 50-1
neoliberalism 105

OECD 7, 36-7, 40, 56, 65, 70, 77, 80, 160
origin of ethics in research 42-4

pedagogik 66, 69, 70-6
performance management 112
performance-based research funding 55
PISA 8, 36, 78, 80, 84, 89-92, 151, 168
policy 3, 11-12, 14-26, 28-40, 54-7, 61-4, 66, 71-76, 78, 80, 83-4, 89, 95-7, 99, 100, 102, 105, 110, 112, 114, 126, 137-42, 150-41, 60-181, 183, 185-88, 190-91
policy agora 7, 14-15, 19-20, 23, 24, 182
policy change 139, 140
policy cycle 164-6
policy development 3, 5, 7-8, 10-11, 22, 24, 140, 142, 151, 154, 161, 163-64, 166, 182, 185
policy discourse 151, 162
policy makers 11, 54, 153, 165, 176, 187
political considerations 54, 167-8, 171, 179
political context 43, 180, 186, 191
political pressures 6, 52, 101, 177, 178, 182, 186, 189
politics 3-6, 9, 19, 31, 41, 43, 44, 45-9, 52, 54, 66-8, 89, 144, 167-69, 176, 180-81, 184, 186, 188-91
politics of educational research 43, 49
politics of knowledge production 41, 44, 52
positivism 27, 33, 74
power 4-9, 10-14, 20-2, 31, 41, 43, 45-6, 54, 67, 119-20, 126, 128-29, 131-33, 135, 137, 138, 141, 175, 177-78, 181
pressure 22, 27, 34, 46, 48, 62-3, 98, 101, 107, 109, 113, 131-3, 136-9, 145, 149, 151, 164, 168, 172-3, 176, 178, 182-3
production of knowledge 25-6, 101

R&D policies 55-8, 60, 62-5
research assessment exercise 95
research ethics 42, 53, 173
research excellence framework 55, 95
research for government departments 138
research impact 94-8, 100, 103, 170
research integrity 103
research misconduct 42, 51
research positions 52, 73, 105
research utilisation 101, 168, 169, 170, 175, 178
researchers strategies 55
research-use stages 171
research-use typologies 169
resistance 36, 49, 100, 176
responsible conduct of research 53
rigorous and ethical research 8
rigorous methodology 185, 188

science 4, 26-7, 29-30, 39-40, 43, 51, 54-7, 62-4, 67-71, 75-6, 78, 95-6, 101, 153, 154, 162, 170
science public policies 54, 63
scientific 26, 28, 32, 33
scientific ethos 67-8
self-deception 47, 49, 52
servant-master relationship 137, 140
social justice 124
social network analysis 58, 60
social research 31, 34, 42, 119
stakeholders 4, 30, 34-6, 38-40, 42, 56, 68, 76, 98, 121, 123, 125, 126-7, 129, 131, 145-61, 76, 181, 183, 185, 186, 189, 190
strategic 13, 21, 24, 34, 36, 56-7, 59, 64, 66, 67, 70, 76, 112, 115, 131, 154, 160, 163, 166, 170, 171, 188

Taiwan 9, 168
Third Way 26, 30
transformative 45, 124
trust 50, 72, 74, 76, 127, 129, 130, 140, 143

utilisation focused evaluation 123

value judgement 98

# eBooks
## from Taylor & Francis
Helping you to choose the right eBooks for your Library

Add to your library's digital collection today with Taylor & Francis eBooks. We have over 50,000 eBooks in the Humanities, Social Sciences, Behavioural Sciences, Built Environment and Law, from leading imprints, including Routledge, Focal Press and Psychology Press.

**Choose from a range of subject packages or create your own!**

Benefits for you
- Free MARC records
- COUNTER-compliant usage statistics
- Flexible purchase and pricing options
- All titles DRM-free.

Benefits for your user
- Off-site, anytime access via Athens or referring URL
- Print or copy pages or chapters
- Full content search
- Bookmark, highlight and annotate text
- Access to thousands of pages of quality research at the click of a button.

**Free Trials Available**
We offer free trials to qualifying academic, corporate and government customers.

## eCollections
Choose from over 30 subject eCollections, including:

| | |
|---|---|
| Archaeology | Language Learning |
| Architecture | Law |
| Asian Studies | Literature |
| Business & Management | Media & Communication |
| Classical Studies | Middle East Studies |
| Construction | Music |
| Creative & Media Arts | Philosophy |
| Criminology & Criminal Justice | Planning |
| Economics | Politics |
| Education | Psychology & Mental Health |
| Energy | Religion |
| Engineering | Security |
| English Language & Linguistics | Social Work |
| Environment & Sustainability | Sociology |
| Geography | Sport |
| Health Studies | Theatre & Performance |
| History | Tourism, Hospitality & Events |

For more information, pricing enquiries or to order a free trial, please contact your local sales team:
www.tandfebooks.com/page/sales

■ **www.tandfebooks.com**